FIELD
OF
MIRRORS

FIELD OF MIRRORS

An Anthology
of
Philippine American Writers

Edited by

EDWIN A. LOZADA

Philippine American Writers and Artists, Inc.

San Francisco, California

Library of Congress Control Number: 2008920113
ISBN 978-0-9763316-3-6

Cover and Text Design: Edwin Lozada
Book Production: Carayan Press (www.carayanpress.com)

Published by
Philippine American Writers and Artists, Inc.
P.O. Box 31928
San Francisco, CA 94131-0928
pawa@pawainc.com
www.pawainc.com

Printed in the United States of America

ERRATA

Corrections in italics.

p. v, 137:	Barot, Rick *Particle* and Wave
p. ix:	*Poma, Edgar* The *Suffer* Brothers
p.3, line 18:	...strength of a *heroine*
p.54: line 2:	from the *course*...
p.55, line 6:	victims *of* blood *baths*...
p.75, line 4:	...Tagalog word *Aywanko*...
p.85, line 13:	Guardian *angel*...
p.101, line 3:	5 years ago, *two months* ago
p.155, line 2:	...ng *angkang* Guerrero...
p.156, line 29:	...where there *were* no...
p.196, line 5:	Gayon din *ang*...
p.253, line 23:	...made it *a* game
p.270, line 10:	...fruits and *vegies*...
p.311, footnote:	...commonly *known*...
p.343, line 4:	around *the* world...
line 6:	...pinpointed *its*...
p.348, line 2:	...in *the* same way...
p.362, line 2;	*Bagong* Alyansang Makabayan
p.364, line 32:	as long as *it's*
p.364, last line:	...their *sons*, Paolo and Anton.
p.375, line 11:	Uncle Manuel *came* in...

Contents

PREFACE

One of the main goals of PAWA is to support Filipino American writers by organizing or co-sponsoring events to showcase their creativity and talents, and through publication. *Field of Mirrors* is the third in a series of anthologies that Philippine American Writers and Artists, Inc. has produced. In the first two anthologies, *Reflections: Readings for the Young and Old* (2002)and *Whisper of the Bamboo* (2004), the featured writers were primarily from California. Our goal for this anthology was to break state borders and expand and reach out to the many Filipino American writers, whether established or just begininning to publish, from the Hawaiian coasts to the western and eastern shores of the US. I had to decide whether this volume was going to present a specific theme, whether to feature prose or poetry. In the end, I opted to give more flexibility and options to the contributor and made it thematically non-specific and open to a variety of genres. The result: a total of seventy-one writers selected featuring diverse styles of poetry, short stories, essays, articles, and excerpt from a novel. Although most of the pieces are in English, there are a few pieces in Tagalog, Spanish, and even Ilocano.

Why the title, "Field of Mirrors"? As individuals of Filipino or Filipino American heritage living in a society in which we are but a piece of a larger quilt, we reflect on our identity and at some time come to an understanding of who we are and the role that our heritage plays in our lives and work. This period of reflection, investigation, and introspection, sometimes life-long, is the "Field of Mirrors." Literary creations from the "field" include issues of identity—immigrant experiences in which our Filipino idiosyncrasies come face to face with the local culture and traditions which at times, result in difficulty, conflict or humor. Stories and poetry are perfumed and spiced with memories, images and elements relating to the homeland or to the unique experiences of being a Filipino American.

Artistry is in constant evolution and the works of Philippine American writers express various phases of their thoughts and ideas. This may include writing that does not focus, or on the page, have anything to do with being Filipino nor incorporate elements connected with the Filipino/Filipino American experience. And yet the work is unquestionably Filipino/Filipino American, for it is the product of a writer, who, liberated by the awareness and appreciation of his or her identity, pursues his or her imagination with creativity without boundaries. This is also within the "Field of Mirrors."

Hence, the "Field of Mirrors" is all encompassing and reflects all that with which we come face to face: our most intimate hopes, fears, sorrows, trauma, pain, joy, reflections, obsessions, creations, revelations—all reflecting who we are, defining us and ultimately compelling us to write and share our creations with others with the hope to enlighten or entertain, to enrich.

The community of Philippine American writers has increased tremendously and being able to include 71 is thrilling, but it's even more inspiring to know that there are many, many more dreaming and creating out there. It is the hope of PAWA that this volume will contribute significantly to the list of previous anthologies that have featured Philippine American writers. The pieces represented in this volume are inspired by personal tragedies, violence, history, cultural conflicts, issues of identity, family, nostalgia, change, travel, displacement, the wonders and beauty of nature, sexuality, faith, love, death, anguish, art—life.

Edwin Agustín Lozada

*A*CKNOWLEDGMENTS

I wish to thank all those who showed interest in the anthology and shared their work that ultimately made this collection possible.

Appreciation also goes to Marie Romero, Karen Llagas, Oscar Peñaranda, Maria Luisa Peñaranda and Allen Gaborro for their assistance and support for getting this project started. The title for the anthology evolved after conversations with Oscar Peñaranda and then with Barbara Jane Reyes. Thank you for your input.

A special thanks to Penélope V. Flores and Manuel Flores for their ongoing support for PAWA and making sure the publication of this anthology would not be impeded by lack of funds.

Thanks also to my dear friends and family that might have felt abandoned at times because of the time I dedicated to completing this project.

Some of the pieces in *Field of Mirrors* appeared in previous publications and are reprinted with the permission of the author and/or publisher.

"The Map of Light" and "Sign Language" were previously published in Amigo Warfare (2007: Cherry Grove Collections, Cincinatti, OH). Copyright 2007 by Eric Gamalinda.

"Once a Winsome Filipino Lass" and "Carlos Bulosan Lives in Me" are from Enriqueta Cartagena Mayuga's *Outspoken and Mute: American Life* (Airleaf Publishing and Bookselling, 2005).

An English version of Patrick Rosal's "As Glass" appears in *My American Kundiman* (A Karen &Michael Braziller Book, Persea Books, New York, 2006) www.perseabooks.com.

The selection of poems of E. Tabios are from *The Light Sang As It Left Your Eyes* (Marsh Hawk Press, New York, 2007) www.marshhawkpress.org.

Rick Barot's "Oakland" is also published in *Ploughshares*. "Return" appeared in MiPOesias.com (Guest edited by Nick Carbo).

Jon Pineda's "Wrestling," "Matamis," "Birthmark" are from *Birthmark* (Southern Illinois University Press, 2004) .

Jean Vengua's "Part 2 from The City and the Garden 2" has been previously published, first in Bay Poetics (Faux Press), and is now is in *Prau* (Meritage Press, 2007). http://okir.wordpress.com/2007/10/27/hoisting-the-sail/

Luis Syquia's poems are from *Fogeater, Poems by Luis Malay Syquia* (Menagerie Arts, 2007).

Victor Gendrano's selected poems had appeared in: *Canadian Zen Haku Canadien, Vol. 3, No. 4, Autumn 2005; Ribbons, Tanka Society of America Journal,Vol. 2, No. 1, Spring 2006; Modern English Tanka, Vol. 2, No. 2,, Winter 2007; LYNX : A Journal for Linking Poets, Vol. XXII, No. 3 October, 2007.* "Pasko Na Naman" appeared in *Heritage magazine, Vol. 2, No 4, December 1988.* They are also in his book, *Rustle of bamboo leaves: selected haiku and other poems*, 2005.

Rhodora Peñaranda's poems are from *Touchstone* (Menagerie Arts, 2007).

Rey E. de la Cruz's "Dear Satu: Letters Tell The Story of Our Lives" first appeared in the March 12, 2007 issue of Newsweek.

Earlier versions of Ben Pimentel's "Lean Alejandro's Midlife Crisis, The short incredible life of a Martial Law Baby" were published in *Inquirer.net* and *Filipinas* magazine. Excerpt from *Mga Gerilya sa Powell Street* is reprinted, courtesy of the author and publisher, Ateneo de Manila University Press, Copyright 2007 by Benjamen Pimentel and Ateneo de Manila University, www.ateneopress.org.

"The Parol: A Bamboo Star of Hope" is from Evangeline Canonizado Buell's *Twenty-Five Chickens and a Pig for a Bride* (T'Boli Publishing, 2007).

field
of

mirrors

Annabelle A. Udo

THE MYSTIC FAMILY CIRCUS

Enter. . .the magic circle of the jesterworld,
a shamanic kingdom of dolphins and mermaids,
gnomes and nomads,
kings and queens,
oddities and odysseys.
We are alive—spiritual beings on a human journey—
children roaming the planet whispering sacred poems
and drinking the nectar of the sun.
From the goblet of the goddesses of Earth, Air, Fire, and Water—
we invite you to the Mystic Family Circus
where the mana of jungle princesses twirl in a mad trance,
clowns flirt with the many shadows of your soul,
stiltwalkers tower into the velvet of the night,
and Rumi readings turn a pearl into the moon.
It is a place where dreams and tribes unite
in space and time
with much love and many blessings.

LOVE SONATA

I have felt love like the rhythm of a deep blue ocean or the scent of
midnight air—as powerful and strong as the notes that have composed this sonata—the one that marks his essence, his nature—so
calm. In this exodus, I've sensed peace and freedom ten times over
simply because what I've always wanted has always been inside of me.

The reality of me is that I want to say, but can only do, the metaphor of "I love you."

> And in this cave, I fly—a beautiful flower tossed into the sky,
> eaten by the wind of the hungry ghost
> who savors her mind like the predator and host.
> I can only swell with the present—indoctrinated by silence;
> Ingested by a lesson that revoked the innocence.
> Love's riddle—a myth made of fear;
> What do we hear when the heart has no sound?
> The moon un-round?
> So within our own madness:
> An elixir of sadness,
> A melody of gladness
> We sleep side by side
> Dreaming dreams with eyes wide
> Bodies entwined with love's suicide.
> Love—oppressed,
> Suddenly undressed.
> His warmth draws near
> Removing the fear,
> And I hear the drum,
> Slowly—
> Numb.

DESERT SERENADE

> The poems of the desert are inscribed in the sand
> With centuries of spoken words written by hand
> Its creator often appears to me
> As sun and moon
> As sky and sea.

These riddles are invisible to the darkened soul
Peering through mirrors in part we know
The scriptures tell us what will follow us home
That which we reap
Is that which we sow.

Inside the oases are the market towns,
Of spicy aromas and dark coffee grounds.
With cosmos and spheres
and a universe with ears
The jars in heaven
contain our tears

The lanterns alight tell us who is home
That in this universe we are never alone
Ancestors watch and carry us back
Filling us with messages
we otherwise lack.

This buzz from heaven is so unique
I have the strength of a heroin but yet I am weak
Dizzy from sipping from my imagination
I am with God
In contemplation.

Born in Portsmouth, Virginia and raised in Stockton, California, *Annabelle A. Udo* is a San Francisco-based freelance arts & entertainment writer and columnist for *Sigaw!/Shout!*, a monthly column for *Listen & Be Heard* in Vallejo, showcasing various Asian/Asian American arts communities. She has performed in numerous venues throughout the S.F. Bay Area and is working on a book showcasing more than 10 years of poems and tales. Annabelle is currently the Events & Fundraising Coordinator for the Asian American Journalists Association.

Patricia Isabel Amoroto

FOOLS AND HORSES

Fools and Horses
Brethren of tubes
Of psychedelic encounters
In breakwater commune
The daily sightings
Brush-off innocence display
Plagued by the comfort of
Fumes...
Crass naïveté.
General Joy
General Storm
General flush
of beauty bygone
Bring in the soldiers
The lake is defrosting
Determine the murmur
Of Echo's echoing
Indeed, in stagnant,
inconsistent drive
and malicious
apprehension
To forgive a child
The prickly thorns
Of conscience commit
A suicide of emotions
'til to hell it submits.

SAINT LITTLE BABY

She came undone
Bruises sturdy as the mountains
How can she heal?
When healing seems to be
Distracted
By another pain, another bruise
Justified
Protruding
Elemental as the water
As the earth.
In crisis she calls upon the Gods
Raising the chalice,
Half-empty
Half-full
Of her own blood
In scattered altars
Her pain breeds storms
The bleeding of her innocence
Stigmata unknown
In fortress of plastic bag chapels
And paper- wrap cathedrals
She conjures solace,
As the other holy mortals
In a mass of fools and horses
Peace be with you,
Be with me, be with her
Make or break
A homily:
As priestly white or
Pop-star fake.
And so the retreat
To pews at the back
To tunes of rosary clicks

And bubblegum smack.
Now the sky is darkening
The Angelus sirens
Everybody stands still
Prayers are fulfilled
In the distance:
Calvary/Golgotha
A sudden collapse
A moment's fury,
Death, perhaps...?

Patricia Isabel Amoroto
Born and raised in Iloilo, Philippines.
Pumping irony since birth.
Metaphor is her lifeline.
Religion-less.

Cristina Querrer

Ako[1]

Ako, I started as a dissident somewhere
between two long planks of phraseologies
languishing between lost prosaic.

Ako, I unearthed my bones in deserts,
in tundras, in islands, wherever
I migrated as a meandering misbeliever.

Ako, then I began to sing songs
from my *barangay*;[2] embedded music most
familiar like fetal murmurs.

Ako, then I began to tend to my
flowerbeds most meticulously, weeding
out rain forests of lost time.

Ako, then I learned to sleep
soundly even when sudden surges
overcame my terrain.

Ako, I woke up to wakefulness,
wonder and incredulity. The seas
feel me, the sky see me. They always have.

1. *I, me (Tagalog).*   2. *Village, town subdivision.*

THERE IS NO LEAVING

To Gabriel García Márquez
(Regarding Your Farewell Letter)

I wrote my farewell letter also
many times in my life on grains of sand,
on various shores.
I still have nothing to give
to conventions. I am just
a woman who has given up
on romance.

Every night, lately, I return to
empty tables and chairs, even
my pots and pans seek attention.
On my back porch, my crimson geranium
lost its life due to lack of affection.
Many dawdling deaths.
But you remind us we have been given
an inestimable world, the bravado
of a baby's breath, insurmountable seas.

You also reminded me
of my Filipino grandfather, Amang,
as I last saw him,
eroded by toiling a lifetime
over an ocean; trodden
brown body and beaten hat
on a small fishing boat that once
bore my name.
You made me remember him
and how much he must have loved me
though we spoke different languages.

Tonight you joined me at my table,
kept me company, read me

love letters from life, lead me back
to the center with roses. I promise
to embrace more, to know that my romance
is happening now. But you see,
I live in a house of memories
of all those who left me behind.
In my house,
there simply will be no leaving
if I have any say so at all.

BEFORE I FORGET

Just in case the leaves turn color;
before my words unfold the awful
truth of how a bitter fruit was once
sweet in our mouths while exchanging
deserts for fertile forests,
algebraic equations for no absolutions.

Just in case the world turns
against us, or was it ever there
for us? Yes, indeed, I say—
it was always there—all encompassing
joys and sorrows that crowd our hearts
so much that we could not prepare
for chances, we vacillate
in between set measures.

Just in case I lose interest,
will I ever? But in case I lose my
sight, my hearing, or all my mobility,
jot it down, right here, right now—
that we were here in earth's bed,
mellifluent, silvery twines, embracing.

TEARS OF THINGS

Truth is,
tears is what I know so well.
Infestation of tulip poplars
infect the eyes, attenuates,
then evaporates. Little
beasts in the foam stay,
abeyant to seasons, it lies
dormant until all fruit
have been eaten. These
steadfast friends to sorrow,
are well-kept, well-fed.
Made their permanent home
in the cellar of my skin,
in the bell tower of my thoughts,
stream of possessed dancers
in the night is all
I hear and see.

LIFE WITHOUT SUGAR

Imagine hard bent days
without saviors. The world
headed by arithmomancy.
A world without Neruda's
neologisms, his leaning into
the afternoons and his talking
about sweetness, always.
Imagine not tasting the granulated
grievances of the gods—gluttony
will get too much, despair
becomes decorous.

What would we be doing
staring into the sugar bowl?
What right would we have?
Delectable the days can be
without processed predicates,
oily fascinations of casual
observers. We are blind
not to savor pure sunrises
from the interstate.
Real chronicles are in cookie
jars, gourmet wrapped
fancies flower in your orchard.
Bestow honeycombed catacombs,
vestiges of casabas and star
apples, all encompassing
succulence surrounds you now:
to be blessed like this!

POET IN SEVEN DAYS

I

It comes in blues,
dark and deep with melancholy.
Tones low and monotonous.
I cannot think above
the clouds. I cannot think
about flowers.
I cannot think past 9 p.m.
So I sleep and slink
into my forgetfulness, shedding
all this nonsense of lasting, for I am
no use to anyone.

2

It's no better looking into
my coffee for a clue—swirling
cream of clandestine charm—
Come hither! Reveal thyself!
The laundry summons me,
my child heckles at my chase and work
grunts at my priority, poetry? This poem
stuffed in my pockets with
pieces of me and miscellany;
proof of my lowly vocation and
residence.

3

Pages numbered, ordered,
perfect. I sleep with
the lights on this time, I rise
a little earlier—alter
the way I live and love by
the philosopher of the day.
Shred all my old bills,
discard irrelevancies. Even
open my desk for a lovely criminal
to sell me illicit descriptions of carnage.
My dog looks up in disbelief,
moans and stretches as the clock
ticks louder.

4

Relinquish asking my coffee for answers.
Surrender asking questions at all.
In my next life I will have no children,
I will come back a man, never

apologizing and abandoning
every chance I get—
'tis the perfect stock for poetry!
Forgive me for these passages,
as I forgive those who never
wanted to know—

5

That there is brilliance the way
dishes are stacked uniformly
and my clothes folded just so, in planning
a future by college Lit courses—
my shoddy attempt at status quo:
to be degreed and dignified.
There are daycare costs and my care note.
But out of all my debtors my biggest expense
is my dues to poetry.
For Lorca sips tea in my living room,
elegance exists at last!

6

Next on the grocery list, cereal
and milk. Perhaps Marianne Moore
can give me tips on dating? Gwendolyn Brooks
can school me on no good men. What if
Frank O'Hara was my uncle—
what life I'd have then!
Here comes a good one, oh where's
my goddamn pen! I curse and blunder
for it lies in the abyss of my purse.

7

There now, wait! My child
asleep in my arms, her breath
in unison with mine—no words,
no theories, no redolent sign.
The day collects like residue on
the furniture—You feel it? I
asked her earlier—the wind? She
in delight of it closes her eyes
and her mouth wide open tries
to swallow air—snippets I put away
in my wallet. Not enough, I know—
but every year's mishap restores
itself right here.

❋

Cristina Querrer is a Filipina-American multi-disciplinary
artist: poet, visual artist and singer/songwriter. Although she
was born and raised in the Philippines, she spent most of her
adult years in southeastern Connecticut then moved to the
Tampa Bay area three years ago to earn her degree in Creative
Writing with a minor in Visual Arts from Eckerd College in
St. Petersburg, Florida.

Robert Francis Flor

SENTINELS

Gothic wings stretched,
Silhouetted cormorants sit
atop harbor pillars
guarding Vashon entry
silent witnesses to each passage.
Like Roman legionnaires
in Galecian castros at dawn
and sentinels through the ages,
they peer over foggy hill and seascape
in search of some elusive enemy.
In these discordant times
their vigilance soothes and
shelters us from critical thoughts
Their presence—a refuge from reason.

THE PLAGUES

We ascend the hill in darkness
through frigid morning drizzle
past the shadowed, sullen
gauntlet of locust people
mired in the mud below.
Lice-plagued men and women
asleep in their stench,
unsheltered and oblivious
to the smell of stale urine
rising from the steps.

Heads lowered,
we avoid their blemished, cattle-boiled faces,
as we leapfrog puddled pavement
to the sanctuary of our comfort cubes.

The day passes uneventfully and
as the primal light recedes,
we descend to the streets below,
cross the flooded septic Styx.
We traverse these same unwashed and fallow
whose lives are spent in traded blood
drinking the death of discards.

Theirs, the endless hunger
of tormented souls,
salved only by begged bread-scraps,
time and death.

We pass without notice
or compassion.

RESURRECTIO

Hola! My name...Miguelito.
You want something to eat?
Second umbrella. See my sign!
Come.

Gracias. Maybe, later.
We must walk first.

Okay. Remember...second umbrella...

Crossing bridge over Mismalloya stream,
we wend our way through avaricious venders,
stroll the neglected concrete path,
watch the ocean grind boulders to sand.
Frigate birds glide like angels overhead.

A solitary cat escorts us up cobbled steps.
Little changed since Huston's film,
the hotel awaits in the humid jungle.
Gated doors prevent our Eden's entry.
Below, the false iguana forever clings to a pole
awaiting any fallen.

Disillusioned,
we descend to the second umbrella,
respite from the purgatory sun.
Waves bathe the shore,
as we sit scanning life's ensuing sea.
We must wait our time.

Under paradise shade,
we share *pescado* and *pan**
while the healing *pelicano* warms wings
and watches while we nourish ourselves
awaiting resurrection.

**fish/ bread*

Robert Francis Flor is a Seattle native raised in the Central Area and Rainier Valley. His father immigrated to the United States in 1932 from Iloilo following his uncle, Baltazar Flor who came in 1921. Robert graduated from Seattle University where he earned a B.A. (1966) and M.A. in Education (1975). He has taught in Seattle Public Schools and at Seattle University. In 1978, he received his doctorate at the University of Oregon in Higher Education and Public Policy. He is an amateur writer and has had poems published in the Tamafyhr Mountain Poetry Review, Poets Against the War and the Seattle Post Intelligencer. He has also written four plays "My Uncle", "The FAYTS" "Pinoys Play Baseball" and "Daniel's Mood." He is a member of the Washington Poets Association and Seattle Dramatists. Annually, he co-produces the Pagdiri-wang Festival's Words Expressed event that hosts readings by Filipino- American writers, poets and dramatists.

Eric Gamalinda

THE MAP OF LIGHT

Because you are indifferent, I can offer each morning
only to starlings and not face their ridicule.
They know the map of light is a burden
shared in poverty. They know that every syllable
is defiance, an act of survival.

Mercy looks for moving targets.
Those who have just been born don't know what it's like
to spend an eternity searching. I will let them sleep quietly,
and hope when they wake we'd have left
enough of the world to live in.

And as the hours pass I will speak in codes again.
In the fisted cold. In the warm evenings
that weaken my resolve. So that those who listen
will keep on asking until all our questions
have circumnavigated the earth.

Someone will release the borders from their tyranny.
When I die my body, a cargo of memories,
will disperse into air. Birds will fly
through me, breathing the words
I no longer remember.

SIGN LANGUAGE

My friend speaks to me in sign language:
This is beautiful, and I'm afraid. The words leap
from her hands, a flicker in the dark. The motor
stutters, jungle mangroves drift and vaporize
to snowcapped peaks. Day fades to night, fades back
to day. Her hands busy, though we've already
lost each other, and she's forgotten gestures
to describe what's become inert, her love
turned perfectly invisible. The water
makes no sound, a furtive blue. We cross
the latitudes. Summer blurs to a storm.
We reach the city in the last long reign
of winter. The cobbled alleys glow. No longer
used to land, our feet drag over the stones.
We know we're heading somewhere, blizzard-bound
on an empty bus. The windows are opaque.
A curfew has been called. The driver speaks
in echoes, a language we have yet
to understand. It's been like this for weeks,
dropping strangers in the same blind-alley town.
The streets are pocked with holes. A man crawls into
an empty vault in a burial wall. He's stolen
votive candles, his twilit cave burns like gold.
The wax rips through the punctured hands
of Christ, another illusion, as sharp
as the dream I see us in. My friend says
he will freeze in his sleep, a gentle death.
She tucks her hands in her pockets, warmth
and silence. This is where our story has to end.
In the square a woman offers us flowers:
a white cloud lifts in her hands. Her face

is a flower's ghost, dirt brown, beautiful once
perhaps. Her children are numerous, fast asleep.
In a while they will walk among us, their palms
spread open to the promise of the world.

The Map of Light and Sign Language are from
Amigo Warfare (2007: Cherry Grove Collections, Cincinatti, OH).

Eric Gamalinda was born and raised in Manila, Philippines,
and has been residing in New York City since 1994. He has
received the Asian American Literary Award for his previous
collection of poetry, *Zero Gravity* (Alice James Books, 1999),
as well as a fellowship in fiction from the New York Foundation for the Arts. He won the Philippine Centennial Award
for his novel, *My Sad Republic* (University of the Philippines.
Press, 2000), and co-edited an anthology of Filipino American prose and poetry, *Flippin': Filipinos on America* (Asian
American Writers Workshop). Gamalinda is also a video artist and has won prizes from the Cultural Center of the Philippines' Independent Film and Video Festival. He has also been
artist-in-residence in various other foundations, including
Civitella Ranieri Foundation in Umbria and the Rockefeller
Foundation in Bellagio, Italy, Chateau de Lavigny in Switzerland, Chateau de La Napoule in France, Fundacion Valparaiso
in Spain, Hawthornden Castle in Scotland, and the Corpora-
tion of Yaddo, the MacDowell Colony, the Virginia Center for
Creative Arts, and Ledig International Retreat for Writers in
the United States.

Luisa A. Igloria

THE CARPENTER

In memoriam, Carlos Angeles

And once again I am reminded
that it is always someone else
who holds the single
taper: the woman shielding
the flame, someone who loves
and hovers close — so
the difficult work might be
done, even in darkness.

WHAT THE DOCUMENTARIST SAID

You make a trip to the capital
purposely to visit museums

and galleries Track lights
shine on slabs of marble

once loosened from the soil
and taken in ships to another shore

The lime-encrusted burial jar
that may have kept the bones

of ancestors   Books
inscribed by priests and lovers

with sermons and messages
The many faces of the Buddha

cracked and loved by lichen
In the lobby you are asked

to fill out forms with name address
gender telephone number academic

institution or affiliation Purpose
occupation age gender email

You could just as well
add height weight build

body racial type Whether
distinguishing marks appear

Distended earlobes or splayed feet
Tattoo marks on arms and chest

Teeth filed to discolored points
from years of chewing areca

nut and herbs... But you don't
The world fills and fills with history

dark as birds and soldiers
winging their way to all the middle

regions of the earth   More often now
the only refuge we have is silence

That part inside the flame—

Paradise

The other country, she can still sometimes see
clear as a new postage stamp held slant against window-
light. The old grandmother remembers the sea-passage,

fields where they burned grass ragged and smoked out
small skulls in the underbrush. Rain plumped the fruit
as they hungered under tin roofs and fed

their bets to the fire. Sometimes they trekked
through red earth, past cane fields to the beach, if only
to watch the moon grow flagrant, saying so little

it was a silence she came to mistake for habit—
light's silver coin, surely being offered and not merely held
over the water, inscrutable

at their feet. More days now she feels she's still paying
for moments she's ever betrayed her desires,
though there is no point calculating how much

time is left, what else could be worth
wanting. *Listen,* she says: *in this life, loss is that so-called
ornament scaling the fences heavy with orchids and bougainvillea* .

Beware its fluorescent and tropical husk, wrinkled
as a bitter gourd's; its seed, only another body soon
buried in earth, waiting for the next hundred years.

ISIS IN QUIAPO

> *I dreamt you found me at last*
> *And in your dreams I turned to light*
> *shed radiance everywhere*
>
> — *Kaze nori*

I am the gatherer
of lost things, the one
who patiently scours the alleys
for clues to your whereabouts

Some days I come across
heaps of leftover food—
warm buns, shreds of a meat
patty bearing the imprint
of teeth; carnations
beginning to smell,
at their stem-tips, of salt
and old excretions

In the rain I peer into windows
of slow-moving vehicles, trying
to remember your shadow

It haunts me even as I string
petals of beheaded flowers—
their dismembered bodies
gone slack and filming
the onyx waters under
the bridge

For all that, faithfully
the river reflects glass and iron,
smoke, the teeming *avenidas**   *avenues*

The moon rising
or sinking,
a stone

⚜

Luisa cA. Igloria (previously published as Maria Luisa Agu-ilar-Cariño) is an Associate Professor in the MFA Creative Writing Program and Department of English, Old Domin-ion University (Norfolk, Virginia). Her work has appeared in numerous anthologies and journals including *Poetry, Crab Or-chard Review, The Missouri Review, Poetry East, Smartish Pace, The Asian Pacific American Journal,* and *TriQuarterly.* Various national and international literary awards include the 2007 49th Parallel Poetry Prize, the 2007 James Hearst Poetry Prize (selected by former US Poet Laureate Ted Kooser for the North American Review); the 2006 Richard Peterson Po-etry Prize (Crab Orchard Review); the 2006 Stephen Dunn Award for Poetry; Finalist for the 2005 George Bogin Memo-rial Award for Poetry (Poetry Society of America, selected by Joy Harjo);the 2004 Fugue Poetry Prize(selected by Ellen Bryant Voigt); Finalist in the 2003 Larry Levis Editors Prize for Poetry from The Missouri Review; Finalist in the 2003 Dorset Prize (Tupelo Press); a 2003 partial fellowship to the Summer Literary Seminars in St. Petersburg; two Pushcart Prize nominations; and the 1998 George Kent Award for Po-etry. Originally from Baguio City in the Philippines, Luisa is also an eleven-time recipient of the Carlos Palanca Memorial Award for Literature in three genres (poetry, nonfiction, and short fiction); the Palanca award is the Philippines' highest literary distinction. She has published nine books including *Encanto* (Anvil, 2004), *In the Garden of the Three Islands* (Moy-er Bell/Asphodel, 1995), and most recently *Trill & Mordent* (WordTech Editions, fall 2005; Runner-up, 2004 Editions Prize). http://www.luisaigloria.com

Luis H. Francia

GREAT EXPECTATIONS

She wants you for the coconuts and rum inside you.
She wants you for a whirlwind trip to the South China Sea.
She wants you for the typhoon in your hair
      And the bright fish of your sperm.
She wants you for vacations she can never take
        To places she can never imagine.
She wants you for the sun in your kisses
For the drummer under your tongue
For the volcano in your blood.
She wants you for the genie that
She believes is inside you, that can
Break her every taboo.
She wants you for the you you
Never knew was you,
For the you you need to die for
Before you will ever be you.

DREAM OF EMPIRE

This way, softer things speak—
woods, stars, keepsakes of ancient art,
land bereft of guile, of gloss.

The lizard's voice guides us,
the hornbill speaks.
We bow to old men in anthills, sleep

with owls, ghouls, and sweet *damas de noche**.

The earth and the tides draw signs for us,
they are our Scriptures, our Torah, our Koran,
and in the readings our lives give

birth to names, each name a dream
and a map.
That way, missionaries untangle

the jungle, they stroke their bilge

bellies, caress our bottoms, as their souls
whisper the desire to be enormous.
Pointing to he who died for our sins,

they claim us as their burden and
their brothers, but they are our cross
and we their redeemers, dying daily

for our six feet of earth.

We have forgotten the names of plant, bird, fish,
we have forgotten our names and our dreams.
Shall we dream then only of empire, the realm eternal?

And I, shall I forget the voice of a boy I once
was, remembered but barely, who whispers in
my ear to bow once more to anthills, to listen in

the afternoon dust for a hint of a bird's call?

*Fragrant flowers that bloom only at night (literally, "ladies of the night").

Shall I open the doors of my days to the jungle
invisible that always surrounds me?
Shall I sing of names that fill me with grace?

Shall I keep company with ghosts, whose
lives map my life's passage, I their
visible son, indivisible from them?

In Order to Save You We Must Kill You

Things are revealed in precints and heard,
whispered and seen in hallways and basements,
bruited about on elegant avenues I daily cross,
that Death will come dressed as a reasonable argument
With a warrant for my permanent arrest.
Concerning my scarred omniscience astounded
by fate, devout and ominous, what
citizen of the white world will believe me,
I, who believe in no god?
Hideous and squat: so many of god's citadels,
Their spires, naves, minarets, and domes
Are gun turrets, their pulpits, forts, their crucifixes,
Crescents, and stars are murderous axes, and
every prayer, every hymn is one dream
less to achieve, one more for
the maw of a salivating deity.
Each says, worship only our Father and no other.
Rather, say I, do not worship.
Blasphemer! Infidel! they hiss.
Oh to merely survive is not bliss,
How far we are from peace!

And the justification for the
Century's benedictions of fire?
That my point of view be obsolete forever.

Savior of No One

Where are you, dissembler, patriarch of language,
wrecker of ghettoes, savior of no one?
Here in the dirt my heart grasps my tongue,
my senses transcend obeisance to unknown loves.
Where are you, master of the
doorless house, avatar inchoate?
Call off your angels and their promise of heaven.
Let me sink into the sea of night,
riding the backs of wolves.
Let poems fill my pockets and a
disorder of rhyme resist my
mind as I slip back into ooze:
Mortal, celestial, elemental.

Luis H. Francia is a poet, nonfiction writer, and journalist.
He has published three collections of poetry, the latest being
Museum of Absences (2004). His memoir *Eye of the Fish: A Personal Archipelago* won both the 2002 PEN Center Open Book and
the 2002 Asian American Writers literary awards. He has also
edited two literary anthologies., including *Brown River, White
Ocean: An Anthology of Twentieth Century Philippine Literature
in English*. He teaches at New York University and sits on the
Workshop's Board of Trustees.

Jennifer Mangantulao Macagba

INHERITANCE: *A SESTINA*

Mother, there is a country
where I inherited the moon's face
and sunken nose that cradle tears
of unspoken words.
There, you loved the caribou yawns
and the ocean's murmur of distance.

But you followed the awe of distance,
riding away from a brown country,
on the waves of ocean's yawn.
Placing faith in the memory of faces,
you wrote letters and only the words
bowed to your family's tears.

When I was small, your silent tears
condemned the distance
but I had to ask: "Speak the words
of a dream country."
"Trace my face with your face
until I begin to yawn."

In my dreams, I visited the red morning yawns
claiming my inheritance of fiercely hidden tears
and an ever-smiling face.
And from my window, I saw in the distance
of dawn, the gentle stirring of a country
and I spoke a language I knew no words.

For I have inherited recovery's words,
mouthing over and over the dying day's yawn.
I have inherited dirty knees of squatting country
men and market women tears
who see Mother Mary in the distance.
I have inherited the sun on my face.

One day I will own the lines on your face,
a sketched apology no word
could capture. One day the distance
between mother and daughter, the yawns
of fatigue will be my burden. One day, your tears
will mark my way back to a country.

Inang Bayan[1], I will come to write the island *luha*[2]
and cigarette *hikab*[3], embracing the cold distance,
madly tracing the impression of my mother's face with my words.

THE LIGHTS OF LUZON

There are nights
in the hut of my conception
when I wrap myself in
banana leaves, mosquito feasts,
red mornings and carabao yawns –
listening to my parents whisper again.

Father played chess,
played hooky,
at the air force base,
where men
took brown knights with white bishops.
One night,
Father got sick of losing.

1. Motherland, mother country   *2. tear*   *3. yawn*

Seeking comfort in Mother's speak easy eyes,
he looked through the linen window
where muted light
fell upon a face
too beautiful to be covered
by the dirt of his country.

Hearing the ocean's tender cadence
it made a man wish never to leave
but he had made their decision – sending
Mother to gather the remaining
Lights of Luzon
into her threadbare bag.

Jennifer Mangantulao Macagba received her B.A. in English Language and Literature from the University of Chicago, and her M.A. in Literature with a specialization in World Literature and Comparative Studies from Northwestern University. She recently spent a year at the University of the Philippines - Diliman where she studied Philippine poetry under Neil Garcia and Gemino Abad. Her work has been featured in *Maganda Magazine*, *Today's Chicago Woman Magazine*, *Kitchen Poems*, and *Aubade Literary Magazine*.

Against the Winter Sky:
The Figurative Use of Winter
in Philippine and Philippine American Poetry

*B*efore delving into a thematic treatment of nostalgia in Philippine poetry written in English, one must first address the historical stimulus of this emotional condition—namely, departure. Beginning in 1905, the first wave of Filipino immigrants was a small group of *pensionados* who were awarded scholarships to be (re)educated in the American system. But in addition to formal "training" came the Filipinos' first encounter with a new season. For the immigrant, winter offers a moment of discovery, and for the poet, an occasion for an utterance of bittersweet awe.

M. De Gracia Concepcion, in the poem "Ili-na" (1925), was one of the first *pensionados* to articulate the problematic concept of nostalgia in its duality—from its roots *nostos*, or "return home" and *algos*, which means "pain, longing." One can read nostalgia as both longing to return home and longing returns the home, respectively an ailment and its temporary salve.

> The scenes are different now.
> The voices are not the same he used to hear.
> He is all alone now in the world,
>   for he feels strange himself.
> Seemingly out of place.
> Seemingly miscarried by the current of time.
> He stands to go. He cannot go.
> For the scent of *azucena** at sundown   *white lily*
> brings back to him
> the long-lost ties of long ago.

Contained in one ambitious poem, the reader is introduced to the four emotional movements of reorientation, alienation, a wistful gesture towards return, and finally, memory's ability to recreate a spiritual landscape of the Philippines and therefore momentarily return the beloved home. In this paper, I will attempt to isolate these four movements that structure the progression of Filipino poems I have chosen. In addition, all of these poems employ the figurative notion of winter in their attempts to enable and disable aspects of the persona's survival in the foreign land of "the States." In these poems, the background of winter supplies the Filipino creative expression a condition of solitude, decay, and survival.

THE REORIENTATION OF "ORIENTAL"

In the first winter poem, Francisco G. Tonogbanua's "Tranquility" (1932), we see a first attempt to pen "the scenes are different now." Tonogbanua writes,

> A field of snow
> Where grackles hold
> Consultation
> About the cold.

There are two things I find striking in this simple, quiet poem in which winter as a backdrop plays an important figurative role. First, there is a tension between the distinctly "Oriental" style and its Western context. By "oriental," I am referring to the simplistic haiku-like form. Because Tonogbanua wrote this piece in America, the location of the winter backdrop is decidedly Western. Secondly, if one were to extend the metaphor of the black birds as Filipinos, the poet is imagining a condition of "Tranquility" created by the Philippine sense of community even in the most alien of environments where cold can refer to the temperature and alternatively, the lack of human sympathy. Exchanging Tonogbanua's tranquil sense of winter (which does not reappear until some years later) for a more problematic winter backdrop, one encounters another representation of the immigrant condition and the figurative condition of winter in Carlos Bulosan's "A Child Dying in a Tenement," (1942). Bulosan writes,

> Dear child, you are among the first to know
>
> the anguish of poverty,
> the cold of winter, the despair of the poor,
> the terror of loneliness.

Because one cannot divorce the poetic Bulosan and the political Bulosan, as activist for migrant rights, the pathos of the poem lies in the destruction of innocence. Here, winter is an unnerving function of this harsh reality and acts as one of the victimizers of the migrant child.

But perhaps the scene is not so different as M. de Gracia Concepcion originally claimed. In Luis Francia's "An Arctic Archipelago" (1985), Francia writes,

> And while from either pole we're
> Half a world and seas away, this
> Might as well be
> An arctic archipelago, where as
> The sun burns the colder it gets.
>
> Where the summer winds are winter's breath
> Making people shiver in heat:
> Everywhere the dark chill of poverty.

Though written more than 40 years apart, in Francia and Bulosan's poems we see a striking similarity or, as Viray elaborates," a candle lit at both ends" (Viray 48). Both speak about poverty and utilize winter as their backdrop, but a key difference between the poems is one of figurative ownership. In Francia's poem, winter is claimed by the Filipino as a representation of his native experience; in Bulosan's, winter as a victimizer claims the Filipino who has been duped by promises of a better life. Here we see the tragic poignancy of the early Filipino migration as Bulosan puts it, "Those who went away never succeeded in escaping from themselves" (Feria 409).

ALIENATION AND THE FRAGMENTED TRAVELER

*H*aving established the potentiality of the winter scenery as backdrop of the immigrant's alienation, a question arises: how does one rectify the homeland as both forever present and forever distant? In Amador T. Daguio's "Bloom of Waters Call" (1954) and Antonio P.G. Manuud's "On the Baltica's Leaving for a Northern Port" (1962), one way to attempt to heal the severed immigrant self is through memory and nostalgia.

In the poems of Daguio and Manuud, we see similar instances of nautical departure and more of an attempt at concrete imagery and metaphorical winter. Daguio writes,

> Though the green isles called back,
> Strange was the wake of my vessel,
> In the night ice of this straight land
> White ferns became my fingers.
>
> My blood whispered; Wanderer, return
> To yellow green aches of rice fields.
> That is why in the dark, my heart
> Finding no home, silence is bitter
> knowledge.

In the poem, the conflict between the persona's internal longing ("green isles called back") and the external reality ("silence is bitter knowledge") is a common theme of homesickness—a romantic and youth nostalgia. What interests me is the way Daguio complicates and enriches the visual details of winter as metaphor, as in "White ferns became my fingers." Frostbite literally disables the persona's ability to write but more importantly, it is a gesture of winter's subversion of life with decay. Green is traditionally the color of nature, and by extension the persona aligns "the green isles" to his natural homeland. In contrast, that which was green and alive has now been covered with frost, signaling and enabling the ferns' decay.

Continuing to trudge through the undercurrents of the transitory persona and his lack of anchorage is the poem "On the Baltica's Leaving for a Northern Port" (1962) by Manuud. Manuud writes,

> Here, though, a colder water once or twice
> May buck a ramming keel—and so let fly
> Splinters of nevermore uniting ice.
>
> And, hearing the rasp of breaking ice, you catch
> A glimpse of love, fragmented, the horror drenched
> With this: the silent twilight of your will.

In Manuud's work we obtain a new image of winter's ice. Here, the "splinters of nevermore uniting ice" can be read as a metaphor for the fragmented traveler. In addition, ice symbolizes the traveler's nostalgic longing for continuity. Manuud's last line implicate that the persona's volition for travel ("the silent twilight of your will") has also determined his fragmentation and horror.

Though Daguio and Manuud did much to deepen winter's metaphor, their description is rooted in the sentimentality of departure. With the emergence of modern poetry, specifically free verse, we see the combination of a less subjective language and the tragic sense of exile. In Donel Pacis's "Photographs of an Exile" (1977) and Ma. Fatima V. Lim-Wilson's "Luzviminda, or Filipinos Make Such Good Maids" (1995), we encounter two specific forms of Filipino exile—the *manongs* and the migrant domestic helper.

In "Luzviminda, or Filipinos Make Such Good Maids," Lim-Wilson writes,

> Tomorrow, they will laugh,
> Building a snowman whose coals
> Are my eyes. Each snowflake I catch
> Burns my tongue, burns away the words
> To the prayer for warding off
> The evil eye's blueness. In vain,
> I try to make angels in the melting

> Snow but my wingless angel waits
> Where I left her at the Customs,
> Clutching a passport long expired.
>
> My thinning shadow
> Crosses the snow bridge of burning
> Coals, walking on bare feet home.

In Luzviminda," a layering of winter images invokes the gathering quality of snow upon snow. But in this poem, each layer of snow is an injury: from dismemberment ("Building a snowman whose coals / Are my eyes,") to wordlessness ("Each snowflake burns away the words,") and finally, complete futility ("angels in the melting snow.") For the migrant domestic helper, to return home is not an option, and to hope, a dangerous exercise.

In Pacis's "Photographs of an Exile," we have a poem about the death of an exiled *manong* and its effects on the persona, here the photographer/nephew. Pacis writes,

> After seventy three years of America
> After seventy three years of Greyhound rides
> Grand Hotels, horses, and nostalgia
>
> He simply died of so many dreams
> That should have been left alone
> By adventurers of his kind. The year
> Before, I said: You can go home again.
> But he chose to die an exile
> Dying in a hospital in winter.
> The week before his death, I began
> To take photographs of him.
> I wrote nothing more about the funeral
> Nor mentioned anything about his grave
> That lies somewhere beside the field
> Of barren trees and winter frost.
>
> Nothing of the cold silent grave of knowing him
> Alive and living in a foreign land.

Because "Photographs of an Exile" is told from the perspective of the nephew, the nostalgia of the *manong* is one generation removed. But more importantly, it is not nostalgia that is the root of the poem but instead, the human condition of grappling with death. Here, winter interacts with both the living Manong and the dead Manong; first, the "invisible fire/ Against the winter sky" speaks the manong's immobility of Filipino pride that burns against his wintry environment. And secondly, as the manong succumbs to death, the winter grave is the location of the manong's permanent state of exile.

In the previous poems, nostalgia functions as an emotional condition that disables the persona. Like Lot's wife in the Bible, nostalgia is a paralysis that runs contrary to the progression that the immigrant seeks. Here, we come to the tentative conclusion: Nostalgia in the traditional way of "longing to return home" comes to an early conclusion that "You can never go home." But as we explore nostalgia's contrapuntal meaning ("longing returns the home"), we find an affirmation of survival and more specifically, an affirmation of writing as an act of survival.

MAPPING A SPIRITUAL LANDSCAPE

Carlos Angeles' "Washington D.C." (1959, 1989) and Manual Viray's "A Winter Walk" (1964) are united through the themes of survival and the figurative use of winter's penetrating chill. In both Angeles and Viray, we see the double meaning of exile, from Latin *ex-salire* which means "to leap outside." In the previous poems, we have seen exile as suffering in banishment, but in Angeles and Viray, exile also means springing into new life. Angeles' writes,

> The hour was arctic, anonymous and gray.
>
> I stood hatless in the cheerless dawn
> Fingering February's frost, its slow
> Fever waltzing through my marrow,
> Its chill piercing my scalded eyes.

> Still I rolled a fist of snow into a ball of ice
> To numb a punishing numbing in my hand.
> What was I to prove in this foreign land?
>
> ...And I,
> Tropic-born, a stranger on these dark shores, felt
> The Alps in my hand crumble and melt.

In "Washington D.C.," the persona stands defiantly "hatless" against winter's "punishing numbing." Although defiant, Angeles's syntax evokes the sense of touch to combat winter's chill. If sensuality is defined by the gratification of the senses, then Angeles's sensuality reaffirms life, and moves the persona to utter the question, "What was I to prove in this foreign land?" Not since "Tranquility" have we seen a persona that replaces longing with belonging—the explicit assertion of identity. Similarly, in "A Winter Walk," Viray ends with the affirmation of enduring life as he writes:

> In this land, winters have always defined
> And always will
> The cold darkness
> In which all the naked and the bundled
> Live even as the evergreens, the leaves
> Move, enduring, stiff, perpetual.

In the nineties, not only do the quantity of winter poems increase but winter's metaphorical power is fully realized, asserting an ease with the subject—a surefootedness with the icy condition. Characteristic of modern poetry, we see a more self-conscious nostalgia as seen in mock letter writing of Fernando Arable's "Letter to the Phillippines" (1975) and Ma. Luisa B. Aguilar Cariño's "Postcard From Persephone" (1994). If one thinks of the pen as a tool that has the power to evoke memory, the pen also has the power to enable the author to return home, as seen in Ma. Fatima Lim Wilson's two poems "Bride of Okura" (1995) and "A Sestina Written in a Cold Land, or There is No Word for Snow in My Language" (1995). From the latter, Lim-Wilson writes,

As the cold enters the house
In the shape of his family ghosts,
I coax myself to sleep. In my mind,
I am making my own trek, a pilgrim
Surefooted in the snow, seeing,
With closed eyes, in all this whiteness:
My son laughing as he calls out
The names of tufted birds, orchids
And thick wasted trees in the language
I have taught him as he leads me,
Running, all the way home.   ·

Here, winter reflects the emotional coldness and alienation of the mother-in-law ("My mother-in-law warms herself / With a single sylla-bled chant,") her inability to communicate, ("Failing to read / the calligraphy of my future,") and an unfamiliarity with Japanese traditions ("where naked men meditate / While immersed in freezing waters.") The poem ends with the persona in a dream state, imaging "my own trek, a pilgrim / Surefooted in the snow, seeing, / With closed eyes, in all this whiteness: / My son laughing as he calls out / in the language / I have taught him as he leads me, / Running, all the way home." The persona's departure from Japan is an illusion but, more importantly, it is language and dreams that mark the persona's repatriation. Regarding Lim Wilson's poem "A Sestina Written in a Cold Land, or There is No Word for Snow in My Language,"

Prettiest phrases axe the air, leaving sapping wounds.
I always slip away, barebacked, on the fish of my tongue.
How I lie, blankfaced as the pages of a dull book.
Swearing on my father's grave, invoking a virgin saint,
I rattle hollow as my ancestors' dried bones,
Echoing back the silent stretches of snow.

In Lim-Wilson's poem, we see that childhood and religious memory is the "accent [of] an alien tongue / speaking" (Santos) and in both her poems, she reinforces language's ability to return the persona to the spiritual landscape of home. For if we were to return to "Photographs of an Exile," the photographs serve as the nephew's letter to the States, and in the process, disables and enables his pain. And finally, in our first winter poem "Tranquility" where we begun the "consultation / about the cold" we are reminded that the immigrant's understanding of a new environment is all the more strengthened by language and conversation. For the immigrant poet, poetry is first made by distance and then remade by language.

In conclusion, the poems that I have chosen reveal that the inability to return home is both a personal tragedy and an enabling force. Nostalgia reinforces the poet's relationship to his past, his home, and more importantly, to his craft. The reason for writing is an attempt to bridge where the immigrant finds himself in the present and where imagination is anchored, usually in the past. More simply, the creative spirit of the immigrant poet is always in transit between the present and the past, respectively the foreign country and the homeland. It is the act of writing that wrestles for one brief moment with the creative spirit in hopes to be born by it, or as Cirilo Bautista wrote in his winter poem "The Archipelago" (1970):

> As the snow
> Flattening the earth now,
> Now I am borne by it,
> Has a single profile.

❧

Al Robles

MANONG GALLO

had a vision when he was only ten years old.
Told his great grandmother what he saw.
She thought her grandson was a little crazy

> "The woman in the sky
> said I was the son of the forest.
> Take care of the trees, rocks, animals,
> insects, grass, rivers, mountains.
> They belong to you; they are your family."

When Manong Gallo was eighteen years old,
he climbed the tallest coconut tree to the moon.
When he looked down, he saw the great pacific ocean.
He said, "*Dagat* [ocean] you think you big and wide?
> But you wait! Someday I am going to cross you.
> And I will see the other side of your face."

JAZZ OF MY YOUTH

i remember jazz of my youth
in the streets of fillmore
crossing over to cousin jimbo's bop city
where the green between his dark ebony fingers
flapped in the cool post street wind
take the A train & slide all the way down
listening to sounds close to the ground
fillmore street bound
jazz comin' 'round
conga tight skins crack
snapping
all day & all morn'
all night session
how high the moon
laying down in the back room
horns blowing to stars fell on alabama
as the night fog squeezed in
wailing sounds echoed in the air
the streets sparkled like stars
all the things you are
jazz of my youth
cruising over to soulsville
stepping over cords
guitar strings cutting loose on tenderly
ten-cent squeezes

jazz of my youth
jacks on sutter
jackson's nook
step back and be cool
head to the back room
thick smoke curling round
a brown pilipino man

blowin' it's almost like falling in love
hunched over a piano
a gray sharkskin overcoat
dark shades
brown fingers runnin' up & down
the ivory keys
dark black hair gleams
with three flowers
charlie abing
the jazz man from stockton
blowing sax & piano
what a rare mood i'm in
it's almost like falling in love
jazz of my youth
runnin' the *mo*
the cool streets
talkin' deep & sweet
i remember you...you're the one that
made my dreams come true...

A Poem About Philip Vera Cruz*

No disheveled weathered grass-minds
Lay dead around the rich grower's ground
Who will touch us
Who will cripple us
We will not sit still
New struggles spring up bursting
Flows over the fields
Thunder cannot move us
Let us all go to Delano
Deep in Agbayani Village

*Filipino American labor leader, farm worker, 1904-1994; instrumental in the creation of the United Farm Workers in 1966.

Let the fish swim deeper
Across the fields
Into the mouth of the manongs
On arrival
I saw poets cried down the grapes
Our conversation
Our love of the Pilipino Chicano farmworkers
We still come back to Delano
We still live by our struggle
We still live by our poetry of resistance
In the dark hours across the Delano vineyards
The struggle against the white growers goes on
I know the things of the manongs
I know the lives in deep melancholy dreams
Empty pockets soaked in old
weathered work clothes
Yet their life of struggle belongs to us
I saw manong cardac and manong Willie
And manong Candioand manong LaCuesta
All of them...all of them...
Circling around us
Laying out things of the past
Marks of brown feet
Hidden dreams and memories still fermenting
Whispering overhead shadows darken
The face and chill the heart of poets

TRAVELING NORTH TO VISIT OKASHI

A diary kept hidden from my eyes
Sprouting up all over
Ten thousand diaries can last
A whole lifetime
Mountains stretch up to the sky

Lost in mist and fog
Wandering from place to place
Stories hang at the edge of cliffs
From mountain to mountain
From river to river
Meeting Okashi many years later
Drinking green tea all year round
Nothing more is said
Will I pass by Okashi again
I left everything behind
Even the winter rains cry out
Heavy winds snapped back
Dreams piled up high
Twisting and crawling around jagged rocks
Waiting for the rains to come
Gathering up the past one by one
Sweet cakes and green tea
A diary full of heavy rain
Songs echo loud and clear
Bringing back everything
Reading poems laid out on tatami mats
While Okashi yawns like thunder
Who knows the poems by heart
Only Okashi—a five year old child.
September is only four months away
My spirit burns like autumn
I'll boil water for some tea
Snow country tales are waiting
To be written down
All my poems are old and withered
Weathered in wind, rain and snow
Laid down tea house after tea house
With del norte redwoods and river rocks
Learning how to sit for tea can bring
Okashi and me together

I'd left my poems deep in the woods
Slipping downhill all the way
Old snow and rain poems
Following the northern river
All the way back home
Waiting to see Okashi
Crossing over six rivers
The dark nights grow longer
Sakurai cries out in the rains
Worn-out wooden getas tilt
My mind far back
How far can a wandering mind travel
No one really knows or cares
When you sit down for tea
Everything stops moving
Even the mind stands still
Nothing more to it than that
Sakurai's belly is full of green tea
His mind is free as the wind
Nothing can hold him down
We traveled south to Big Sur
Crossing over the ice-cold river
Gathering twigs and branches
The roaring sound of the river
Kept our minds going
Three of us sitting near a riverbank
Sakurai and Kunio piled up stones
Bending down to fill a pot with rice
Scooping up hot steaming rice
Slurping up buckwheat noodles
Konnyaku leapt between heaven and earth
Echoing sweet Okashi tales of the past
Sweeping up river poems
Mushashi's laughter cuts through wind and rain
A long tradition of koans and mondos

Recorded in mountains and rivers
Musashi knew Okashi's heart and mind
Like a tea bowl
Life in the Konnyaku days was crazy
Drinking tea all day and night
Writing poems and eating rice
Is there more to life than that
Dreams speak louder than words
Heading north to visit Okashi.

Al Robles was born in San Francisco, California, into a large family of twelve. He has lived practically his whole life in the Fillmore area. A poet, he has taught in schools and prisons.

Since the early 1970s, he has been a member of the Kearny Street Workshop. As a poet-oral historian for the San Francisco Art Commission under the CETA program, Al Robles has worked closely with the manongs collecting their histories and stories in Manilatown.

Enriqueta Cartagena Mayuga

ONCE A WINSOME FILIPINO LASS

A magnum, an acid, a lyric,
A scalpel, a pipe bomb, a chant
— my life, a commingling of all,
Missiles and litanies,
Missals and trajectories —
        only you can tell
        from these array —
        what I have become.

Possessed by contrition,
        I veer to the Deity while
Mammon wrestles
        with this divine intrusion,
I have come a long way —
        transfused by the laser beam
            of disarray —
        caught in the nexus
            of dueling powers.

Sequins and ribbons
            are my beginnings,
        sheltered by the parasols of the earth,
There I blossomed
            in the bungalows of the old,
        shaded by the protective, tropical palms.

At the crossroads of my life
    tattoos and chains
        have usurped my innocuous throne,
    raw wounds and harsh keloid
        have emerged from the carousels
           of my voluminous rage.
I am a brazen reminder
    of a contentious path—
    A living carnival of fire,
    A continuous rush of flash floods,
        of passions—belligerent
        and for a time, unanswerable to no one.

In the mud hut of my domain,
    my inner voice whimpers and whispers,
        low and clear—
    my murmuring soul
        ponders:
How come this pagan end
    to a sweet and wholesome girl—
        one time a
           winsome Filipino lass.

CARLOS BULOSAN* LIVES IN ME

From the carcass of your youth,
    from your doomed fairy tale,
        ashes of your exploits
           ignite and awaken me
           encroaching my comforts,
You haunt our plastic lives
    permeate our generic planes,

*Pioneer Filipino American writer, 1913-1956. Author of "America Is In the Heart" (1946).

long after you are gone
from the coarse you set afire
to spur our timid lives.

I feel your seething rage,
punctuating the social milieu
which you were unable to escape,
your furrowed soul, half famished
floundered in the survival game
—in your new found land.

You pried the nooks and ghettos of America,
naked and miscast
in the gamblers den
of forgotten men
and ill-fated women.
The railway transient that you were
in the tumbling boxcars of life
—nowhere to hide.
Dreams ruptured, your spirit ravaged,
longing for the motherland,
for the impoverished barrier of your birth
which you naively exchanged
for the lures of America.
Your dignity all but gone
no vestigial virtues to tout,
Hunger and iniquities succumbed
to the nefarious side of men.

Deprived beyond control,
thwarted at every turn,
Unwanted, unkempt, unemployed
unskilled—but not forever,
The acid from your churning gut
propelled your love of books.

You stood apart from all—
  distinct from your fellow men,
  rovers, unwanted migrants.
Pummeled and brow beaten,
  you rose after each fall,
victims to blood bathe, racism
  and prejudice—
    but unfettered no more.

You foxtrotted at every turn
  your mind enlarged beyond
   the requisites of the Gods,
Somehow, a bread crumb
  would suffice to pacify your appetite
   and snuff the pain
    that has bleached your soul.
Your rhythm was for a tomorrow
  that didn't await you,
You aspired for a decent job,
  a beautiful mate,
  a house, respectability,
   all meant for
    the established citizenry,
You face a society that didn't
  delight in your kind.

One day you're choked
  on your own sweat and phlegm,
Short lived your contused life—
  but too long to bear the smudge
  heaped on the soul of a transplant,
Too much to bear for those
  who never fitted the culture
—for those who are
always on the run.

You were saved—as your time ran out
from this earth,
no more enslavement and hunger
and racism—
and finally at the home of the angels.

In your time, in this earth
in America—
you didn't stand a chance—
you almost did—
Your legacy is the shining light
of faith for me,
I salute you
Carlos Bulosan.

"Once a Winsome Filipino Lass" and "Carlos Bulosan Lives in Me" are
from the author's book: Outspoken and Mute: American Life
(Airleaf Publishing and Bookselling, 2005).

Enriqueta Cartagena Mayuga was born in the Philippines on December 18, 1937. She has a medical degree from the University of Santo Tomas. Her residency and fellowship training was at Harlem Hospital, Rochester General Hospital and at the University of Texas in San Antonio. She is a diplomate in Obstetrics/Gynecology and has been in private medical practice for more than three decades.

She is the author of *Immigrant at Peace – A Woman Physician Reflects* (1997), *Spring, Autumn, Sunset* (Black Forest Press, 2001). Her poems are published in seven different books of anthology in the United States. Her current book, *Outspoken and Muted: American Life*, reflects her contemporary view of life in America culminating in September 11, 2001. She lives with her husband Simeon in Pasco, Washington and has three grown children and three grandchildren. She still has an OB/GYN practice and works as a consultant with a minority health clinic.

Korina M. Jocson

A Lesson from an Elementary Principal

in school
i never use
wooden rulers
for art class
their edges
remind me
of lined scars
on my knuckles
marks
since age five
that insist
to heal
as disfigured
cursive letters
still tremble
sometimes
just to write
my name

PLANE WITH A VIEW

Lights everywhere I look lights orange red yellow lights
Pair of pubescent eyes never danced as wildly as melody
Philippine Airlines descending toward a sea of LA lights
Entire families engulfed by a city unknown to newcomers

July transforms the Pacific Ocean into a mere darkness
Valley mountains in the distance become a fresh mystery
As countless indigo blue reels us toward destination
I gaze upon colors more melancholy than yesterday

We must be near the captain's voice pervades the cabin
Calming the beating of hearts forever silencing dialects
Flashes of my familiar world in laughter games and stories
Diminish in lights signs announcements forms declarations

Somehow somewhere in these lights epitomizes a settlement
A piece of steady terrain to hear the same laughter and stories
Sounds of rain on tin roof voices of elders constant reminders
It is time and everywhere I look lights orange red yellow lights

❧

Korina M. Jocson is a postdoctoral fellow and visiting scholar at Stanford University. Her interests include mixed media literary arts, cultural politics, and literacy education. Her publications, including articles, essays, and poems, have appeared in various scholarly journals and edited books. She is the author of *Youth Poets: Empowering Literacies In/Out of Schools* (forthcoming), and is currently completing her first volume of poetry, *Dahil Means More Than Because.*

Elsa Valmidiano

Overseas Female Worker

I am not allowed to be a woman.
I am not allowed to be a mother
where the world requires me to leave my children,
to work elsewhere,
across the ocean from them,
where money is made,
but not for a better life.

I am not allowed to be a mother,
not allowed to tell my children Aesop's fables before bedtime,
  scold them to eat their vegetables,
  tell them not to take drugs,
  not to have sex before marriage,
  sew their fallen buttons from shirts,
  repair zippers,
  cook warm *pakbet*, *tinola*, *paksiw*, *guisado*
  and laugh with my children at the dinner table and when they
  just come home from school.

I am not allowed to be a wife,
making love to my husband every night,
having sweet conversations before we go to bed
and when we come home from work,
giving each other massages,
bickering with each other,

and then kissing, kissing,
so that we get lost in each other.

I am forced to migrate
where the money is more
on the other side of nowhere.

I am going nowhere,
as I am leaving my children,
     my heart, my love, my soul,
          who are dying, starving,
and I must send money, right away.

And where I go,
will I be able to go home,
     write letters,
          send e-mails,
              make phonecalls,
          shower my children with wonderful presents
          like pearl necklaces, Barbie dolls, Playstations, Nike
          basketball shoes, Ivory soap, and Pantene shampoo?

I worry, my children worry, my husband worries.

Over there, over nowhere,
will they feed me,
clothe me,
pay me,
beat me,
rape me,
torture me,
will they send me home
in a body bag?

I will take on the face of your maid,

your nurse,
your nanny,
your cashier,
your waitress,
your telemarketer,
your topless dancer,
All of these,
Some of these,
One of these
At least,
At least one of these.

I leave,
my children grow up without me,
becoming lawyers,
 doctors,
  club owners,
   engineers,
    drug dealers,
     dope addicts,
      strippers,
       porn stars,
        revolutionaries,
all of them motherless children,
my children,
whom I love
while I cannot be a mother.

Understand, please, there is no money here.

I will be traveling far,
very far,
like a female Ulysses, leaving her Telemachus, and my husband
          Penelope,
will you wait for me,

even for twenty years?

Understand, I will be traveling to
Saudi Arabia,
  Switzerland,
    Austria,
      South Africa,
        Iraq,
          Israel,
            the United States,
           Lebanon
War-torn countries, world-class countries,

And I will return to you
Within a year
Within 50 years
In tears,
Old and haggard
With money
Without money
With gifts
Without gifts
Naked
Clothed
Whole
Dismembered
In a body bag
In a wooden coffin
In a nice dress
All of these,
Some of these,
One of these
At least,
At least one of these.

In the Philippines as of 2006, some one million workers were exported from the country and 75% of all overseas new hires were women, mostly as household help (maids, cooks, nannies). Three coffins per day on the average return to the archipelago bearing the bodies of dead domestic workers, while thousands more are subjected to physical and sexual abuse, slave-like work and living conditions, unpaid wages and 12-16 hour work days. Many are even restricted in food and liquid intake, so that they live in perpetual slow motion starvation and thirst. — from the GABRIELA Network's findings, published 2007, www.gabnet.org

Born in the Philippines, and immigrated to California while an infant, **Elsa Orejudos Valmidiano** is a poet and writer. While holder of a law degree, her passions primarily lie in her literary and humanitarian endeavours. She continues to be an avid supporter of GABRIELA Network while also finding time volunteering at various feminist and pro-choice organizations throughout the Bay Area. She currently resides in Oakland and can be reached at evalmidi@yahoo.com.

Cora Monce

APPRECIATION
FROM AFAR
Part 1

REFLECTIONS OF MOM

There once was a lady
I used to know
She had a baby
You should see her glow

She had six more
It became a chore
For her life was a lore
Having babies was her role

She worked all day
Away from home
Away from her babes
She was all alone

Her babes asked
Mom where are you?
She replied unabashed
Taking care of you

Where are our hugs
And kisses too?
How come we hurt
And can't find you?

Don't worry dears
Wipe away those tears
Mommy was here
All those years

I loved you all
Every one of you
Just from afar
That's all I know

APPRECIATION
FROM AFAR
Part 2

BROKEN MIRROR

There once was a lady
I knew very well
She had a baby
You should see her glow

She had two more
It became her role
For her life at the core
Being a mom, nothing more

She worked all day
From a new home
Away from her babes
They had no choice

Her babes asked
Mom where are you?
She replied unabashed
I am here for you

Where are our hugs?
I come to you
Where are our kisses?
I love you too

Don't worry dears
Wipe away those tears
Mommy is here
All these years

I love you all
Every one of you
I love you from the heart
Nothing can keep us apart

APPRECIATION FROM AFAR
Part 3

MY OWN REFLECTION

There once was a lady
I knew her inside and out
She had a baby
You could see her grow

She had two more
They became her extensions
For her life was their world
Their spirit was her existence

She worked all day
Clearing up the past
Closer to her babes
She was whole at last

Her babes asked
Mom where are you?
She replied unabashed
Turn around—peek-a-boo!

Where are our hugs?
I open my arms
Where are our kisses?
I draw you closer

Don't worry dears
You lived what I lived
We are here for each other
Till eternity

There is no doubt
We love each other
No matter where we are
Our hearts are together

Cora Monce was born in Manila and grew up in Stockton, California. She holds a BS in Biological Sciences and an MBA. She has worked in education, medical, biotech, business, and bioenergy. What brings her most pleasure: being a mom and writing. She is the author of *Daisies for Mom* (Heart House Publications, 2007).

Michele Gutierrez

REFLECTION INTERNAL

I look in the mirror
and imagine the history
inside me
hair black as ink
spilling wounds and scars
onto brown parchment paper skin
inscribed with the stories of memory
eyes with tears churning
oceans walked across by so many
tides rising and falling
crashing upon unfamiliar shores
I look in the mirror
and see the history
inside me
auburn lips quivering
volcanoes ready to erupt
tongues afire with molten lava
spilling forth from deep within
a sunken belly baring stretch marks
spanning the rice terraces of Banaue
to the grape fields of Stockton
through the jungles of Mindanao
I look in the mirror
and witness the history
inside of me
knees of mothers and daughters
callused from kneeling in prayer
scattered across the Diaspora

asking for deliverance
feet tired and worn and aching
blistered and cut from fleeing
bombs built of rhetoric and mortar
devastating spirits and villages and bodies
veins throbbing with blood
of those who've lived and died struggling
each beat a reminder from generations
still yet to be born into liberation
I look in the mirror
and feel the history
inside of me

Michele Gutierrez is a 26-year old Filipina American born and raised in Southern California's Westside Long Beach community. She believes in the power of culture and art as a powerful tool for healing, growth and change for both people and communities. Both her parents were the first in their respective families to immigrate from the Philippines. Michele has been involved in working for community empowerment and social change since high school, working on issues ranging from access to education to reproductive justice. She graduated with degrees in International Development and Asian American Studies at UCLA where she produced and directed the documentary *Broken Promises*, chronicling the lives and of Filipino WWII veterans fighting for equity after being denied recognition and benefits by the United States government. She is currently the grassroots media activism coordinator at the Center for Media Justice. She enjoys reading sci-fi adventures, canine companions and writing random ideas in little notebooks.

Melanie Medalle

LABAN*   *fight, struggle

The black of my
Hair
Drowns willingly into the soft music of
Yours,
As we lie there in the dark
Indistinguishable,
Our bodies interwoven
Like layers and layers
And layers of woven thatch.

Our parts melt.

I arch back like a wave facing west,
                              facing home.

The sun greets me

          and the wave breaks.

                              Unity.

My hand is on my belly.
Already I cradle the child inside:

*Malaya**   *Freedom
      our creation
      our hope
      our greatest protection

This is our reason
And only true intention.
Manapa'y mamatay kaysa sumuko.

I would rather die than yield.

Ang Masa
[the masses]

The land is sweet.

You are the land like I am.

You are the rain that calms.

We are the rain that feeds.

Melanie Medalle was born in San Francisco, California. After traveling on service projects to Kenya and Thailand, attending undergraduate courses in Southeast Asian and African history, dance, and literature, she moved her studies in life and the academe to Hawai'i where she now resides. A political science and women's studies major, she addresses the striking continuities between race, gender, and the environment, in specific contexts of militarism, globalization, and social inequality internationally. In her upcoming masters' work, she plans to continue this research track with emphases in comparative politics and ancient Philippine anthropology. Both her literature and research revolve around the interconnections between all physical, social and spiritual phenomena. She believes, without reserve, in the healing powers of words, food, laughter, music, the relentless beauty of the natural world, and all other things born from love.

Susan T. Layug

BANANA BLOSSOM

Puso, we call you—pendulous heart that bleeds
a dewdrop globe of invincibility that, when caught by mouth
at the precise moment of letting, becomes *Mutya*—
muse and amulet, womanandman pearl that conquers fate,
kapalaran—the transformation secured under the wave of tongue.

Crimson, sinewy as abaca filaments your skin
is dusk and dawn guarding rows upon rows of fingers
—fruits awaiting ripeness inland, while farther
out to sea, the *Habagat* wind wails the *alamat*, myth
of a daughter cursed by her mother to eternally grow
hands of use to others.

I wonder
if Mother,
seeing you now
with your thousands of hands
scrubbing thousands of kitchens
as useful as the fork and knife,
as handy as the urinal,
as functional
as a Leap Pad preschool gadget
as purposeful
as an O-mouthed blow-up doll
I wonder—
Is she beaming?
Or is she cursing
herself, wishing
she had bitten
her tongue, instead?

INTERPRETING INES'S DREAM

Three candlesticks: blue, white, yellow waiting to be lit.

> They are the kerosene wicks of your days, improvised
> from your caftan hemp of the occupation years. Raising
> your head and fingers to the smoke-grey bombers, you
> marveled at their maneuvers, their bird-of-prey form.

Your father's stick taught you just so
to read and write the litanies. Tired
of the lighthouse games and betrothal suicide
stories, you lifted your soul
to the Lady of Voyages.

> They are the bamboo torches edging
> the crag shore of your crosshatched tablets —
> the sapling rice stalks you wrote,
> erased too soon by monsoon winds.

Your one-room marriage with
the incandescent city gifted you
with the crib-dead Emmanuel
you swaddled, on the doctor's advice,
like a healthy newborn
on your jeepney ride back home,
avoiding the morgue costs and co-passengers'
suspicions with your stone face

> They are church votives you burned
> your fingers scoured
> from sunrise laundry to sunset weaving
> nets, baskets, lives

At 62, a widow, and on a foreign land,
you still wanted to learn how to read

the Pledge of Allegiance.
Your husband would have you do, too, he—
a guerrilla, whose post-war escapes
yielded victories of other names. The Virgin
has so many names, herself: Mother
of Perpetual Sacrifice, Mirror of Unflinching
Faith, Tower of Eternal Bondage...

They are your candles, suppliant for
redemption, hailing penance for
your departed husband's, son's, father's
omission of your selfhood, childhood,   woman—
They are your wax-bead path to transfiguration.

How apropos now,
when you have evolved to
dream in color,
that you should still raise
your eyes and hands
for your ward-souls'   indulgences!

Handbook

Chapter 1: How to Become

Leave your *hinabi** and lice-picking,   **weaving*
your thatch-roof tales of Maria Makiling. Pick up
patch quilting instead—the velvet soap
operas, patterns; the lush silky lives
of shampoo ads, texture. Stitch
with proudly-Made-in-the-USA threads
your top-of-the-line Prada-y-Gabanna and
your tapestry or rug

is an eloquent
*Chabacano**   **Filipino-Spanish creole*
of stateside
-ness.

CHAPTER 2: HOW TO KEEP

If your criss-cross
view of the world
leads you to a crossfire
abandon immediately
and take shelter
in the thought that you don't have
to trudge the *pilapil* * of leeches, larvae -   **dike*
lording uncles, salacious cousins,
gossip-hungry neighbors who
passed the buckets
when your rubbber-tire-and-plyboard
city condo caught fire,
find solace
in your newfound
singular
self.

CHAPTER 3: HOW TO FULFILL

Take your tongue
to the University of P's and F's
Elongate your o's (or else your nose)
Remember when buying a house
a one-and-a-half bath is always preferable
to one or the common *kasilyas**   **outhouse,*
by the river no more laundry paddle   *toilet*
—it served its purpose—
nor the palm landing

on your little
one's
ass.

CHAPTER 4: HOW TO (UN)MAKE

Dip don't dip your pan-*amerikano* children
in your coffee novenas Saturday nights
are mahjong videoke nights better yet miss
misis miss little mr./ms. gay lola
philippines midwest ilokandia jambalaya
see how easy chachacha to stage
such success you are you
are not you
any longer you
are still you
yoo-hoo
who?

Susan T. Layug has poetry published in *Our Own Voice Literary Ezine* and *Apocalypse 14*. Her personal essays have won first prizes namely, The Don Carlos Palanca Memorial Awards for Literature and The Ray Bradbury Creative Writing Contest. Her work has also been read on Chicago Public Radio. Susan T. Layug lives and writes in Chicago.

Jennifer Almiron

I am She

"*I* want one, I want two. I want to. *Iwanko*."
She was very experimental with words. She loved when a coincidence made a "pun"—when she could match sounds without matching meanings. The Tagalog word "Iwanko" (which meant "I don't know") sounded so much like the English expression "I want to."

I want to eat my favorite book.

Before she could read all the words in her beginner's book collection from the *Disney Animated Reading Series*, she was convinced these colorful pages would taste great—as good as they looked. Her imagination made edible the reds, the sky blues, the happy sunshine in the green trees. She put them all in the bathtub, while her sister was still in it. After cooking the buoyant, brightly colored books, she took to eating, one by one, the pages of the Sorcerer's Apprentice, her favorite one. She already knew the best things in books could be found in mischief.

She was always good at spelling tests. She liked the way words looked on the brown handwriting paper, set between the layers of dotted lines and straight ones. Words looked like the music on the staff but they had different sounds, different meanings.

"S, H, E, L, L"	"shell"
"B, E, L, L"	"bell"
"F, E, L, L"	"fell"
"F, E, L, T"	...felt

Felt. I felt sad. I felt my...dog.

The meanings of words didn't touch her until she had to write them herself, in stories. Montessori School, Primary I: Math, Spelling, Sociology, Science. Her favorite was spelling. It wasn't the actual spelling that challenged her but the arrangement of the words on the line. The task of making them sit the same way, in the same angle, with the same spaces in between each word consumed her with each exercise. She would always use up all the eraser, chaffing the like-newspaper page. The "t's" never stayed straight, and its appearance on the page would always be enclosed in a halo of rubbed-off "t's." Her pencils were sharp. She wondered how she could make erasers longer and less rough.

She began writing stories in large looping cursive about horses and summer houses—all the things she wished she had, all the adventures she had heard of, somewhere. She would write plays that were really fairy tales set into voice-parts. She would make her bunkbed a puppet stage, draping a sheet over the back as the background and the front as a curtain. Her dolls were judiciously cast as characters in fairly tales. The language of imaginary people in their imaginary, but predictable lives, was in her command. There was very little her status as "oldest" kept her from. "Her sister was always an animal in the enchanted forest, she made the best impersonations of the "Big Bad Wolf."

In Catholic school, before she was kicked out and sent back to Montessori, she was in Sister Clementine's class. She wore a uniform, and loved to watch the cursive charts above the blackboard as if they were alive, looping their sound into space like a high-pitched song, vital and lilting. It was another way to shape her words. Everything had to be perfect, like God.

Stand up-Sit down
Share-Repeat after me
Yes! No!

Things were confusing, especially when speaking to and about God. Her mother used to be Catholic, but converted when she met my dad, a preacher's kid from the mountain province. Her mother insisted the nuns were good teachers. Her father relented. They all tried to be more Catholic that year. When she didn't say the right prayers, it was primarily because she didn't really know there were any. She said poems out loud instead, but softly.

> *I shot an arrow in the air,*
> *it fell to earth I know not where.*
> *For who has sight so keen and strong*
> *that it can follow the flight of a song.*

Sister Clementine always caught her poetry. It was unfortunate that her assigned seat was right beside the teacher's, on account of her "A" last name. Her reciting the poems had nothing to do with her conflicts with theology but with her aversion to the repetition of hallowed, hollow words. The poems had music in them and they danced around in circles and circles and circles.

Her last day at St. Paul ended in the Mother Superior's office. After forgetting her lunch money on a "hot lunch" day for the third time in a row, she was told to turn in her tartan skirt before Friday. Her father told her that she wasn't Catholic anyway. She was relieved until Sister Clementine died of a heart attack two days later. *Hail Mary full of grace, the Lord is with thee...*

Things started getting complicated. She began to doubt she was on the right track. She began to question her experiments, her words. She started to favor her violin. Every weekend she went to the city to play with other children with stringed instruments. She enjoyed the wordless company of children who played the music with her. When she played in the orchestra she had the sense that she was both alone and connected, moving in a single wave of sound through the pieces, despite the different voices, registers. In one moment she would be playing with a stillness, a near silence, and in another she was moving through runs, playing as loud as she possibly could.

She didn't deal well with numbers: addition, subtraction, long division. There was always a wrong answer. She hated looking for the single, one, right answer. That would mean the end of possibility, not the beginning of it. The uniting powers in the language of math left her speaking in tongues. A whole class and one answer was the closest thing to blasphemy she ever witnessed. To think there was only one word, one number after all that work. The word problems were the worst, full of number-tricks in word form. She knew math would never be English. Spelling did have tricks of its own, but nothing like the beguiling characters of "sums products and quotients." In college she took Math 5 but not Math 6. Math was too much about continuing, about "carrying it over two places." She didn't like long divisions. Long. Long. Divisions.

After a while, things began to get easier. All she had to do was change! She tried to reinvent herself to be more open-minded. She joined team sports. "Play by the rules, the rules of the game. You can do better than that. Stretch, pass!" However, the more things changed, the more they began to shape her to be like everybody else. While at Hackley, the prep school in Westchester, New York, she had to remain pure within herself, even if that meant being alone. She didn't wear catalogue clothes, no flannel. She was the teacher's pet. The coach's dream: she knew her own speed, and could use it. College coaches sold their schools to her; she knew she was wanted—but didn't know what she wanted. College noticed she was not white and not always— studious. Still, she was a prep-school and above-average kid.

She was used to testing the rules in high school. She challenged the dress code by wearing pants on a cold day—though skirts were required in late March. She received detention. Two hours of stuffing pledge letters to Hackley alums. In towns like Westport and Montecito, she put the labels on backwards.

She wondered about being different. About how she smelled. Did she smell worse than her Sikh friend, Joti? Worse than the Black girl, and her cocoa buttered hands? She wondered about being herself. She had no idea what traits were particular to her Asian self and her middle-school, athletic, musical one. For example, the ESL kids whose fathers were huge corporate sponsors of everything—were not like her. Was she a white girl, deep down inside?

When she left for college, she applied to live in the Asian Culture house, ready to face her difference. That didn't work. She became friends with the Italian guy who moved in next door. He lived in

Massachusetts.

She tried to escape the molding hands of intellectual superiority. But her admission into Amherst College had changed her. She was the only Filipino admitted. In four years. Said the grand but balding Admission Director. She celebrated in wide grins. Not sure what he meant. What she had become was a person she was not sure she knew.

Jennifer Almiron is an English and Music major from Amherst College, currently living in Los Angeles. She was born in Brooklyn, New York, in March, the month her father and mother first saw snow.

Charity Ramilo

BROK-E (N) ENG;LISH

Broken English
Replay
Same old thing
History repeats itself
Broken language
Barrier to cultural consciousness
Brother
Who calls me Miss Charity
Wanting better opportunity
Yes, ma' am, I mean miss
Smiles
Accent or not
He speaks eloquently
Telling his story
My brother's, sister's, family's, their culture, our culture
"your broken English will get you far"
piercing my ears as my heart bleeds through my eyes
born here
my tongue still feels broken
going home to the Philippines
my tongue feels broken
when you speak of
my brother's supposed broken tongue
that's my *tatay*, my *inay*, my *lolo*, and my *lola*
you insult
I wait to not let
My anger get the best of me
No, I must speak

I must say
To you, means nothing
But to me and our world of culture
Means everything
I speak in hopes to open your mind
To think before you speak
To encourage
And not be discouraged
Or so disheartened
To positively reinforce myself
I must fight with my words
Of courage
Limited tongue
Your limited mind
To do something about it
Instead of whine and complain
Use my ancestors' wisdom
That are mere whispers in your ears
As you deny truth
Diamond tongue to cut through your ears

I must break your glass ears
Language barrier
Justifies
Try one more time
To make it the last time
I will not do anything
Broken silence
Silence is broken
Educate
A soul that is broke(n)
Must be put back together
Must be refilled
Education
To that sound replay

'Til you listen to the message
To that sound replay
Till you listen to the message
To that sound replay
'Til you listen to the message
Till you understand

Born in San Francisco, ***Charity Ramilo*** is an artist as well as a community activist through the power of spoken word, music, art, and dance. Currently, she teaches at the Filipino Education Center Galing Bata Program in San Francisco. She was co-editor of the Yellow Journal, an Asian American Studies Publication at SFSU. She has been featured at various community gatherings including Mango Mic, Rizal Day, Locus, and Bindlestiff Studio. She is pursuing a Music Credential and a Masters in Education with Special Interest/Concentration in Filipino/Tagalog Bilingual Education.

Vanessa Verdadero Kenyon

ODE TO ROSE AND THORN

Did not the thorn betray your protection
To shield your petals of harsher prey
To warn such suiters of the need for attention to
detail, as pricks to flesh produce beads of sanguin
gems on fingertips?
Did not your image amplify the very contrast
to a closer look at life's odd array of
imagination—conceptualized play of photographic
optimism—all to convey your delicate nature of
how thorns of protection can pierce soft
leafy petal still in bud; to captivate the notion of
unexpectancy—*as you accompany many on journeys of
poetry.*

ORISHAS

I place before you my offerings as to calm waves of confusion
Mimicking purposes of what may or may not be truth
Eleqqua, I would like to take your soulful medicine and
spread it across the wounded and weak
Taewo-Kainde, guide me to your hacienda and there we will
recollect the very shells I lay out

16 Paths, each one a child to which there are equal amounts of
mother and father, female and male all derived from
Obatala, creator of mankind

Sometimes I want to live like *Ogun,* and protect as did the
Maferefun warriors
Or better yet, let our most wishful and compassionate orisha
—*Oya,* bless those parents and return to them their dying
children—
let the rains carry them together

As our hearts beat, let the drumming magnify into fire, into
La palma grande, into thunder, into war spelling out warnings
Eshango, as you stand on ashes of conquest I too would
Barter gifts of prophecy for music and dancing all because
that is your calling, a reflection of my own

Yemaya united with *Ogun,* you are powerful though you live
in solitude upon lagoons of hidden things between woods of
drenched struggles all to be carved into orisha on a string
sold for $1.00 at the markets.
Yes, your value is more than the art and many may never learn
you—
your meaning

Beauty Queen

Wrinkles lace her face, body, hands and soul.
Scars beautify her existence.
She is 8 decades of history,
Not yet learned to many;
A relic for religion she has...
Fought the devil in her questions of
Why, how, who and for how long does this story live?
She is breakfast,
Lunch,
And Dinner,
Wrestled out from struggle;
Life giver,
Guardian angle compressed into
One four-foot-eleven beauty queen never given a crown—
Whose eyes look out like glazed almonds.
Her smell is familiar, whole and dated—
Dated back to the very first time she entered the room,
With her high cheek bones and blackened hair—now grey,
Whose soul cannot be extinguished with any amount of hate or
Rage set before her.

Ask her of her scars,
The one across her face from childhood tomboyishness
Or the iron, or her calloused feet from
Those long standing days,
And her arthritis in hands and fingertips;
From hand washed clothes and sun fresh laundry.
Let her show you her garden-full of exotic veggies;
Then ask her how she fed them with afternoon conversations,
Accompanied with daily visit as she smoked her tobacco;
As she read and reread all the books she found
on the living room shelves.

Ask her to explain how she knows just how much salt,
Or onion,
Or water to put into a pot of life.
Please ask her before she can no longer say,
"*Anak*,* you've never asked me, showed interest or watched me,"
For her history of history is your way home.
It is your legacy.

*child

DEDICATION:
TO MY MOTHER['S] LAND

Strong-willed, loved and respected is the person who has most changed my life. Deprived as a child of many material things, yet culture, custom and sense of self were her riches. My mother taught me virtues, which to this day I hold strong. She has given me life. In this labyrinth of a world, she has given me the path to follow and has directed me to the staircases I must climb. She is my silver lining in all the clouds after the heaviest rains have fallen. She is like an oyster that tries to avoid the troublesome sand yet can still produce a pearl from a single grain of hardship.

Vanessa Verdadero Kenyon, is a first generation and dual heritage Filipino American raised in Vallejo by a single immigrant mother. She is also a first generation college graduate with a BA in Psychology and a BA in American Multicultural Studies from Sonoma State University. Writing, based on some element of struggle, be it life, ideals, or the rediscovery of self, has always served as an outlet for her personal expression.

Ernesto V. Epistola

FOR ANNA

Did I ever tell you
That I came from a country
Where there are many old stone churches
With towers for huge bells?

When I was a boy
I climbed the creaking wooden steps
Up many a belfry
Through the smell of bats
Mingling with the aromas of fiestas
Interspersed with the odors of baptisms
And of funerals
To the platform where I could touch
The bells.

With a knife I would carve my name
On the aged patina into the glitter
Of the biggest and most ancient
Of the ancient bells.

There were always
A few other names already there
With dates of a few hundred years
And initials of lovers long gone.

Someday I shall go back
To that one bell
Where I had carved my name.

An old man told me once
That the bell would call out your name
If you carved it on the right place
And I thought I heard it call mine
At Angelus time when I was young.

And I shall add yours to mine.

Quietly we shall wait to hear
The bell call our names together
Over the lakes and the valleys.

When it does
I shall turn to you
And say
    See, it really works.

And you would smile.

A retired professional musician, music educator and photographer, **Ernesto V. Epistola** earned his undergraduate degree in music—cello performance, and his BA in English Literature at the University of the Philippines. As well, he has a Master's degree from the School of Music at Yale University.

A Palanca Literary Award winner for one of his plays, he is now working on the second printing of his biography of the eminent Filipino composer, Nicanor Abelardo. He is also preparing his fourth book of poetry, a collection of haiku and photographs.

Although his symphony orchestra conducting, his string-orchestra clinics, and adjudicating engagements are now limited, he still performs as a chamber musician and a recitalist. He lives in Sarasota, Florida with his wife Anna Clare, also a retired music educator and a professional flutist.

Lewanda Lim

A Peace Corps Volunteer

She came to a storm-sick island
To the brown folks it seemed
a Hollywood star stepped out of a screen.
Her long, golden hair
the grandmothers touched
At last, a real blond American.

Drank beer with men at the *sari-sari** store.
The barrio buzzed with gossip.
Had to learn island ways
Spoke their tongue, ate their food
Lived in a thin thatched hut and
got attached to the people
who sang songs of woe and glee
told tales of hard toil.
The toll of feudal ties and colonial yokes
made history clearer to her now.

Skirting bureaucrats and shady dealers,
she set up a health clinic
Helped the women understand
fate can be in their hands.
She did more but wondered
was it better for her kind
to stay away instead?

The men wanted to marry her.
They dream of coming to America.

*small variety store

A Bus Ride on the Avenue of the Americas

The young man comes up the bus
Sits on the blue connected seats
Meant for the old and frail
His old gray suit reluctantly accommodates him.

His cheap dark glasses unable to hide
a jocund self, revealing itself
in the warm explosions of a Caribbean accent
as he tries to connect with the jaded driver

He lives in the Bronx, he says
A hundred bucks rent a week.
Not bad. Good landlord.
But he's afraid to walk the streets
Was in the Marines
lived in a ship
a town of five thousand men.
Good old days. Misses them.

Now he wants to eat in a restaurant
owned by his hero—de Niro.
An old lady shouts her Brooklyn
"It's in the Tribeca—know what it means?
It's the triangle below Canal."
She tells him how to get there.

A graying man in front of me
looks around
eyes me with a hint of recognition
He whistles a native tune
I wanted to tap him on the shoulder,
greet him in our language.
But something held me back.

I knew then
a part of me
has turned to jade.

SUMMER

Prickly pine greens
Supple knives of willows
Proud asterisks of spruce
Clumps of maples and oaks
The unruly verdancy of the Adirondacks
surrounds me as I glide
through the high salad days of summer
and I am marinated,
soaked to the edge of drunkenness
as the season's pungencies
invade my senses.

Always, as I watch the unfolding
of summer
my eyes grow green
at nature's profligate display
 a   peacock flaunting
his spectral spectacle—
shimmering, flapping, swaying, sitting.

This is my summer secret
this delicate intoxication I reserve and savor
For this season is short, too short
for my tropical remembering
before that icy whiteness
impales me again.

SECOND GENERATION

For my children
I cook rice everyday
and salted baby shrimps
on open-window days.

I steeped their tongues
in a basket of native sounds.
On their young brown heads
I painted my childhood.
Tropical lushness, succulent papayas
pink guavas, orange mangoes
red bananas, torrential rains
choral frogs, ponderous carabaos
paradise farms, nature spirits
and malevolent witches.

But now, sharp lights
are blurring my ethereal sketches
Their tongues stumble through
half-remembered phrases.

So I cook rice and salted baby shrimps
They will not taste forgetting.

SMALL GESTURES

Call me when you're near the edge.
Come to my house and
I will steam rice cakes for you.
They are white and sweet.

I will make tea;
its amber simplicity
I will pour
into cups without handles.

We will sit together
warm our fingers around
golden phoenixes, birds
waiting on porcelain walls.

We will sit still like Buddha
as jasmine vapors rise
to collect broken promises
and consign them
to the winds.

Lewanda Lim is a visual artist working in different mediums
and genres. She is known for her historical and political paintings, depictions of Philippine market scenes and unique fabric
collages. She started writing poetry in her late forties and has
been published in two anthologies: *Going Home to a Landscape,
Writings by Filipinas*, edited by Marianne Villanueva and Virginia Cerino and *From the Listening Place* edited by Margaret
Blanchard. She lives with her husband, Antonio, in Gahanna,
Ohio. They have two grown children and a granddaughter, all
living in the Boston area.

Shirley B. Dimapilis

Fancy Wind Chimes

Waving in the air
They twist and turn
From the threads of tiny strings
A tinkle of tiny music it brings
With a repertoire of sounds
Amid decibels attuned abound
To tiny tympanic wave lengths
Gently shaking with the breeeze
On flights of fancy in a special space
After catching light of the torrid sun
Even any slight breeze is fun
To flights of birds and dances in the wind
Hear the songs and beating of the metal bells
A chorus of cylinders that call and swell
As we enjoy the cool air and breeze
Wind chimes ever ready to blow with ease

Shirley Beltran Dimapilis is an author who writes about the Filipino American immigrant experience in California. She is a retired public school teacher who continues to sit in several San Franicsco commissions and boards.

Luis Cabalquinto

BIRD BRAIN

A speckled pigeon sails down like a kite
from a maple branch every afternoon

and waddles behind me to the door
when I come home about the same hour.

I think it's one from the big flock
I fed rice grains all winter long out front

when, for weeks, snow stayed on the ground.
I don't feed the birds as often now

and most of the flock are long gone.
Why not this speckled oddball one?

Here's what I believe: it hears and marches
to snappy songs my heart's been whistling.

Hum

With all the lights out, the house
takes on the color of buffalo fur.
It has been very quiet, the others
gone out to a party or some other
unreported nightly business.

Close your eyes: listen to the low whirr
of the midnight New York City outside—
a hum that seems to come from
beyond the reach of the farthest discovered
planet, like coded messages from the outer edge.

You feel weightless in the wooly dimness,
buoyed in space by the cool clarity of your thoughts.
It's like being on stage for an opening season—
this self-knowing intoxication that, in its excess,
admits to dark undertones—from being human-born,
from having too often badly lived.

But taut moments like these grow impatient
with negations and encourage the mind to indulge
in the night's exuberant languages.
And as you pick and choose, the body, too,
inebriates itself into the most intense dialect

Then, mind and body coupled, the self aligns
with the hum of the room that enlarges into
the larger room of the galaxies: like the
orchid bud at your window, swollen and opening.
In the whirring dark, the self's full blossoming
is once more providentially approached.

THE DAY AFTER

for Sean Lugano, who died
in the WTC horror of September 11

This morning, outside
my window,
the light is just
right on an oak
branch, leaves
moving
in the wind
just so—

as if
no tower burned
and fell, nor any
human died.

What this
is really saying
though:
it's now upon us,
left to live,
to move on—

with the wind's laughter,
with the kindness of leaves,
with the heart's unflinching light,

every gifted day—
as if they
had not hated us
and you had not
too early died.

❧

Luis Cabalquinto writes poetry, fiction, and non-fiction in three languages: Bikolnon, Tagalog, English. He is the recipient of many writing awards, including the Dylan Thomas Poetry Prize from the New School University, a poetry award from the Academy of American Poets, a Lifetime Writing Award from the Arejola Foundation of Naga City, Philippines, and a writing fellowship from the New York Foundation for the Arts. Last year, he received the Gawad Balagtas award from the Writers' Union of the Philippines.

Cabalquinto has published five poetry collections, including *Bridgeable Shores* (Kaya Press, New York) and *Moon Over Magarao* (Univ. of the Philippines Press, Quezon City). *Manhattan Mahal*, his latest poetry book, is coming out this year from the University of the Philippines Press. He lives in New York City and in his birhplace in Magarao, Philippines.

Edwin A. Lozada

SLEEPLESS IN MANHATTAN

Metro: waiting for the E-Line
John, Jill, José and a few hundred more gather to be transported
then a strange reincarnated transformation
of an overture from Bizet's Carmen dispensed from an electronic
trumpet
mingles with the whispers and silences adrift in the station
someone's attempt to inspire generosity
and charity
from the soon to be
passengers anxious to get to
somewhere
who will soon be masses huddling yearning to breathe free

Walked in to an antique shop once manned
by a Mr. Aggarwal, a gentle man in his late 70's
5 years ago
he had a set of Indian miniatures
exquisite, extravagant brush strokes in gold...
Maybe they still had them
I stepped in, a young man now runs the shop
I ask about the old man fearful of the answer
How is Mr. Aggarwal?
  My grandfather.
  He passsed away in April
From what? I ask
  From no illness
  There was nothing physically wrong with him
  He was rather happy and then
  just stopped breathing one day

At a conference a poet speaks about his father's regret and sorrow
as he moved on to another world
A writer spoke of death closing in on a young man entrenched in war
Dead ancestors are remembered, jokingly
but full of tenderness

Passed by the cemetery of St. Paul
old tombstones
form the landscape of its garden
Visitors sit on benches around the stones
whose engraved names that once marked
the graves
have eroded like the memory of those who once claimed them
now anonymous
liberated from formalities and labels that dominated them in their
lives
and sometime after
now quietly blend
with the verdant and yellow autumnal
surroundings
Right across,
these silent stones contemplate a site targeted
           more than once
for extinction

A friend I haven't heard from in a while calls on the phone
and tells me about the cold weather in Denver,
how his once colorful garden has become overgrown with weeds
work has distracted him from his passion and that
and that,
          "oh by the way, I wanted to tell you
             my father has passed away."

I cried acrid tears feeling my friend's repressed pain
reminder of my own partially unvoiced anguish

It's November 11, 2006
Sleep does not arrive at my bedside
5 years ago, 1 month ago
over 2700 perished just across the hotel where I am now
I am numb
Pain, incalculable, radiates from the emptiness
that dominates the hallowed grounds
it is but an annexation of the old graveyard just across it
countless good-byes, *I love you, I'm sorry, forgive me, if only...,*
        I miss you,
I need you, I worry about you, take care...
undelivered to their destination
resounding, echoing, reflected in the million pieces of broken glass
and in the agitated earth: grief, tears, pain, futility, desperation
mix and melt in the dark thick air

it should be left alone, perhaps turned into a memorial park
but oh no, too damn valuable a real estate for that purpose

I have this thing about the number 5
It's my special number
born on the 5th, in the fifties
my name has 5 letters and it starts with the 5th letter of the alphabet
and I happen to be in this hotel, #55 on the block

I lie in bed thinking it's November
yes, it was my grandfather's birth month
I have kept his ring with a yellow gemstone
citrine, a healing quartz that brings hope and strength to the bearer
I can't recall the date when he died, but I do remember feeling
dazed as we heard the final verdict in the hospital
suffering ongoing lapses of sadness as a result
of the unwavering finality of the last breath

I do remember that the year he left this earthly dimension
Jonathan, a precious baby, was born into our family

KANSION
in Ilocano

Agtaytayab
Purao
Nga kalapati
Ti rimwar
Diay nabanglo
Nga sabong
Purao ken kiaw
Diay nakaturog
Nga kalachuchi

Agtaytayab
Purao
Nga kalapati
Diay puso na
Agliplipias
Ti kansion
Kolor ti rosas
Ken gumamela
Nga awan pay
Ti nakangeg

Papanam ngay
Billit
Nga naulimek,
Sika
Ti makapagtalna
Diay langit?
Sinno ngay
Ti makangeg
Dagita regalo
Nga rumrumwar
Diay pusum?

CANCIÓN	SONG
volando va	in the midst
la paloma	of flight
blanca	a white dove
que salió	emerged
de la flor	from the perfumed
perfumada	amber and ivory
alba y ámbar	blossom
de la plumeria	of the plumeria
adormecida	lost in slumber
va volando	watch it fly
la paloma	as white as the clouds
blanca	the dove
su corazón desbordado	with a heart
derrama	overflowing
canciones	with song
color de rosas	color of roses
e hibisco	and hibiscus
que todavía no	none yet
se han oído	has heard
¿adónde vas	where do you go
ave callada	bird
y mansa	so quiet and meek
tú	you who can
que apaciguas	appease
el cielo?	the heavens?
¿quién sino tú	who but you
oye	can hear
los obsequios	the gifts
brotando	coming forth
de tu corazón?	from your heart?

Nakadanon
Idiay karayan
Ket inungwanna.
Idi kuan nagpukawen

Didiay karayan
Agkankanta
Napunpunno ti sampaga
Rosal, rosas
Ken gumamela

TEMBLORES SECRETOS

en tu abrazo
cada gota de mi sangre
se transforma en un sol nuevo
tocar tu piel franca y suave
despierta una sed olvidada
del calor carnal deseos nacen
oscuros, ocultos, embriagadores
nuestros, sólo nuestros

manos calladas, atrevidas y aventureras
buscan ensueños y suspiros perdidos
sobre terrenos calurosos y ansiosos
el ritmo ensordecedor de nuestros volcanes
de donde brotan el dulce vino rojo que nos sustenta
ese ritmo, este ritmo que nos rige y que nos llena
te llama, te atrapa y te devora
nos borra el pasado y el futuro ya nada importa

una caricia
un beso

a la faz del río	towards the river
llegó y se acercó	the dove drew near
dejándole un beso	kissed its water and then
y entonces desapareció	disappeared
el río	the river
cantando	singing and flowing
colmado de sampaguitas	with gardenias
gardenias, rosas	jazmine, roses
e hibiscos	and hibiscus

SECRET TREMORS

in your embrace
each drop of my blood
becomes a new sun
touching your frank and smooth skin
awakens a forgotten thirst
from the carnal warmth desires are born
dark, hidden, intoxicating
ours, ours alone

hands, silent, daring and adventurous
search for lost dreams and sighs
over warm and anxious terrains
the deafening rhythm of our volcanoes
from where the sweet red wine that sustains us flow
that rhythm, this rhythm that governs and fills us
summons, entraps and devours you
erases our past and the future no longer matters

a caress
a kiss

rumor de brasas
los secretos se liberan y se revelan
en las fugitivas chispas rojas de crepúsculos estivales
que al azar se aventuran y llamean
por las tinieblas tibias que palpitan
debajo de nuestra piel que se estremece
despertando, despertando danzas nocturnas

ha llegado el diluvio de un perfume primitivo
aniquilando la razón
abriendo un mundo infinito de fantasía reprimida
piel encendida y ciega que te ilumina el camino
del paraíso prohibido que tanto, tanto deseas
y por unos instantes
tu mundo
de antes
se desvancece

murmur of embers
secrets liberated and revealed
in the fugitive red sparks of summer twilights
randomly venturing and becoming ablaze
in the warm darkness that pulsates
under our trembling flesh
awakening, awakening nocturnal dances

the deluge of a primitive perfume has arrived
anihilating reason
opening an infinite world of repressed fantasy
blind and ignited skin illuminating the way
to forbidden paradise that you so much, so much desire
and for a few moments
the world
you know
vanishes

BLUE

He was tired from the torturous and seemingly interminable day—
like every day that he can remember since that cruel morning
light came crashing in like a school of ferocious metallic sharks breaking the fragility of his not yet fully awakened shell protecting his already illusory existence. He was ready to withdraw from the buzzing,
yelling, honking and quivering of the city. He was ready to close his
eyes and dream of the possibility of forgetting the countless instances
of indifference or contempt that slapped his already numb façade.
Ready to tune out everything from that day and from the day before
and the many days before those days and find his way back somehow
to a time when he was far from where now he seems doomed to me-
ander, an unrecognizable specter, only occasionally befriended by a
pigeon, a stray dog or cat.

Perhaps as the debilitated sun folds his billowy, orange-red silk cloak and hides it in a secret corner, as the desirous evening begins to blossom with alluring fragrances and innuendos, and as the quiet expectant moon prepares to make her discrete and graceful entrance, perhaps he will dream and awake to a dream that he once had, or thought he had, in which there was warmth, an occasional trickle of joy invading his countenance and a sense of order and peace. Yes, order. Yes, peace.

In the dream he recalls having had memories inhabited by happy characters. He believes he was one of them. Maybe he will magically open that luminous door that was once revealed to him in a hallucination and pass on to another dream, and never again awake to the predictability of his relentless and infernal daily non-existence. He was ready to escape through the enchantment of sleep.

He serenely crawls into the dusk-filled solace awaiting him under his deep-sapphire blanket and soon feels the familiar instant unconditional warmth it provides. Covers his beleaguered head. Closes his fatigued eyes. Huddles and draws himself to the fetal position. Ready to be reborn.

"Not so cold this evening." He thinks. He drifts.

On California Street, I walk past him: an anonymous, impervious blue mass on the sidewalk against the freshly painted, immaculate white wall of a Bank of America.

Edwin Agustín Lozada, inspired by José Rizal and other Filipino authors who wrote in Spanish from the 19th century up to the first half of the 20th, writes primarily in Spanish to continue that tradition. He also writes in English and Ilocano. In 2001, he received a San Francisco Individual Artists Grant in Literary Arts for his first book of poetry, *Sueños anónimos/Anonymous Dreams* (Carayan Press). His second book of poetry is *Bosquejos/Sketches* (Carayan Press, 2003). He is president of PAWA, Inc.

Patrick Rosal

As Glass

When these sons of Buenos Aires call to me
from across the street in the formal idioms
their fathers use to ignore the beggars of Recoleta
and the ubiquitous feral dogs I understand
just enough to switch my bag of fruits
from one hand to the other and put *El Clarín*
between my elbow and my flab then fling
their summer-toughened leather ball
back half way to the field and they all rush
toward me to be the first to retrieve it
I go back to my hard-floor flat in Palermo
and phone my dad back in Jersey: *Papa* I say
Of course at first he doesn't recognize his own
name or even my voice for I am speaking to him
with an affection whose prepositions
point in all the wrong directions
It's simple: We don't loathe one another in Spanish
the way we do in English For once we are laughing
at the same time From *Qué hay* to *Adiós* We end
by wishing each other to God
and the boys—I can still hear them teasing one another
in lunfardo down the street Maybe
they aren't too young to despise
their fathers Maybe they can already taste
a petty venom in their mouths in the prayers
they pretend to say before they sleep

For the moment I love my dad more in this
Castillian (this dialect of conquerors
this larcenists' parlance) I love him more than I will
in English in the many years to come in the American
slang I'd rather spit at his feet
the one I stutter into my lover's hair
the one boiled into my tendons
I'm eloquent in foolishness and rage
I should tell you what you don't yet know
about my father's English: it rises
from his ankles to his torso and limbs
like molten glass It stiffens when it cools
and this is why he and I can glare at one another
for decades without moving—all the lexicons
of sadness and delight fill the body turning
cold and hard around every muscle and bone
a crystalline filigree twisted around the capillaries and
and metacarpal nooks stopping themselves
in the esophagus duplicating precisely
the full latticework of the unseen So if
flesh sinew and gut—this human crucible—
were to fall away (as it must) what's left is the clear
anatomy of a man's invisible-within—
cast in the most fragile human language gone
77 years unsummoned: the whittled wooden fans of his childhood
calesas rocking over Vigan cobblestone
hand-carved rosary beads the curious Chicago cold
the solitary cough from a Brooklyn pew
soup and cots and elevators and burnt offerings
and 400 years of horse shit poured hot through his veins...and I—
I am there too sitting in a chilly apartment in Palermo
listening to the fading howls from the football field
the bold charity of a foreign tongue sweetening

in my mind the image of this quickly aging man
who used to whack me and my brothers silly with his leather belt
and every word of every tenderness I have failed to speak
is already rising through my knees
as glass It is old and it is pure
It is not free from bitterness or grief
It is heating my very fingers as I write this
I want to learn to love my father more fluently
even if it means—in English—
I should shatter into the body of my father

From: *My American Kundiman*
A Karen &Michael Braziller Book
Persea Books, New York 2006
ISBN 978-0-89255-330-3
www.perseabooks.com

COMO CRISTAL

Spanish version of "As Glass"

Cuando estos hijos de Buenos Aires me gritan
desde el otro lado de la calle en los lenguajes formales
que usan sus padres para ignorar a los mendigos de Recoleta
y a los perros callejeros en todas partes, entiendo
apenas lo suficiente para pasar la bolsa de frutas
de una mano a la otra y meter *El Clarín*
entre mi codo y mis michelines y entonces se lo arrojo
de vuelta su bolón—rendido por verano—que aterriza
a la mitad de la distancia al campo Se lanzan hacia mí para reclamarlo
Regreso al piso de madera de mi departamento en Palermo
y telefoneo a mi papá en Nueva Jersey: Papi digo yo
Por supuesto al principio él no reconoce su propio

nombre ni aun mi voz porque le estoy hablando
con un cariño cuyas preposiciones
apuntan a todas las direcciones equivocadas
No nos aborrecemos en español
como nos aborrecemos en inglés Por ahora nos estamos riendo
juntos Desde *Qué hay* hasta *Adiós* Terminamos
deseándonos que cada uno vaya con Dios
y los chicos—todavía les oigo burlándose
en lunfardo hacia la mitad de la calle Quizás
no sean demasiado jóvenes para detestar
a sus padres Quizás ya puedan probar
un veneno minúsculo en sus bocas en las oraciones
que fingen decir antes de que se duerman

En este momento yo amo a mi papá más en este
castellano (este dialecto de conquistadores—
idioma de ladrones) le amo más que le amaré
en inglés en los muchos años que vienen: en los vernáculos
norteamericanos que preferiría escupir a sus pies
lo que tartamudeo en el pelo de mi amante
lo que es cocido en mis tendones
Soy elocuente con rabia y tontería
Debo decirte lo que todavía no sabes
del inglés de mi papá: surge
de sus tobillos hasta su tronco y brazos
como vidrio derretido Se anquilosa cuando se enfría
y por eso él y yo nos podemos mirar enfurecidamente
por décadas sin movernos—todos los léxicos
de tristeza y deleite rellenan el cuerpo haciéndose
fríos y duros alrededor de todos los músculos y huesos
una filigrana cristalina alrededor de los vasos capilares y
en sus escondrijos metacarpianos deteniéndose
en el esófago duplicando con precisión
la celosía plena de lo invisible. Pues si
la carne, la fibra y la tripa—el crisol humano—

fuera a deshacerse (como suele deber) lo que se queda es la clara
anatomía del interior invisible de un hombre—
fundida en el idioma más frágil que va sin ser evocado
por 77 años: los abanicos de madera tallada de su juventud
calesas meciendo sobre los guijarros de Vigan
rosarios cincelados el frío curioso de Chicago
la tos solitaria en un banco de iglesia en Brooklyn
sopa y catres y ascensores y ofrendas quemadas
y 400 años de estiércol de caballos...y allí estoy también—
sentándome en un departamento fresquito en Palermo
escuchando a los aullidos atenuándose desde el campo de fútbol
la caridad audaz de una lengua extranjera dulcifica
en mi mente la imagen de este hombre que está rápidamente
                                                    envejeciendo
él que nos golpeaba a mis hermanos y a mí con su cinturón de cuero
y cada palabra de cada ternura que no logré hablar
ya está subiendo por mis rodillas
como vidrio Es anciano y es puro
Y no es libre de amargura ni de dolor
Mientras escribo, esto está calentando mis dedos
Y de esta manera yo sé que pasaré mi vida
esperando hacerme añicos en el cuerpo de mi padre

LAMENTO DEL GALLO
by Aracelis Girmay and Patrick Rosal

querida gallina caída
cuéntame la historia de una semilla
que contenía
todo el universo en una espina
que picó el ojo
de la noche

me das sed y seda

y no te vas
y no te vas

y si me enseñas
la ventana de tu boca
te seguiré
por las multitudes de mentirosos
que dicen
no iré
no iré

ay gallina
dime algo de tu vestida tan amable
y como robaste la voz de otra ave

animal tú eres
animal tú eres
tan bravona

se cree que las estrellas fueron hechas
por una sola clave

y me haces buscar
por las ruinas del corazón
robándolas de los dientes de esa tierra

y aún escucho las susurraciones p'arriba
y no te vas en seguida

y no te vas
no te vas

querida gallina caída
sueñas sin ignorar el frío
ni el agua ni cuchillo

los lobos aúllan los versos más secretos
no hay nombre que niegue ese sonido completo

rompe los cristales con tus lamentos
las torres de arena y de cemento

manda a los gobernadores que bajen
entre las alas y tu penúltimo viento
te prometen una bala o una canción
te las prometen
te prometen

y no te vas

Rooster's Lament
by Aracelis Girmay and Patrick Rosal
(English translation)

beloved fallen hen
tell me the story of a seed
that held
the whole universe in a thorn
that pricked the eye
of evening

you give me thirst and silk

and you don't go
and you don't go

and if you show me
the window of your mouth
i'll follow you

through the multitudes of liars
that say
i won't go
i won't go

oh hen
tell me something about your delightful costume
and how you robbed the voice of another bird

animal you are
animal you are
so brave

it's believed that the stars were made
by a single key

and you make me search
through the ruins of the heart
robbing them of the teeth of that land

and still i listen to the whispers above
and you don't go

lovely fallen hen
you dream without ignoring the cold
nor the water nor the knife

the wolves howl their most secret verses
there is no name that denies that complete sound

smash the mirrors with your laments
the towers of sand and of cement

order the governors to descend
among the wings and your penultimate wind
they promise you a bullet or a song
they promise them to you
they promise

and you don't go

Patrick Rosal is the author of *My American Kundiman*, winner of the Global Filipino Literary Award, and *Uprock Headspin Scramble and Dive*, which won the Asian American Writers' Workshop Members' Choice Award. His work has appeared in many journals and anthologies. Twice on the faculty of Kundiman's Summer Writers' Retreat, he is currently Visiting Professor of Creative Writing at The University of Texas, Austin.

The inheritor of Eritrean, Puerto Rican, and African American traditions, *Aracelis Girmay* writes poetry, essays, and fiction. She holds a B.A. from Connecticut College and an M.F.A. in poetry from New York University. Her chidren's art book, *Changing, Changing*, was publisehd by George Braziller in 2005. A former Watson fellow and Cave Canem fellow, she has published extensively in journals and literary magazines. Girmay leads community writing workshops throughout New York and California. She currently lives in New York.

Nick Carbó

Like the Dogs

"...the majority of the souls in Manila—like the dogs—are mongrels, or *mestizos*, as the word is, and the saying goes that happy is the man who knows his own father."
—Joseph Earle Stevens, American entrepreneur 1894

sim.i.le [L. fr, neut. of *similis* like, similar] 1 : a figure of speech comparing two essentially unlike things and often introduced by *like* or *as* .

soul [ME *soule*, fr. OE *sawol*, *sawl*: akin to OHG *sela*, *seula* soul, ON *sala*, Goth *saiwala*] 1 : General George Washington
2 : Thomas Jefferson 3 : John Quincy Adams 4: Benjamin Franklin
5 : Grover Cleveland 6 : William McKinley 7: Commodore Perry
8 : Captain Alfred T. Mahan 9 : Theodore Roosevelt
10 : William Howard Taft 11 : General William Armstrong Custer.

dog [ME dog, dogge, fr. OE docga] 1 : We mongrels believe these truths to be self-evident: *a.* All dogs are created equal under the stare of the Great Breeder. *b.* We can lick our testicles because we can.

LÚCAR SILERO

Lúcar Silero
mató a su mujer,
sacóle las tripas,
las llevó a vender.
¿Quién quiere tripas,
tripas de cordero?
Mentira, embustero,
que son de tu mujer.

LÚCAR SILERO

Lúcar Silero
butchered his wife,
he removed her intestines,
he took them to the market.
Who wants some intestines,
intestines of young sheep?
What a lie, you filthy liar,
those intestines came from
your wife!

LA NOVIA DE PEPE

La novia de Pepe
se mea, se mea en la cama,
y Pepe, y Pepe le dice:
Cochina, cochina, marrana.
Péinate, péinate esos pelos,
lávate, lávate esa cara,
mírate, mírate al espejo
y verás, y verás, ¡qué guapa!

PEPE'S BRIDE

Pepe's bride
wets her bed, she wets her bed,
and Pepe, and Pepe calls her:
Dirty girl, dirty girl, filthy swine.
Comb your hair, comb those unruly hairs,
wash that face, wash that dirty face,
look at the mirror, look at the bright mirror
and you'll see, and you'll see how beautiful
you really are.

Nick Carbó is a writer of Filipino and Spanish heritage and the author of three poetry collections—*Andalusian Dawn* (Cherry Grove Collections, 2004), *Secret Asian Man* (Tia Chucha, 2000), and *El Grupo McDonald's* (Tia Chucha, 1995). He is also the editor of three anthologies of Philippine literature—*Pinoy Poetics: Essays on Filipino and Filipino American Poetics* (Meritage Press, 2004); (co-editor with Eileen Tabios) *Babaylan: Fiction and Poetry by Filipina Women Writers* (Aunt Lute Books, 2000); and *Returning a Borrowed Tongue: Filipino and Filipino American Poetry* (Coffee House Press, 1995). His criticism and essays have been published in *The Encyclopedia of Modern Asia* (Scribners, 2002), *Melus, Poets & Writers Magazine*, and *The Anchored Angel* (Kaya Press, 1999). His visual poems have been exhibited at Harvard University's "Infinity" visual poetry group show, The Studio Alternative "Poem as Image" group show (Armonk, NY), and the Atelier-Hans Fereyabends Studio & Gallery "Poetry Meets College" group show. His sculptural piece "Credit Score" is collected in the Museum of Contemporary Art, North Miami and his piece "Medicine Cabinet" is in the collection of the Ruth & Marvin Sackner Archive of Concrete and Visual Poetry.

Eileen R. Tabios

The First Face Transplant
—*after Imee Marcos*

A dog mauled
              her

Surgeons repaired
her with someone else
                        's face

The face donor is rumored
to have committed suicide

Successful surgery
But she can't purse lips
                    into a kiss

                 that kiss

SCUMBLE-D
—after "The Bounty" by Derek Walcott

I cannot remember the name of that mountain city
but it trembled

                it is near XYZ
a town with hyphens

Now, so many deaths

                the only art left—
the preparation of grace

"FIND" IS A VERB
By Nick Carbó and Eileen Tabios

Bowdlerized books of history—
those pages where she flamed
aghast at marmalade and toast

—colored fricative verbs. Instead
belly bulged from blackened goat
with privilege ascribed to charred skin

the pensive prepuce would not
touch. Allow pastiche, she cooed.
"To collage is to include the world."

SKIM THE SHEEN
By Nick Carbó and Eileen Tabios

Let me take your Homonhon shoes on
a tryptic walk through betel nut Avenues

while we listen to ghosts singing
as they skim the sheen of the Abra River.

Let Maria Clara's nape hairs stand
like cormorants by the water

when Gabriela Silang orders, "Stop
flirting. Use your *panuelo** to bandage a wound."

This is the red W of the sound
of downtown revolutions,

the 21st century opera
bled from faces burnt by noonday suns,

a carapace running down your
logos moons

as you stone clay-footed authors
of history texts: "see Dick run!"

At 388 mph the postcolonial dime
is dying dusty.

I know now what matters most:
the fidelity of your eyes on me

which I cannot step into twice
and be the same sumptuous stare

(you see how even Greeks
crack marble lips to join the fray?).

*shoulder shawl/kerchief

If only I would dare eat
this eurocentric speech.

But why lapse to bitter needs
when my lips would rather form "Mahal"* *love*

and your amber feet turn
into lahar lansones pies.

My love, the mangos have ripened—
throw out that marinade of vinegar and salt.

DIE WE DO

Die
we do
as much as

we
live. Then
we write: right

what
we lived
when we write.

The selection of poems of E. Tabios are from:
The Light Sang As It Left Your Eyes
(Marsh Hawk Press, New York, 2007)
www.marshhawkpress.org

MORIR HACEMOS

Morir,
lo hacemos
tanto como vivir.

Entonces,
nosotros escribimos:
corregimos aquello que

vivimos
cuando, así,
nosotros lo escribimos.

*Translation into Spanish
by Rebeka Lembo*

Eileen R. Tabios has released 14 print, four electronic and 1 CD poetry collections, an art essay collection, a poetry essay/ interview anthology, a short story book and a novel. Recipient of the Philippines' Manila Critics Circle National Book Award for Poetry, she recently released *The Light Sang As It Left Your Eyes* (Marsh Hawk Press, 2007). In her poetry, she has crafted a body of work that is unique for melding ekphrasis with trans-colonialism. She's also edited or co-edited five books of poetry, fiction and essays. She is the Poet Laureate for Dutch Henry Winery in St. Helena, CA where, as a budding vintner, she is arduously and long-sufferingly researching the poetry of wine. Her poems have been translated into Spanish, Italian, Tagalog, Japanese, Portuguese, Paintings, Video, Drawings, Visual Poetry, Mixed Media Collages, Kali Martial Arts, Modern Dance and Sculpture.

Paolo Javier

22

hungry sky humming   a kid   gloom over all   so put-off

& he stumbles to weld whose attitude ang bilis   one daft punk percolator

stolen noone unwitting   the call   colonial

why rim them   void rights to

owing to usual flippantry   bear the daze Kaleidoscope Lit   toilet INRI

you weave sick muses child in a manger   duraan mo   jack-off   hate hidden bench   opportuning

forged an abyss   the sheer madness priestly messages

Papal ruin sky owing metals   emphatic men put-off   more counting   your galling sky

empire's aid lay flock Gaul towards Thebe's engine   padded ruse mockingly   summary waste

Huns weave away   width invalid   summary space an entrance

you're born with reason   aesthete & fascism Louis' France   lost tanks   sell out a moderate heatseeker

burned into ink   retire the Somme   Simon, Theodore, &   museum of babble sense

de Legazpi's imago ye gods of horseshit alive next door   Alvin, I prefer the real, yo

leaden referents   unfamous deaths   demand open ideas

double your madness   tangina nyo

24

A-List ruse   whose attitude ang bilis   covert

hokum ruses   channels   sobs erupt   whose hostile oceans
to rest easier   witness to ordeal   exhume Orion enemy ruse   de Legazpi's imago

amnesty disheartened terrorist   the all-time hater owes you
Odyssey notarized   coerce poem   dictates of the time hydra
Forrest Hills   briss hurried   DiPlo arrayed   regain odds Taurus

rest if Percival will avail her   A-List ruse as steerage ill-use striated

conscience aver favor to ascend a treatise early ruse ye gods of horseshit alive next door

this taunt's daughter   tell it   on whose common seas you bed her   Telos

mired pabling   Royces race   habeas will interest   eye of the fish
& may tire this heart here   the all-time hater's ode   a dumbbell country
Forrest Hills précis   Fallujah   new ruses

Army sauce ta-dah   luddite kids spelunk atoms   volumes formalize aluminum
no Esso station here Wisconsin tough bred profiteer museum of babble sense a ruse

35

a gust combs through Iraq corrals armies two-color sphere an ornament
hey Moses averred us to deliverance here mere walls no talking nice this hour
look at us stubbed to rob a dour mind de Legazpi's imago bite mga alimasag
pasensya na lang, Leda   this Elysian noise solicited   aver cadence
aint got with Thrace   Thebe   museum of babble sense   Louis' France
death hinimay   buckle agenda dare we hustle the challenge   hand of god
hindi Rizal to lesser foe touching   ye gods of horseshit alive next door
make us want it kung di man ornamentalists o call em fisters commode gestalting
matching asses wanting o glistening spirits justice combing eye of the fish I chew off
declare it Tecumseh lynching Detroit assembly combing through Illiad
assuming Cami forensic bilinguals   whirling Indio I prefer the real, yo
assuming Cami to liberate Ahab the redneck invention of licentiousness
meanwhile I sedate King Lear   meanwhile I base no detection
Saturn amend one frigid autumn comet all hail Pegasus o Penelope elope

---

Paolo Javier is the author of *Goldfish Kisses* (w/ artist
Ernest Concepcion, Sona Books), *6o lv bo(e)mbs* (O Books),
and *the time at the end of this writing* (Ahadada), which received
a Small Press Traffic Book of the Year Award. He edits *2nd Ave
Poetry*, and lives in Brooklyn.

Bienvenido C. Gonzalez

I QUIT

BEAT A BAD
    HABIT
BY REDUCING
    ABIT
DAILY EVERY
    BIT
TILL YOU RID OF
    IT

PERSEVERANCE

IF AT FIRST YOU DON'T
SUCEEDE
SUCCEDE
SUCCEED
TRY, TRY AGAIN.

MONEY TALKS

A FEW SAY   "HELLO"
SOME CRY "SURPRISE"
MOST BID "GOOD BYE"

Bienvenido C. Gonzalez is a wordsmith who has created neowords and logos principally as a hobby. He is currently experimenting with poetry in art form under the name WIZ-ART Micropoems. This current collection is from his PARA-PRAISES or tributes to old and original sayings.

Alberto Vajrabukka

[N]Ako...

an afternoon of creativity and sharing.
potluck . picnic . pau hana   5 nov oo

PROGRAM

one	*PM*	*~ eat! eat!*
two	*PM*	*~perpormanses*
four	*PM*	*- klin up e!*

PERpORMERS
In no particular order, but alpabetikal ~ sorry ha, if you aren't listed

Christy Beavers & Lilia Ramos
Emanuel Benisano
Joel Cruz
Take the shackles of my feet (pumps) So I Can Dance
Marco Antonio Chavez
Friends2
Rodney de Jesus
Sitting Piece
Daniel Cavaltera, Jose Tacloban, & Jojo Teodoro
· Untitled, (video)
Bryan Roy Lucena
Bringing It Back
Aileen Medina
Bryan Nicolas Pangilinan
Epilogue
Ariel Sacote
Jose Paulino San Pedro Tamayo

THANK YOU DEAR FRIENDS FOR BEING HERE, AND BEING THERE.
love,
Alberto Vajrabukka, *da birthday boi*

DARK SISTAH

sweet dark sistah
othas
took us as lovers
brothers
or tried to smother
and otha
our brownness
but you were always
there
wicked
witty twin

Paul
as in in Paulino
not "pawl"
the shortest distance between two points
was a runway
two strides and you crossed the room
clasped my hand
took me under your wing
warmly firmly
our nation was born
and our parents began wondering
what were they sending us to college for

If I had known tagalog back then
I would've thought
sarimanok
no not chicken
but bright phoenix
legendary
sign of good fortune
no wonder
I misheard your name as
Power

I would watch
as you played out
those who tried
to kick their tired game
with you:
"do you know how to make rice?"
tick tock
clocked
what are those chickenhawks
to a *sarimanok*?

skooled
with new toolz
n skills
chin up
walking tall even in heels
feeling it's ok
to swish lisp n snap
with you at my back
it's all about context
not contests
right miss chanté?

but more than your lola's *lumpiya*
and mahjong with moms n pops
when my own family flew the coop
you gave me a place to rest
nestled in your understanding
nourished by your strength

BITE (V. 2.0)

Bite! Take this body between your teeth.
And roll those lips over it.
Flesh caught. Skin taught.
Gnawing desire.
A lesson in cause
and effectiveness.

Bite! The silent tongue of affection.
Simply
not hickeys, nor the New World.
Sink in
splitting the double helix into
the tart of an open palm
hardness of sea spray
scents of fire
colors of a sigh
thunder of a lime

This plush of breath is your welcome.

❧

Alberto Vajrabukka draws his inspiration from the cultural clashes and synergisms of having a Filipina mother, a Thai father, and a California upbringing. His work has appeared in *Maganda Magazine* (issues 11 and 12), the chapbook *Too Mixed Up*, and the anthology *Queer PAPI Porn*. He lives, writes, and dances in San Francisco.

Rick Barot

GOYA'S DOG

What did I know that they didn't give me?
Even the house-shaking storm
seemed one more background of their conjuring,

our house a crystal globe in the tropical dark.
Inside, our puzzle pieces shaped the night into another place:

a castle with turrets, white as a swan.

It wasn't a mere storm but a monsoon, one kind
of cognate for the wind and rain
that brought the trees' faces to our windows.

At first the cheer of my mother in the kitchen,
my father caught at home. Then the electricity gone,
the candles stood up on bottles.

Childhood, a house defined, set apart.

Gold and lavender, like that wall of Goya's painting,
where the spaniel looks up. Only his head is visible,
staring at something we can't see.

It must believe in the heaven held above it, the gilt scuffed
but still fresh to sight.

Once, my father took me to a field.

A ring of spectators brewed around two horses
that had been brought there.
A third, a mare, was in heat, neighing at the side.
It was held by a rope while the two stallions raged

for wanting her. The circumference of the crowd grew
and shrank around the fighting.

Foaming teeth, hooves, brown dust raising its own storm
over the brown horses.
My father was everywhere and nowhere.

His hand on my head, then he was lost among the quietly
expectant others, his white shirt indistinct,
remote as the snows of a later country.

Goya's Dog was first published in "The Threepenny Review."

Oakland

The street went up a slight rise and then angled up
toward the left, like a raised arm. There were four utility
poles on one side: each pole was a T with two crosses,
with the wires coming from each pole and extending
out in a messy radiance of black lines to the houses
and buildings of the street. The wires illustrated how
everything on the street was connected in this one way:
a web of electricity flowed through all the structures
like blood. On a gray day, you looked up to the electric
wires like the spines of an umbrella, on blue days
you forgot them because what you noticed were the trees'
green over you, and the blue past that green. Our house
was on the right side, middle of the block. In the first
half of our life in it, it was a cream-colored house
with blue and red trim. Later, we had it painted a light
olive and a dark green, the colors of river stones.
The yards used to be a jungle, but at some point we spent
a summer hauling things out and planting. A pergola
which the potato vines took over: a continuous mass

of little white flowers. Lavender bushes in a long row
on one side of the house, roses in a long row on one edge
of the side yard. The roses had always been there,
the cleaned yards now showed them to good advantage.
At the back: the apple-pear tree with black arthritic
branches, the sour tangerine tree beside it, and beside that,
the holly tree with pricking leaves. On the patio
was an old claw-foot tub converted into a flowerbed:
dwarf agapanthus, more lavender, daisies that never took.
Directly across the street, the house that I still think of
as Paul's, though he's been dead at least five years.
I had seen them take his body out, unceremoniously,
in the middle of the day, on a gurney. His daughter
and her family live there now. A few years before that,
his wife had died, a heart attack while in the shower.
This would be the very first death. And before our house,
built sometime in the 1920s, and before all the other
houses on the street and in the neighborhood, what
houses stood? Few enough houses, anyway, so that you
could see the way down to Lake Merritt. But our house.
The very house. Our house that is now as *madeleine*
to the larger mind of the place, and to my mind also.

"Oakland" is also published in "Ploughshares."

ARTICLE AND WAVE

For example there was the afternoon
        I walked into her room

and she had been tied down
by the granddaughter meant to take care

        of her. The granddaughter,

who was my teenaged aunt,
　　　　explained with no apology

that she had been digging at the rashes
which by now covered her

　　　　arms and legs, resisting
the Calamine administered to them.

I would have been five or six, she close
to ninety, bird-small and

　　　　bird-gray, her face an eroding
gray image, eyes and bones.

This shows that memory can be particle.

　　　　That it is a certain justice
administered in time, the shape of it

exact in mind, long after the dispersed
fact. For years after that,

　　　　there seemed only waves
depositing their silt, then taking away

what they first gave: the manzanita tree
we made a kind of house,

the wire from a fence that pierced

　　　　my cheek, the killed pig's acrid
screaming from someone's backyard,

things coming to mind
then pushing past the mind, memory as

　　　　its very opposite, a sea
unmarked by any particularity, a sea

of nothing. I remember coloring a picture
while my grandmother and aunts

swore to each other, not knowing
                what to do about the old, dying

woman in the other room. I did not

know if a lesson was intended in my
                being allowed to stay there,

to listen, to see. What I remember is that
when I looked back at my picture,

                I decided that it was finished.

Rick Barot was born in the Philippines and grew up in the San Francisco Bay Area. His first book, *The Darker Fall*, was the winner of the Kathryn A. Morton Prize in Poetry and was published by Sarabande Books in 2002. His new book is *Want* (Sarabande, 2008). His poems and essays have appeared in numerous publications, including *New England Review*, The New *Republic*, *Poetry*, and *Virginia Quarterly Review*. His work has also appeared in many anthologies, including *The New Young American Poets*, *Asian American Poetry: The Next Generation*, and *Legitimate Dangers: American Poets of the New Century*. He has received fellowships from the National Endowment for the Arts and Stanford University. He lives in Tacoma, Washington and teaches both in the Program for Writers at Warren Wilson College and at Pacific Lutheran University .

Jaime Jacinto

ALTIPLANO

Dear Family,

At 16,000 feet our blood thins,
the poor turn desperate and all that we own
can disappear as easily as our innocence.
How could I have been so stupid?
Thinking only of comfort, for that window seat
closer to the grey ghost light of the altiplano,
its ice blue peaks, magic and so still
they could turn into poems or these words
scrawled on a homesick post card.

Only a few seconds. That's all it took.
Just enough to distract me. No one has eyes
in the back of the head. The others, the ones who live
here knew better and hugged their tattered bundles
watching me as if to say too bad, you had no chance.
They'd traveled this train before. But I was the
El extraño* sitting there by the window,   **foreigner, stranger*
an easy target, daydreaming like a child
who chased the loose change from a blind man's tin cup,
his coins rolling down the aisle.

I replay the scene to learn their art.
So first you shake the loose change

in your cup, bump shoulders
up and down the aisle until you stand close enough.
Then spill your cup, scattering coins like
breadcrumbs for the starving who are not
pigeons but indian villagers.
Ask for forgiveness from the señor
for being so clumsy, and maybe he'd think
you were just another beggar.
Watch him stoop like the rest, just as the blind
would, palming the dark space before them
until you see it, the fat wallet in his back pocket.
When he bends, nudge him just a little from behind
and keep saying that you are sorry for
disturbing him. He'll believe you and then
the rest is all yours.

Vow of Silence

*V*ow of silence. Lifetime of prayer and abstinence. Nothing would tempt her away from the holy life, though when Don Alfredo, her father, had heard of her intentions, he cursed out loud, for days roaming the compound in his solitary anger, slamming doors, banging his fists on the dining room table, tipping over chairs, in short, like a child lost in a tantrum, disturbing the peace of his beloved kingdom so that the entire family as well as the maids, the errand boys, even Tonio, his personal driver and confidante fled his presence which grew more unbearable each day. His jaws clenched tight, the furrows on his brow deepened, and still his body seethed though weeks had passed since his eldest daughter divulged her longing for the spiritual life. A life of celibacy and humility before God, to whom she would dedicate her entire being, for the greater honor and glory of God the father, and not her own, she would whisper to herself, giving in on occasion to the spiteful resistance that made her father's favorite. Ironic but true nevertheless, which did nothing to dampen his pain and embarrassment or the horror of family shame for Don Alfredo's plans for Luisa did not include a vow of chastity or rosaries to be recited inside a walled convent. How could this be? Impossible, he repeated one night, slamming the small brown vial of medicine on his bedside table. His dreams dashed, he wondered where he had gone wrong, or better yet, who was this flea-bitten scoundrel that had laid waste to his master plan.

Ma.Isabela Bautista Garcia, fondly referred to as "Chinita", being the eldest daughter of Don Alfredo, was not only the favorite among his eleven legitimate children — she was also the most talented, beautiful, and the most intelligent of the seven daughters who bore his name, Luisa being the first to be raised like a proper aristocrat's daughter, schooled by Spanish nuns, fluent in the Castillan tongue, versed in the rules of etiquette, so well-groomed that her beauty matched her wit and courteous conduct, prizes that would bestow all the wealth a man could need or ever want. Or so Don Alfredo always thought. But his plans had never accounted for the xylophone player who appeared one day in a nearby village and eventually made his way to the capital where Don Alfredo's compound occupied its place among the fields of buffalo grass and walled homes.

He was, after all, a European, pale, red-headed, thin and angular with a steep furrowed brow and a wispy red mustache which made him appear more debonair than he really was. His name was Lázaro— Lázaro Fulgencio Montes, a xylophone player who, for several years since his arrival, had roamed the countryside along with his ragged band of musicians, musical accompaniment to the circus of midgets, pantomimes, lame horses, spitting camels, dancing bears and arthritic trapeze artists, all of whom inevitably appeared on the eve of some saint's feast day on the outskirts of town, perhaps near the cemetery where their neighbors, for the duration of their nightly extravaganzas were the unwanted, the lost, and the unforgiven of the villages and boomtowns of our island country. They were all, no, we were all casualties of some twist of fate, runaways from a string of bad luck, bad debts, and unlucky cards or throws of the dice.

Lázaro loved every moment of his wanderer's life, having abandoned early on hope of returning to his native land. He was born on a winter afternoon in a tiny mountain village on the southern coast of her majesty's realm, raised just like any other boy descended from a line of mercenaries. Centuries before, his forefathers, gristled, gums bleeding, their long bushy beards afflicted with lice, endured an ocean's passage to the other side of the world so that they might be granted a title from the Queen and her royal family, thus erasing forever any traces of their peasant roots, the generations of goatherders and cheesemongers, forgotten, erased from memory because of what the New World promised.

It was poverty, rocky soil, scraggly harvests, and the monotonous taste of parched bread and goatsmilk that drove Lázaro's ancestors away from the meseta towards the sea, closer to the hazards of crossing an unmapped ocean, to travel where many believed was the edge of the world, where ocean became a dark abyss and all one could think of were visions of an untimely tragic death, the sea serpents, equatorial typhoons, treacherous reefs, relentless winds and most of all, the unmerciful madness which accompanies months of solitude and nearly 300 years later. They say that a man will weep for his homeland when faced with the possibility of never returning home. This never crossed Lázaro's mind, even when faced with the memory of shipwreck and its aftermath, the weeks marooned at sea, floating on the salt soaked timbers of Nuestra Señora de la Concepción, once a graceful galleon bound for the port of Manila.

Eventually, he would become famous for the chronicle he would later write, about his life in a distant land. And it would begin like this:

"I traveled across a dark-blue sea and that voyage, I first thought, was my undoing, a voyage farther than the sun's shadow, more distant than the roads of childhood, more treacherous than a sea-serpents revenge and more mysterious than the curve of a new moon. But after years of wandering the coastal villages of the archipelago, I found her, or rather, she found me, and I was struck by lightning and lost all my good sense to my beloved."

Excerpt from: Ficciones Repentinas, Making Kuwento

Isabela, La Sufrida

*I*sabela suffered in the heat, when the days grew so hot that birds fainted and dropped one by one from the sky, a heat so intense that memory left a bitter taste on her tongue, and solitude became both cure and punishment. On days like these, she thought, disasters could not be averted or denied, so all that she could do was to perform the rituals of the day as if completing some sort of penance, her prayers whispered into an amulet that contained the relic of some minor saint.

That summer, Isabela could not find the cure for the suffocating dreams that woke her, often just before the first mockingbirds signaled sunrise, the yellow morning light entering her room, greeted by the swirling dust motes that floated above her bed. If it were not for her pet dogs, two gargantuan English mastiffs that slept at the foot of a tarnished brass bed, she would have remained beneath her tent of gauze, content with her own solitude, reclining in the melancholy that filled her room with a fragrance of camphor and cedar wood.

This bed was her own sanctuary, a landmark among the chaos and unfamiliar territory that was the world outside her window, its sounds now intruding into her private reverie, its silence broken by the crowing of a neighbor's rooster, the ticking antique Swiss clock and its swinging pendulum, or the roving packs of dogs that barked in the streets below her open window. What do you have to lose she thought to herself, now that her children were far away in another country and her husband lost in his fits of gambling and opium binges in the Chinese district. Today would be like other days, living in a trance, somewhere between past and future, while he was astray, wandering through his psychic limbo, distracted as he was with the machinations of a fumbling mind, fixated on the inventions of a dreamer, blue light bulbs, birdsongs kept in a cage, a window filled with summer clouds, and portable thunder, maps for reading people's faces, a measurement for intellect, emotion, and will, lessons for training the intuitive, charms for the superstitious, holographs of distant memories.

Excerpt from: Ficciones Repentinas, Making Kuwento

Jaime Jacinto splits his time between the SF Bay Area and Hilo, Hawaii. He is the author of *Heaven is Just Another Country* (Kearny Street Workshop Press).

Barbara Jane Reyes

A LITTLE BIT ABOUT LOLA ILANG

*D*uring the war, the old women would still go outside the house to smoke their hand-rolled tobacco, after cleaning the suppertime dishes. But in order to not be seen by Japanese soldiers, they learned to flip their cigarettes so that the lit ends were inside their mouths. They flipped their cigarettes with their tongues so fast, and we kids would try to copy them, singeing our own tongues in the process. Your Lola Ilang, she used to do this, and I tried to copy her. It hurt! It hurt so much when I burnt my tongue! Yes, your Lola Ilang, she used to cook the best *pochero*, and visitors thought it was a little weird, to cook banana with bok choy. You use the *saba* banana. No other kind is sweet enough. Do you know that when she died, everyone had already forgotten how old she was? We asked her a few years ago, and even she had forgotten. But I was saying about the war. No, the women did not want the soldiers to find them and capture them. You know what the soldiers did to the women here. The Japanese buried so much gold in our hills. This is because our northernmost provinces were the last places they set foot before their ships left, after their emperor surrendered. They stole this gold, Spanish gold, from our churches. You know, not too long ago, some of the Japanese who had gone into hiding were found in the hills. They were so old. They never knew how the war ended.

AUTO/BIO

(1) 12 JULY 2006, WEDNESDAY 9:27 A GMT-08
Speaking with Papa, two months before his ninety-fourth birthday.

There are four of us eleven still alive. Rosalia was ninety-six when she died. She is the mother of Teresing. Julio (he is in Mindanao) is one hundred and one years old, he drinks one San Miguel Beer per day, and he walks like a frog.

He gets up from the sofa to demonstrate. Legs spread wide, bends low at each knee. Spine virtually parallel to the floor. Hands behind the back, clasped. Takes a few steps, and laughs. Goes back to the sofa and sits.

At least Julio can still tie his own shoes.

Now Victor who was formerly in Australia is now Dean of the College of Engineering. Dominador is a Physics teacher in La Union. Lakay Sipi is the father of Bienvenido. In Seattle, there is the Sabado family. Their grandmother is the sister of my father. My father is Concordio. On the Garcia side, there are the Bambaos, Sabados, Sorianos, Luadas, Martinezes. Lakay Sipi married Leona. Your Manong Gene's grandfather was the brother of Concordio. My sisters' surnames are Jularbal, Madrid, Mendoza. I was told we had a sister who died in infancy. They told me her name was Tecla. *My fingers are cramping; I am scribbling so furiously in my Moleskine.* Julio is the father of Jonathan who is the father of Arthur, who is a military man. You met him once when you were at Diliman. Braulio is the father of Jonas, who is the father of Mary Jane. Doming and Bong are on the Adviento side. The Rabinas are Advientos. The grandchildren of Ambrosio II still called us cousins. One married a soldier. They lived in Malacañang Playground.

"Papa, I don't know how to write all of this."

You are the poet. You can write this.

Papa is the youngest of eleven siblings. He is ninety-three. These are their names, in birth order: Ildefonso, Trinidad, Rafael, Herminagilda, Rosalia, [Tecla is not counted among these.], Ciriaco, Braulio, Julio, Alfredo, Pedro, Eustaquio (this is my Papa).

(2) 25 March 2007, Sunday 12:34 P GMT+08

He shouts at the television. Manny Pacquiao is running for Congress. "This is why there is no progress in this country! A boxing super featherweight champion with a third grade education thinks he may run for Congress."

For three days he contemplates the concept of sharing in its various contexts. We ask for translations, and this is how it is with him. Accuracy is important. Response is important.

He is ninety-four, and he is dying, and that is all there is to it.

There, we discuss irrigation. There are piglets, and squash vines. The farm is in the shape of a diamond. In the grooves between the rice paddies, slick mud. I bring him his walking stick. He holds my shoulders with both of his hands. I help him balance. I never knew how much taller than he I was. American grandchild. How beautiful is this which he has grown. Healthy seedlings, swaying.

It is an infection, and then the antibiotics make him sicker. It is not an infection, and so he discontinues the antibiotics. Then he is ambulatory, lucid. He is coherent once again.

There is sharing space, sharing food, sharing idea. We forget we'd asked him in the first place. It has kept him awake, not knowing the proper translation.

It is an abscess, and then it is a tumor. It is in his liver, and now it is in his lungs. The MRI cannot make up its mind. Now it is not in his lungs. He is ninety-four. *Pabayaan mo na lang*, he says. He foregoes biopsy.

Now he cannot eat. We try, with rice, mangoes, smoked fish. The cans of liquid nutrition, he knows they are a good idea. He just cannot stomach it.

He cannot eat, and now there is a tube needled into his arm.

Nananaginip siya[1], his nurse tells me. *May mga bata sa tabi niya. Naglalaro.*[2]

I think we must be those children he dreams, my sister and I, playing at his bedside. There are no children here. It has been thirty years since our first trip back.

Ngayon? Natutulog pa siya?[3] It's late. I think that it is harvest time on the farm. I think that what has been left fallow will now require fertilizer.

Now that he cannot eat, he cannot stand, nevermind the intravenous pain medications.

Now that he cannot eat, he cannot think, nevermind the hallucinations.

He is dying, and that is all there is to it.

(3) 29 JUNE 2007, FRIDAY 9:27 A GMT-08

Eustaquio Garcia Pulmano, MD died last night. He fell into a coma, and he never climbed out.

He was ninety-four.

---

1. He's dreaming.   2. There are children playing at his side.
3. Now? Is he still asleep?

call it talisman *(if you must)*

here, the blind old man tapped this marking into my left arm and breastbone. he used his tapping stick and his sharpened irons. these are leaves and grass blades. these are sunbursts of flower petals, the flitting eyes of moth-wings, of cicadas. this here, the soothsayer and her see-ing stones. the glass eye with which she viewed the heav-ens. above her mountain village, the stars arranged into hunter and bow, arrow aimed at mighty lawin.*   *hawk

this is not thunder. no, only men are marked with thun-der. he marked my flesh with the swirls of our village stream. here, on my right shoulder. what i see is no stream, but a blade which women conceal beneath their skirts. even today, we do this. though it is not proper, the elders say, for women to be marked for war.

it is no secret. women did indeed fight alongside the men once. few talk about it these days. the black robed and hooded ones who carried more curses than prayer, so feared armed women, they branded it savage and sinful —women who tucked skirts between their legs, wielded knives and tilling tools, then returned home to nurse their babies after washing clean their bloodied hands.

no, daughter, these are no talismans upon my flesh. the blind old man wished to give me markings in the pat-terns of my father's fields, for he walked my father's lands, from new growth's edges to the greenest center. every sunrise in wordless prayer. many years, he did this, never once opening his eyes. but by the time i grew old enough to marry, all his fields my father lost to the fire, and to the papers of the wealthy, not of this land but of grey cities far away from here.

he marked my flesh with the swirls of our village stream, though its cool, sweet water, its bubbling no longer gives us music. it has long since been fenced and dammed, but by whom, no one who ever shows himself. its music we have all of us forgotten. and the flowering trees that once dipped its branches into the water to drink have all withered. there is no sense in my very body carrying a reminder of all that is lost to us, for no healer of scars, and no magical markings could save any of it. this is no stream, no. it is the curve of a warrior blade.

this is how my flesh was marked with the ash of burnt coconut husk and sugarcane, so that i could marry. but all the young men had neither land nor wealth, and invading armies came with bayonets and bullets. sun worshippers, harboring no love for things of this land.

when my grandfather's father was still a young man, an army of white ghosts came to our forest. but our men took their heads with ease. running dogs, whimpering, they were. cowards. and even the lowlanders, some marked with the talismans of their own elders, some who had grown their hair down to their waistlines, hid in our forests with rifles and the sharpest knives. they fought those white ghosts for many years, until those white ghosts numbered so few, they boarded their steamships and they fled.

but these sun worshippers, they were cruel. they used the young women as whores, slid loaded pistols between their legs, gave them sores and fevers which none of our medicines could cure. the sun worshippers also took heads, but left these to rot where they fell. no hunters were these, but mercenaries, beasts. this is why the sun wept a sky the color of black pearls. this is why he weeps still.

he took me, from the river's edge, where i washed clothes for the missionary's daughter. he took me, gripped between his fists. i feared that if i tried to escape, i would fall, pierced by the sharpest bayonet. i knew for sure i would bleed, for i had lived my entire life in my father's house and had never before touched man. when the soldier came with his vulgar words, i leaned farther over the edge than i should have. but so venomous, his words. upon the banks of the river for which my father was named, there, the soldier took me and took me, and the river could do nothing. i knew my brothers too could do nothing. there, i was torn.

my child, your father's eyes. my child, one day you will curse his name.

Barbara Jane Reyes is the author of *Gravities of Center* (Arkipelago, 2003) and *Poeta en San Francisco* (Tinfish, 2005), for which she received the James Laughlin Award of the Academy of American Poets. Her work has appeared or is forthcoming in *Asian Pacific American Journal, Chain, Interlope, New American Writing, North American Review, Notre Dame Review, Tinfish, XCP: Cross Cultural Poetics*, and elsewhere. She lives with her husband, poet Oscar Bermeo, in Oakland, CA. Her author website is http://barbarajanereyes.com.

Ceres S.C. Alabado

STORY OF THE LEPER SPY

Joey was a charming Spanish Filipina mestiza who married a doctor of the Guerrero clan of Manila.

After a few years of her marriage, her fair skin began to burst with lesions and swellings. She was diagnosed to be sick with the dreaded disease: leprosy.

At that time, leprosy was incurable and could be transmitted through contact with the infected person. So people shunned being seen or having contact with Joey.

On the war front, after the surrender of Bataan and Corregidor, and the escape of General MacArthur to Australia, Filipino and American guerrillas continued to fight the Japanese invaders all over the Philippines — in the cities, in the mountains, underground.

General MacAthur was still in over-all command from Australia. The guerrilla fighters in the Philippines were communicating with him, sending and receiving messages and information secretly.

The Japanese suspected this and began to set up checkpoints all over the country. They checked everyone passing through, from the cities to the provinces, to the mountains and back.

Women were stripped naked to find out if they concealed messages to and from the guerrillas.

Joey Guerrero often traveled to her family's farm out of the city. She would carry a basket full of goodies like cigarettes, soap, and biscuits for the overseers of her farm. The Japanese laughed at her closely, they whispered to one another: "She's a leper! Don't touch her! Throw away those goodies!"

And they let her pass through freely. They would have nothing to do with a leper!

Si Joey ay isang kalugod-lugod na mestisang Kastilang Pilipina. Maybahay siya ng isang doctor ng aklang Guerrero sa Maynila.

Pagkaraan ng ilang taong mula ng siya'y mag-asawa, namutok sa kanyang maputing kutis sa mukha at buong katawan ang mga mistulang nagnanaknak, mapupulang sugat at pamamaga. Ang diyagnosis ng doctor: siya ay may sakit na kakila-kilabot na karamdamang ketong.

Noong panahong iyon ang ketong ay di nagagamot at lubhang nakahahawa, naililipat sa ibang tao sa pamagitan ng pakadikit sa sugat ng maysakit.

Kaya nilalayuan, iniilagan ng mga tao si Joey.

Sa labanan ng gera, pagkaraan ng pagsuko ng Bataan at Corregidor, at pagtakas ni Heneral MacArthur patungo ng Australia, nagpatuloy ang laban sa mga nanalakay na Hapon, ang mga gerilyang Pilipino at Amerikano, sa lahat ng dako ng Pilipinas. Sa bundok, sa lunsod, at lihim na pagkilos.

Ang Heneral MacArthur ay siya pa ring namunong opisyal mula sa Australia. Ang mga gerilyero sa Pilipinas ay kumukontak sa kanya, sekretong nagpapadala sa kanya at tumatanggap ng ulat at impormasyon mula sa kanya.

Naghinala ang mga Hapon at sinimulan nilang magtayo ng mga *checkpoint* sa buong kapuluan. Siniyasat ang bawat taong dumaraan sa *checkpoint*. Mula sa lunsod, sa probinsiya at sa patungo at pabalik galing sa bundok.

Hinuhubaran ang mga babae upang siyasatin kung may tinatagong mensaheng galing sa mga gerilya o ibibigay sa kanila.

Madalas magbiyahe si Joey Guerrero tungo sa bukirin ng kanyang pamilya sa labas ng lunsod. Dala nito ang isang *basket* na punung-puno ng mga sigarilyo, sabon, at biskwit para sa mga katiwala sa bukid.

Bibigyan ni Joey ng mga dala-dala niya, ang mga sundalong Hapon paglapit niya sa *checkpoint*. Tuwang-tuwa ang mga ito, tawanan.

Ngunit nang lumapit sila't aabutin ang binibigay ni Joey, nagbulung-bulongan sa isa't isa:

Ketongin siya! Huwag lumapit sa kanya! Itapon ang binigay niya!

When the guerrillas heard about this, they contacted Joey right away to ask her if she could do some work for them. Joey was more than happy to be able to contribute her share of freedom fighting for her country.

From then on, Joey would carry in her basket not only goodies for the farm but pieces of paper with messages to the guerrillas at certain points. She would slip into her bra, maps and drawings of Japanese military installations, or information of the troop movements to be sent to MacArthur.

When the American troops had already landed in Luzon, the northern island of the Philippines, and were making plans for the final assault to retake Manila, they chose a route based on reports furnished them by guerrillas as the safer route to take.

The Japanese discovered these plans, and immediately saturated the road with mines and troops to trap the Americans.

The guerrillas were frantic.

The problem was how to get this information in a very short time to the American troops who were now ready to march to Manila. All checkpoints were heavily guarded.

Joey Guerrero! She could cross the lines without inspection.

In a matter of hours she was ready with maps and directions hidden under her chemise and bra.

Her face, legs, arms swollen with sores and scars, she just breezed by the sentries who promptly shooed her away.

"*Kura! Kura!* Out! Out!" They shouted at her.

Alas, they never suspected that she carried a most vital message of the last stages of the war. Message from the guerrillas for Mac Arthur's troops not to take the planned route, to change to another passage where there no Japanese defenses.

For this, and other heroic acts of Joey Guerrero, the leper courier and spy, all through the four years of Japanese occupation, General Mac Arthur decorated her with citations:

"For saving many American and Filipino lives in the battles of the World War II in the Philippines."

At agad-agad tinaboy at malayang pinadaan si Joey. Ayaw nilang makisalamuha sa isang ketongin!

Nang mabalitaan ang pagyayaring ito ng mga gerilya, agad nilang kinontak si Joey upang itanong sa kanya kung papayag siyang magtrabaho sa kanila. Malugod na tinanggap ni Joey ang alok na gawain upang siya'y makaambag ng kanyang tulong sa paglaban para sa kalayaan ng bayan.

Mula noon, ang dala-dala ni Joey sa kanyang *basket* ay hindi lamang mga samutsamot para sa katiwala sa bukid kundi mga mensahe ng mga gerilya, nakasulat sa pira-pirasong papel. Isinusuksok niya sa kanyang bra guhit sa papel ng mapa at drowing ng mga instalasyong militar o impormasyon tungkol sa paggalaw ng tropang Hapon na ipapadala ng mga gerilya kay MacArthur.

Nang lumunsad ang mga kawal Amerikano sa hilagang bahagi ng Pilipinas sa Luzon, at sila'y nagplano ng kanilang huling pagsalakay upang bawiin ang lunsod Maynila, pinili nila ang isang ruta na ligtas at di mapanganib ang daan, batay sa *report* na ipinadala sa kanila ng mga gerilya.

Sa samang palad, nadiskubre ng mga Hapon ang planong ito at kaagad nilang pinuno ang daan ng mga mina at tropa, upang mahuli sa bitag ang mga Amerikano.

Balisang-balisa ang mga gerilya.

Ang problema: paano nila mapaparating ang impormasyong ito sa pinakamadaling panahon, sa tropang Amerikano, na noo'y nagmamartsa na patungong Maynila. Lahat ng *checkpoint*, tiyak na mahigpit na ginaguwardiyahan.

Joey Guerrero! Makakaraan siya sa *checkpoint* na walang inspeksyon.

Sa loob ng ilang oras handa na siyang lumakad, ang mapa at direksyon nakasuksok sa ilalim ng kanyang kamison at bra.

Dahil sa namamaga niyang mukha, binti't braso na tad-tad ng sugat at peklat, mabilis siyang pinagtabuyan ng mga guwardiya.

"*Kura! Kura!* Sulong! Sulong!" ang sigaw nila sa kanya.

Aba e, hindi nila pinaghinalaan na ang dala ni Joey ay isang pinakamahalagang mensahe para sa huling yugto ng gera. Mensahe mula sa mga gerilya na isaiwan ang unang planong ruta ni Mac Arthur, at palitan ng ibang daan kung saan walang depensa ang mga Hapon.

Dahil sa pagsagawa nito, at iba pang nagpakilala ng kabayanihan ni Joey Guerrero, ang ketonging mensahera at espiya, sa buong apat na taong panahon ng Hapon sa Pilipinas, siya'y papuring hinayagan ni Mac Arthur at binanggit ang ganito:

"Sa paglitas niya sa maraming buhay ng mga Amerikano at Pilipino sa labanan ng Ikalawang Pandaigdigang Digmaan sa Pilipinas."

❦

Ceres S.C. Alabado is PAWA's founder and a past president. She is also the founding president of the Children's Literature Association of the Philippines, Inc. Her published works include *Beautiful Dreamer* (Sulu books, 1995), *Kankong 1896* (Pamana Inc., 1969), *Multimedia Multicultural Children's Literature in the Philippines: A Historical Perspective, Donald's Dreamcatcher* (Sulu books, 1999), and others. She lives partly in Canada, California and in the Philippines.

Jon Pineda

MATAMIS
from Birthmark

One summer in Pensacola,
I held an orange this way,
flesh hiding beneath
the texture of the rind,
then slipped my thumbs
into its core & folded it
open, like a book.

When I held out the halves,
the juice seemed to trace
the veins in my arms
as it dripped down to my elbows
& darkened spots of sand.
We were sitting on the beach then,
the sun, spheres of light within each piece.
I remember thinking, in Tagalog,
the word *matamis* is sweet in English,
though I did not say it for fear
of mispronouncing the language.

Instead, I finished the fruit & offered
nothing except my silence, & my father,
who pried apart another piece, breaking
the globe in two, offered me half.
Meaning everything.

WRESTLING
from Birthmark

Before the season, we were already pissed,
our bodies tightening around ribs, our eyes,
like panthers, sinking into shadows.

We had given up food, sweat until
the air around us was heavy. The only thing
we cared about was winning.

At our first match, I wrestled a guy
I had met summers ago at a Filipino gathering,
some first communion or baptism.

By a man-made lake separating the neighborhood
in two, where most of the children had wandered,
a few of the boys pinned my shoulders against a tree

while one punched me. I could say it was because
I was only half, a mestizo, but that would be too easy.
We were just boys, happy in our anger.

When they let me go, their eyes clouded as the lake,
I didn,t say a word. Years later, when I pulled
the one who had punched me down on the mat,

I watched the clock as I locked a breath inside his throat.
He could have been my brother, his hair the same
coarse black strands, his face filled with my shadow.

I held him there in front of everyone.

BIRTHMARK
from Birthmark

After they make love, he slides down so his face rests near her waist. The light by the bed casts its nets that turn into shadows. They both fall asleep. When he wakes, he finds a small patch of birthmarks on her thigh, runs his finger over each island, a spec of light brown bundled with others to form an archipelago on her skin. For him, whose father is from the Philippines, it is the place he has never been, filled with hillsides of rice & fish, different dialects, a family he wants to touch, though something about it all is untouchable, like love, balanced between desire & longing, the way he reaches for her now, his hand pressed near this place that seems so foreign, so much a part of him that for a moment, he cannot help it, he feels whole.

RETURN

1.

We found ourselves gone
into the crowd on Bourbon
Street, a river with its current
of tourists breaking the invisible
levees until certain things drew
us in, someone's wife undressed
among college students quick to
drape camera flashes across her skin,
and the man struggling to cover her
with his wrinkled suit coat
is her sad husband, you imagine.
His smile appears only an apology.
It is almost January, and the wind
lingering in the distant marsh grass

gathers to speak its name over
the woman's nipples sharpening
while people nearby disappear
into themselves, an easier descent
among the alleyways lining the empty
church, its rusted grates meshed
with the stench of piss and blood,
and how we all emerged then into
Jackson Square, the Baby about to drop
and signal the end of one year,
the beginning of another. Finding
your spot within the crowd, your hand
holding onto your wife's, you find
there is always a hint of sadness
that hangs back from any considerable joy
and waits, your mother's sure words like
a prayer through life, "Remember laughter
turns to crying." Before the hour
slides into place, you decide you will cherish
the temporal, holding onto each other's face
to steady yourselves before the embrace
of the moment passes on. You enjoy
a kiss among the crowd of others
cheering through jazz and blues,
drunk on Hurricanes.

2.

Outside, in the sun, a Louisiana winter
hums within bristled palms, you overhear
someone a table away say "Filipino Necktie"
and swipe a single fingertip across their throat.
Others among them laugh, and it is gruesome,
you think, how silence then follows.

It settles over the food set before them.
A woman's slim fingers slide over the neck
of an opened bottle, which she struggles
with a few jolts to release the ketchup,
its dimpled redness spills onto her plate
of fries and catfish, and when you return
to the conversation, among your friends,
they are smiling casually in their hunger
to be understood, the lull having gathered
about you all, you want to tell them a story
about your father, one he'd waited until
you were grown to inherit, how,
when he was young, stationed in Norfolk,
a few of the Filipinos from his ship would
spend weekends at a dancehall in Oceanview,
and many times over, the nights would end
with white sailors starting fights with them,
those young Filipinos in their custom-
made Hong Kong suits, slick as snakeskin,
their black hair primed with pomade,
they had to know they were dangerous
for girls would come those nights wanting
only to dance with them and so, one night,
my father says, before the dance, those young
Filipinos fashioned thick chainlinks around
their necks, under silk shirts, metal pressed
heavily against their skin and covered
marks left by a mother's rosary. When
the white sailors cut in with their worn routine
of violence, my father says, smiling, as if
he wasn't there, "those Filipinos pulled off
their chains and began swinging them at the other
sailors' legs," the music then had stopped
and the only sound it seemed to him
was the popping of bone into the void

where faces of those girls, wide-eyed,
have long since vanished.

"Return" appeared in MiPOesias.com
(Guest edited by Nick Carbo)

Jon Pineda is the author of *Birthmark* (Southern Illinois University Press, 2004), winner of the Crab Orchard Award Series in Poetry, and *The Translator's Diary* (New Issues, 2008), winner of the Green Rose Prize for Poetry.

Karen Llagas

TANNINS

Inside this vineyard, someone is fashioning
a door to ruins, to once viaducts
and colonnades.

A deep-colored failure is fermenting in the fruit:
to know *how* is to move away
from the light that holds you, and holds you
by being mysterious.

I'll explain it as being shown how to love
something before it's understood,
standing here, staving off sadness
in what is enduring and nameless.

Because the subdued light in the photograph
became sympathetic to your questions,
you took a plane back
to a dialect that could no longer recognize you.

Childhood is provincial like that.
It's a small bird making ripples on a lake
before disappearing. Your own *Leptis Magna*,
at the edge of becoming sand, to be collected in jars.

The tannins are in the seeds, we hear someone say.
You ask if there is something in the sugar
that remains inedible. How deep do you
keep the bottles so that the light

and heat can't follow?
Those stains in your hands,
until when will they remain?

The Muse Speaks

Turned sideways, as you asked, I am more
masculine than exuberant, my breasts almost
coy. We hold no secrets here, I told you,

and still you insist I guard this circle
of women and their stories, the dog
with his island of stories. Come closer.

Tell me what you see. Dirt, the crimson
of my lips? The mango trees' swagger?
The glisten of coconut oil in my hair?

The sun bleaches our laughter, and even
more, our sorrows. You ask, *is it ever
dark here? Is it ever cold?* O infinite

afternoons, O profound boredom.
All I've known is brightness until you came.
Here, I give you back the charcoal you sketched

me with, the one you left by the bed that night.
You told me very few colors can be seen
at once, what matters is what separates them.

I dreamt of the light in Arles, the sepia snow.
But that world is mute for you now, as it will be
for me, once you leave. You don't know me,

and I've shown you everything. Come, let me
feel your palm again, show me the texture
of bricks. Make me smell smoke, pressed linen, coal.

FROM A LIGHTHOUSE KEEPER

You must know how to navigate the different
kinds of darkness. Not to trust the moon:
though brilliant, she is faithless. You must need
very little sleep, and write long letters. Sometimes,
the Pacific insists on being cadmium.
What derivatives would you take then?
So you play solitaire and sing lullabies with the wind.
You think those buoy lights are a god's
stubby fingers. Very good. Now become
something other than fallible. Accept that waving
the lost home is, at the moment, best done without men.
We find the mirrors able to concentrate better without
being gazed at, and the kerosene, left on its own,
will sweeten and effloresce. You must know
how to navigate the different kinds of darkness.

Karen Llagas is a first generation immigrant based in San Francisco. She has an MFA in Writing from Warren Wilson College and has read her work widely in the SF Bay Area. She works as an intepreter and a translator.

Sarah Gambito

IMMIGRATION 88

I write with my dogs. So they don't observe the
creepy crawlies of their doubts shimmering in the
background. I write because I'm pack leader. I want
them to stay the course. Whether it's for water or
better boyfriends. My will is theirs.

It's important that I know our old love. That I slide
down on the bathroom floor in front of our original
country. There was a map on his wall with everything
pinned to where he had been. I felt each location. I
listened with every ear I had. I slid to the floor. I said
this is where we are going to go.

Sarah Gambito is the author of *Matadora* (Alice James
Books, 2004). Her poems have appeared or are forthcoming
in *The Iowa Review*, *The Antioch Review*, *Denver Quarterly*, *The
New Republic*, *Field*, *Quarterly West*, *Fence* and other journals.
She holds degrees from The University of Virginia and The
Creative Writing Program at Brown University. She teaches
at New Yor University and Baruch College and is co-Founder
of Kundiman, a non-profit company serving Asian American
poets.   http://www.kundiman.org

Jean Vengua

THE CITY AND THE GARDEN 2
(Excerpt)

2.

I took as beginning the warm bricks of the French Hospital my birth
day and instructed my hands to a place, time, entry into the world.

I mean that I got older and returned to where I wanted to be.

Telling a story to myself, as usual, and thinking this is memory.

And then to think it and to see in the choir's morning practice the gathering,
and to hear in it in rounds and small corrections, over and over under the
vaulted ceiling and the old saints.

You. I told no one else the details. How walking on Green Street I will ro-
manticize a small store like a Joseph Cornell box full of objects where "East
meets West." That is to make beautiful where the dissonance begins to tear.
The city is ripe for that artifice. There are grey mornings, so anyone is willing
in moments to search for happiness among damp newspapers and mortar.

I have a sense of what "Filipino" means and I carry it outwardly, but there is
also *that* gathering and we have names for it, that is, we. It is not a constant,
what I think I am disappears and emerges in time.

To that end we obsess about food and draw a circle around it and smile.

I walked slow when alone, trying to find all the parts that fit. Together with
friends, we walked quickly and the meals were rushed and talking.

We are concerned with the events of the day, with preserving identity and with its dissolution. The *patis* tastes fishy and I think I am this taste.

Together we hear the hesitance and watch how y/our eyes flick on and off. At the table over Pad Thai we have many fears and comfort ourselves.

Asserting and pulling back to include and smooth over arrange and rearrange our selves to each gesture or some emotional chord; it is worthwhile work. By turns and in rounds we are angry, indifferent and in love.

Yesterday, I asked myself if I knew beforehand how the dying at Laguna Honda would change me. The going out and disappearing. There were cartoons and faces and things to remember on the walls. His face shiny and the hollows pouring into the eyes and around the smooth sockets where he begins to go. The tropical garden and the almost forgotten Spanish flowering into. Like this.

Are to say memorials, we say, of life. I no longer know you are of a race or a location. Only, the door was open to green leaves where they tended, and the stones were wet. I tell it, and they will tell it when the city grows older and like this, I cease. There are names on cards and a stubborn remainder of outlines, a skyline, or a face. To draw you in. It's like this.

Jean Vengua
Location: Central Coast California
Job: Editor/writer, sometime college instructor
Dog: Gracie
Desserts: Chocolate truffle cake & rice pudding gelato
Dinner: Philippine Adobo w/rice and raw tomatoes on the side; green mangoes w/bagoong; anything Italian or Greek; anything Mexican sans cheese.
Bird: Great-eared Philippine Nightjar
Dance: hokey pokey
Published: in *Moria*, *Fugacity*, *Otoliths*, and numerous anthologies including *Geopolitics of the Visual* (Ateneo U.), *Ping-Pong* (Henry Miller Library), *Bay Poetics*, *Pinoy Poetics*, *e=x=c=h=a=n=g =e=v=a=l=u=e=s* (interview) and *Babaylan*. Co-Editor with Mark Young of the *First Hay(na)ku Anthology* (2006), and the *Second Hay(na)ku Anthology*, forthcoming 2008. She is the winner of the Filamore Tabios Sr. Memorial Poetry Prize; her poetry book is entitled *Prau* (Meritage Press, 2007), and chapbook is *The Aching Vicinities* (Otoliths Press).

Juliana Seneriches

AUTUMN PRAYER

God, you stopped me dead on my tracks
when I passed by the window all ablaze
with You: the whole frame fully filled
with gold melting into red into orange
into brown, burgundy into yellow;
yellow edged with red; light green
edged with brown, breeze and morning
light playing with the spiky tufts;

A blue jay flies in, a leaf wafts down,
as all I could do was silently write
this pray'r!!!

NOON BREAK/ALL MY BLUE JAYS

It started on a Sunday encounter, nay, accost by a wet scraggly nestling off the nest from the front yard cherry tree, wobbly hopping towards the front walk and me! What to do? I backed up hurriedly, got to the phone, dialed a Berkeley Bird Rescue team, there, boldly printed on our phone book. "Is the bird's tail black?" —No.— "If not, the tail shall grow within two days, and the bird, a blue jay perhaps, shall be able to fly on its own. In the meantime, its parents shall bring it nourishment. Don't let anybody touch the baby bird and keep away the neighborhood cats and dogs until the bird's wings are strong enough to fly." That morning, I was in touch with the whole neighborhood; to my surprise, no one laughed me away. True to the prediction, the parent birds hovered over their young, noisily warning when people approached, flapping it towards the bushes. They had food in their beaks; while the wings formed blue and true. The dogs, cats were in the house, while the children were out, dutifully away from the bird family, curious and tickled by a drama they could all understand. That same day's night, I stepped on my brakes suddenly! There was this birdling, hopping towards my car and me! On the third day, while I was in the garden among the roses, it tried its new found wings and flopped into the pool. Exasperated, I skimmed it out of the cold chlorine waters.

Three short days (they did seem long!) of introduction and today, I have three fat blue jays in my garden, eating peanuts off my hands, noisily flying to my window sill as soon as they know I am home for lunch!!!

THE SOUNDS OF EVENING RAIN

Loud gushing down the gutters,
soft hypnotic patters on the roof
and splatters on the concrete drive.

Crashing thunders, silent lightning,
winds wishing through the palms,
creaking through the bamboo grove,

In unison,
     in crescendos
          and in whispers,

then, when silenced, the hoarse frogs
     and chirping crickets start!

Juliana Seneriches is a writer, poet, and a practicing physician (psychiatry) from Pleasanton, California. Julie divides her time between living in California and Iloilo, Philippines where she directs a medical mission project of bringing Filipino American doctors to treat the poor in the home country.

JP Catenza

IN THEIR SOCIETY IT IS FASHIONABLE TO LOOK LIKE AN EGG

All the city birds
in angle less turns

ever taking off
each other's nemesis

for crumbs and puddle water
no dowry no colorful skills

scavengers of the old city
colored like cracked pavement

hop along to the pigeon school
learn from gulls

to quit flying underfoot
mime the state bird

and resurrect a love affair
with the myth

that blood provides
it is a burden myth

but birds must make
something with young wings

A Forest Full of Bears/
An Alley Full of Thieves

In the morning
I wake up late for the sunrise

and read a six o'clock sky
by its shade and attitude

to gauge the cold
I spy with farmer's eyes

the people at Washington Square
a furlong of shawls

is zero degrees
my city quantified

in cab rides, bus stops
and lonely measures

of street lamps
a rhythm of

surrogate moons

Two Thousand Years Old

Don the new days
of season less years

let the heart migrate
and outgrow climates and clichés

when the years become
too awkward to pronounce

we will mark the date
according to mood.

JP Catenza is a writer from Boston, MA. Born on Christmas
Day 1981, his parents came from the Philippines to the US in
1970. JP is the last of their seven children. Catenza has been
writing poetry since he was 16.

Rey Escobar

TULI - #1

In 1984, Dr. Salvacion pulled down my shorts and asked
what kind of "style" I preferred, would like and could live
with. would I like the american, straight, well groomed,
with a rounded collar look. or the dutch, shy one's best

Friend, with a thin, rounded lip. or the german, helmet
hard, thick style, with oval tongue look. I wanted to
choose "none." to keep my little brown brother of sugar
cane skin hanging like a limp vine collared around the

Ratiles tree that bore small, colorful and sweet tasting
jamaican cherry fruits. I wanted to choose "none,"
but Dr. Salvacion expressed his need. my need.
our need to have a look. a definition.

The need to define a "style" I must choose. a style. belief.
infectious scalpel rinsed in alcohol, handpicked,
and just ordered for my rubbery foreskin
that had edged closer to a callous toughness.

That at age ten, would have required more than just a
beat down building courage from my father, than a
bigger scalpel from Dr. Salvacion, than louder and
much more frequent taunting from Mister Ignatio:

> "O ano, pinatulian na ba yan?
> Takot yata.
> Baka bakla...."*

*So, has he been circumcized already? He seems scared. Perhaps he's gay.

So I picked the closest skin I felt kin with: white collared
german, thick tongue, helmet hard, lashing gestapo
genitals, which later in life, I described to my wife
as her very own:

Guapo* gestapo, little brown brother general, bone hard   *handsome*
and stubborn general MacArthur's: "I shall return."
like a nymph rock that broke a shoring wood. I watched.
myself. undress.

My shorts pulled past my legs, down to my ankles and
then off to the floor it floated. my t-shirt, half rolled up
to my empty stomach. the need to eat waiting. the need
for ice on a promised coca-cola drink growing. the need

For Mang Purong's salty ice cream, the cream he scooped
into his cone, the one surrounded by icepicked blocks of
ice. the one that chattered my upper teeth against my
lower teeth when I licked them.

The one cone that battered my back and twisted up my
spine like a cold icepick pressed then punctured cold
into my summer's body, my hardening bones,

Hardening eyes, neck, head, skull, all hardening because
of his ice cream. salty cream digested and seemed to be
spitting out of my mouth as Dr. Salvacion

Stroked away my salvation. my cock stroked by his warm
rubbery hand. fingers sweating through. and with one
look, he smiled and tapped my grown stiffness.

"O bakit ka tumitigas?"

I watched naked from the waist down. as the other
hand slipped into another glove. as the scalpel is picked.
as his rubber cold fingers keyed my shoulder.

And with gentle prompt, pushed my shivering body to the
bed. white sheets crumpled stiff. I watched, still naked from
waist down. his nurse joined us, listened. him intoned.

And she began to stretch the lip of my cock. I watched, as she
stood bedside, just below my knee. I watched as she stood,
beauty behold. thin fingers inside white papery

Thin gloves. thin and soft fingers tugging wet paper. her thin
lips half puckered. her slit eyes watching, slightly slanted.
thin smile shaping on her as the scalpel carved.
As she gave me courage. as she gave me stiffness. as my hand
gripped the bed's handle bar. As I watched her back.
and forced a smile. my own slant eyes watery.

My own lips reddened as if her sudden kiss painted my lips with
her lipstick. she must have been twice my age. I was nine. I knew
then how far my hard on would last.

❧

Rey Escobar was born in Lucena City, Quezon and at age 13
he emigrated with his family to the U.S. in 1988.

   He lives in Oak Park, Illinois with his spouse Christine, a
journalist & freelance writer. He is currently pursuing a Bachelors of Arts in Poetry at Columbia College in Chicago. He
is a father of two. Ezra (he loves being called 'Boogie') is a six
year old cellist & unschooler. Lucie (she loves being called
'Bumple') is a beautiful two year old strong-willed wanderer of
the world around her.

   The selection in Field of Mirrors is from a collection that
he started to piece together: his "TULI" poems --reflections
related to the physical, social, spiritual, emotional, political,
religious, subject/theme/idea of circumcision; and his upbringing, his cultural and immigration experiences etc. as they
relate to the the word itself.

Elmer Omar Pizo

Corrected version for parts I & II

Viagra

I.

*W*hat good does it do to a man, 69 years of age, widower for the last ten years, retired from his full-time job building houses and his part-time job customizing cabinets and fences, walking with the help of a cane (rheumatoid arthritis hasn't stopped from stamping its authority over his left knee), to get back to P.I. to marry a lass 40 years his junior, defying in the process all kinds of pointed questions and hassles from the U.S. Naturalization and Immigration office needing proof the marriage isn't fixed or for convenience, and that their union is consummated before he can bring his girl back to Hawaii after a 3-year and a half wait? For heaven's sake! More often than not, the story of this kind of marriage doesn't end in *"And they lived happily ever after."* "See you in court!" is the usual line, when after three years of permanent residency, the girl secures her much-coveted prize: U.S. citizenship.

II.

*G*etting to the core of his action, either by prying into or by furious digging of how things are now unfolding in his personal life right after his good friend set him up for that girl, it remains difficult to understand why this "being taken advantage of" stuff is not his main concern. Aside from reaching that stage where he doesn't know how to handle the romantic side of love anymore, such as giving away small packages of sweet nothings with a couple of light kisses on the forehead and cheeks, one of his main tools of the trade (as he considers it as such), once formidable and up to par in meeting any kind of challenge, but now with very few windows of opportunity, sad to say, is reduced to a *jack* that can no longer lift! Him, indulging in bowls of shark fin soup and soup #5 (a concoction of stewed testicles and penises of sacrificial goats), tons of live oysters, crushed Spanish flies and powdered Korean ginseng roots—not to mention those reams and reams of x-rated magazines and used DVD's —yet, all these failed in their collective effort of resurrecting the *dead*!

the girl has

Elmer Omar Pizo

Wnat good does it do to a man, 69 years of age, widower for the last ten years, retired from his full-time job building houses and his part-time job customizing cabinets and fences, walking with the help of a cane (rheumatoid arthritis hasn't stopped from stamping its authority over his left knee), to get back to P.I. to marry a lass 40 years his junior, defying in the process all kinds of pointed questions and hassles from the U.S. Naturalization and Immigration office needing proof the marriage isn't fixed or for convenience, and that their union is consummated before he can bring his girl back to Hawaii after a 3-year and a half wait? For heaven,s sake! More often than not, the story of this kind of marriage doesn't end in *"And they lived happily ever after."* "See you in court!" is the usual line after   secured her much-coveted prize three years after her permanent resident status changed: a U.S. citizenship.

II.

Getting to the core of his action, either by prying into or by furious digging of how things are now unfolding in his personal life right after his good friend set him up for that girl, it remains difficult to understand why this „being taken advantage of„ stuff is not his main concern. Aside from reaching that stage where he doesn,t know how to handle the romantic side of love anymore, like giving away small packages of sweet nothings with a couple of light kisses on the forehead and cheeks, one of his main tools of the trade (as he considers it as such), once formidable and up to par in meeting any kind of challenge and doesn't pass too often any window of oppor tunity, sad to say, it's reduced to a "jack" that can no lor lift! Him, indulging in their collective effort of resurre the dead!

III.

A day before his much-anticipated trip, one of his clos est friends, deeply concerned about his sexual well-being, brought 10 packs at 6 each of the blue pill for him to take once he's already in P. I. facing the inevitable. The following night, at his rented room in Kalihi 3 hours before his sched uled check-in at the airport, his will, now too weak to resist the overpowering strength of his curiosity, "The hell with it! Come what may!" he said, tearing up one corner of the packet then popped not one but two pills into his mouth. (*If only he took the time and paused for a moment to read the Warning por tion printed in small case, all could still be well with him.*) Before he could swallow the pills, regret, coming out of nowhere, stepped in, hyperextended its arms and blocked his throat with such force, his Adam's apple broke in half causing him to cough, gag and choke! At 50 mg. a pill, absolutely, they're very potent. Although he was able to spit them out, the pills' coating already melted! His tongue, at first, felt numb. After a few seconds, like an overfed cucumber, it has grown swol len, erect and stiff. When he attempted to say some words, nothing came out except a garbled kind of sound and those unexpected showers of spit! How messy and quick, the suc cession of events were as panic made its move to take over. Running outside the house barefoot, in his loose underwear and muscle-hugging shirt, his trembling hands pointed at his exaggerated tongue coated with saliva foaming from the back up to its tip. All that you could hear from him: a monkey-like *uh-uh-uhh* sound punctuated by his billiard ball eyes about to pop out of their sockets! And yet, onlookers were at a loss, still couldn't figure out what exactly was going on with him. Him, being in that altered state; and me, being of no help to him whatsoever even with this sweating bag of ice I intended to wrap around his tongue (to alleviate its suffering). I could only say with much regret, his stiffness lasted for hours and his muffled cries for help lasted for almost forever!

Elmer Omar Pizo, originally from Asingan, Pangasinan, is a 17-year resident of Ewa Beach, Hawaii. He is an Inspector for the Department of Health, State of Hawaii. Some of his poems have been included in the Bamboo Ridge Press anthologies (http://www.bambooridge.com) and in the *Hawaii Review* (Dept. of English publication of the University of Hawaii-Manoa).

Lora Mendoza

SENT

10.

There is a beast living at 3138 River Street. It will not leave. It sleeps next to the Head of our Household. Lays its bony neck upon the very same mattress. It is definitely female. At five feet and nine inches, she can touch the ceiling and clearly see above store counters where I cannot. She has already spawned a boy from another carrier. He is 12 years of age and can only play three chords on the guitar. To acknowledge him is to consider the pimplets on my chin as mini gift baskets filled with love from the gods.

11.

It is hopeless. I've already spent all the patience in my body just thinking about being patient with her. Flagrant mistakes mark her stay. One—serving *adobo* with brown rice. Who dares to ask your newly acquired family to eat it in this manner? Why don't I shove the *adobo* meat up against a bran muffin and dip it in soluble oats. I know what the stale purgatory of my future tastes like: plain brown rice with chicken *adobo*. Two—hug people when they cross the threshold of our door. Especially the oldies. Lolo and Lola didn't endure this long for a soft handshake. Embrace the flesh. Three—stop encouraging teenagers to sign up for the Princess Urduja Festival. Having taken any number of East Asian Women's courses at Berkeley does not make a beast an expert on potential candidates.

12.

Boo to the beast for her spaghetti without sausages. And I am not the only one affected as I hear the Head of Household ask her if she could set aside sausages in a bowl for those who wish to add them.

13.

I never said I knew anything about Princess Urduja. There are subjects I haven't gotten to yet. After some light internet research, Princess Urduja was a great Filipina warrior who may or may not have existed. Experts say she is a myth. On Monday morning a competition application is taped to my door.

14.

She's planted birds of paradise in the front yard where the yellow roses perished. Nobody watered the damn things. Sometimes I swat the beaks. Look closely and passers-by can spot the black marks of poorly drawn slanted eyes and teeth on them. They end up looking like sharks. I miss the yellow roses.

15.

The beast overheard me calling her a beast. I'm not sorry. Well, I'm sorry this had to be written down and exorcised from a somewhat guilty conscience.

16.

Lumpiang shanghai is not to be called "petite lumpees" and *pancit* should so not be described to others as a derivative of chow mein. I want to slam a basketball in her face.

17.

I heard my name when I turned the corner. The beast underestimated my ability to capture her airy, proper voice ten feet away. She thinks if someone walks out of a room they can't hear you. On my desk she found a newspaper article about people committing suicide by jumping off the Golden Gate Bridge. She says this is a strange thing to hang on to. Head of Household says nothing. He knows I could have been working on a speech for the forensics team.

My expository speech is about dust.

I like reading the newspaper and inhaling the strong stink off the pages. Plus, it irks the beast to find grungy newspapers next to the toilet.

18.

Kneeling on the couch, the step-brother plucks out suspicious look-ing gray hairs out of his mother's curly brunette hair. This is gross. Step-brother nitpicks over every inch of scalp. She sits with her back against one end and spins a basketball endlessly on her middle finger. Supposedly a point guard in high school. Step-brother earns a dollar for every three he tweezes from the root successfully. Head of House-hold comes home to discover the two, falls onto the cushions and convinces the step-son to work on his grays next.

19.

Today I put on the Head of Household's steel-toed work boots and stomped on the birds of paradise. Green beaks smashed. Yellow-or-ange feathers disintegrated. Stems bent at acute angles. I left the hose running in the yard. Then I ran off to Anita's house for the rest of the day. I was asked for at 9:03 p.m. and I returned by 9:26 p.m. Wimp. Head of Household is transferring out in three weeks. We're moving 1,751 miles away.

> "Should toss them out."
> "No. I'm gonna put them on Plevin's desk." The man tucks away the bundled paper into his jacket pocket.
> "Now you're saving them? For a scrapbook or what? Come on, the people know it's supposed to be dumped out," says Jay.
> "I finally opened up a couple. Damn if I didn't feel sick for throwing the earlier ones into the recycling bin."
> "Not likely that Mrs. San Tomas is going to see them."

The man lifts his baseball cap off and smoothes over his thinning white hair. "Don't throw them away if you see more letters out here next month. Right Jay?"

"Fine."

The man slips his cap on and he nudges Jay to the side. He continues with his work. The bronze vase holding a dried out yellow rose is tipped over a garbage bag and the flower disposed. He twists the vase back into its spot on the thick marble headstone and pushes the wheelbarrow over the freshly cut grass.

Lora Mendoza has a B.A. in Communication and has studied at The Writer's Studio and UCLA Extension. She currently lives in Northern California.

Luis Malay Syquia

Selections from
Fogeater, Poems by Luis Malay Syquia
Menagerie Arts, 2007

MIDNIGHT

from Pan Asian Holiday Tour, #IV

Sorcery of snakes has caught me
Naïve and unaware...
dragon disappears...
I hear the ripple of ocean
                              Submergence
listen to a king cobra hissing
ready to strike
above my head
Still
i sing to the enduring enchantment
of eastern eyes
weeping in the wake of wasted lives
amidst the ignorance and dull oppression
                              of human joy and
                              sorrow...

KINDNESS

He was
homeless
dirty blonde rheumy-eyed
lazy crazy wino
don't want to work—or can't
possibly a disillusioned vietnam vet

sitting day after day on kearny street
passing him by hundreds of times
trying to ignore him seemingly
beneath my contempt or sympathy
one late afternoon
an old chinese woman
possibly a recent immigrant
unexpectantly squats down in front of him
she hands the blue-eyed beggar
a carton of hot, steaming chinese food
he accepts it greedily gratefully
bowing in an exaggerated manner
the woman walks away
without expression
without ceremony

PIANO LESSONS

my godfather
my "ninong"*
professor Calixto Llamas
my piano teacher
quick-steppin' ballroom
dancer— still whirling
the young and not-so-young
ladies around and around
still teaches them
new steps to keep time
and to dazzle
the eye

tito calixto
the man i used to fear
in my youth

i remember his bony
knuckles rapping
discipline Discipline
into my skull
on wednesdays or saturdays
every week my sisters and cousins
& i would expectantly fearfully
wait for him to come
whoever was the first
brave or foolish
to take piano lessons
would report back to us
waiting/telling us
whether he was in a good
or bad mood

he looks more fragile now
like a delicate piece
of wrinkled jade
his step is still nimble
but the insistence of age
has made it slower
i see him sometimes
grippin' a brown shopping bag
full of cut-rate groceries
thin whispy white hair
wizened eyes
cackling laugh
his back starting
to stoop like a comma

he's a smart old man though
saved up enough coin to go
round the world again—whirling
whirling around and around

unmarried
my mom said that his
sweetheart broke his heart
long time ago back
in the islands
still he plays virtuoso piano
travels dances
laughing laughing

tito calixto
eighty-four years old
my mom told me the
other day tito calixto
just became a u.s. citizen
—and got mugged
on his way home

WISHES

the swelter
of a swollen
summer expectant
ready to
burst—
a water
balloon full
of flying
fishes flying
dreams flying

Luis Malay Syquia was born and raised in San Francisco. *Fogeater* (Menageris Arts, 2007), his new book of poetry , is a compilation of poems written over 30 years and reflects the experience of growing up brown and Asian in America.

Victor P. Gendrano

JAPANESE HAIKU

(Tagalog)

ospital silid hintayan
ang plastik na mga bulaklak
palaging bukad

(English version)

waiting room
the plastic flowers
always in bloom

pinagbiling bahay
puno ng halakhak
ng mga bata

sold house
children's laughter echoes
from its bare walls

Canadian Zen Haku Canadien
Vol. 3, No. 4, Autumn 2005

JAPANESE TANKA

chopping onions
enough excuse
to shed my tears
as I cook for myself
this New Year's eve

Ribbons, Tanka Society of America Journal
Vol. 2, No. 1, Spring 2006

(Tagalog version)

di lang sibuyas
sanhi ng pagluha
kundi sa pangungulila
pagluluto sa sarili
ngayong bagong taon

scent of jasmine wafts
through her open door
this sultry evening
she calls him to say
don't be late coming

the torn jacket
and worn-out cane
lie near a trash bin
his chuckle still echoes
from the empty bed

Modern English Tanka
Vol. 2, No. 2,, Winter 2007

Korean Sijo

Aloneness

the visiting son laments
his loss of their backyard tree

where as a teen he carved a heart
to express his very first love

his widower dad explains
twice there I tried to hang myself

Alheizmer Disease

as I brush mom's golden hair
she keeps talking to unseen friends

she accepts me now as a friend
in the hospice where she lives

sometimes I wonder if she knows
I am her least-liked daughter

LYNX : A Journal for Linking Poets
Vol. XXII, No. 3 October, 2007

Pasko Na Naman

Sinalubong siya ng lamig ng hangin
Halos mapatakbo nang hindi ginawin,
Danga't simbang-gabi't dapat manalangin
Upang patnubayan sa ibang lupain,
At mapagtiisan hirap ng damdamin
Sa pagkakalayo sa anak at giliw.

Udyok ng dolyar na makapangyarihan
Umalis sa lupang bayang sinilangan,
Tulad din ng iba'y iniwan ang mahal
Naiwang pangako'y babalik din naman,
Oras makaipon ng sapat pambuhay
Sa kanyang mag-ina't matandang magulang.

Kahit na ano lang klase ng trabaho
Kanyang pinasukan, kahit ang totoo,
May pinag-aralan at isang maestro
Nagsimula siyang isang mensahero,
Sa gabi'y janitor inaasikaso
Nagpapahinga lang sa araw ng Linggo.

Matuling lumipas ang mga panahon
Linggo'y naging buwan saka naging taon,
Marami-rami nang perang naiipon
Ngunit isang araw siya'y naparool,
Natutong mag-poker, Las Vegas at mahjong
At sa blondeng Kana natutong pumatol.

Pati mga liham ng kanyang asawa
Hindi na masagot, di na mahalaga,
At madalang na ring pera'y magpadala
Sapagka't sa dami ng sweldong kinita,
Gayon din and dami ng kanyang paggasta
Wala ring maipon, minsan ay kapos pa.

Ngunit isang araw biglang naospital
Sa kanyang trabaho'y nawalan ng malay,
Presyon ng dugo ay lubhang mataas daw
Ang hatol ng doktor ay magpahingalay,
Kung hindi ay baka bawian ng buhay
Sa sakit sa puso baka matuluyan.

Sa pangungulila sa sariling silid
Walang kaibigang sa kanya'y sumilip,
Kay-dami n'ya noon na tinatangkilik
Ni anino ngayon ay hindi lumapit.
(Habang mayroon ka'y maraming kapatid
Kapag naghirap na'y sarili ang sakit).

Muling nagunita ang kanyang pamilya
Kabiyak ng puso, ang bunso at ina,
Bulong ay patawad sa pagkakasala
Kusang pagkalimot sa tuwi-tuwina,
Mahabaging Diyos patawarin sana
Magbabagong buhay ang aking panata

Ng siya'y umuwi sa pagka-ospital
Malamig ang simoy ng hanging Amihan,
Mga palamuti't tugtog sa tindahan
Ay nagbabalitang malapit na naman,
Ang Paskong dakila sa sangkatauhan
Luwalhati sa lahat at kapayapaan.

Ngayong simbang gabi'y malamig ang hangin
At ang mga tao'y lakad ay matulin,
Ngunit payapa na ang kanyang damdamin
Sa Sanggol na Hesus wagas nanalangin,
Na sa Paskong ito'y muling pagyamanin
Ang pagmamahalan ay panatilihin.

Heritage magazine,
Vol. 2, No 4, December 1988.

Victor P. Gendrano is a retired librarian from the Los
Angeles County Public Library and presently living in Lake-
wood, California. He obtained a BS from the University of the
Philippines and an MS from Syracuse University in New York.
He was publisher and editor of *Heritage Magazine*, an English-
language quarterly that ran from 1987-1999. He is the author
of *Rustle of bamboo leaves: selected haiku and other poems*, 2005.

Almira Astudillo Gilles

THE BASKET

The rough hands that wove this basket,
twisting and knotting strands
of abaca and hemp
belonged to my grandmother.

She took two kinds of rope,
one sand-colored, the other dark
like her hair; she tugged and pulled
until her fingers grew calloused.

She knotted strands
of hemp and abaca,
humming two melodies
not knowing she had twisted them
into one.

Her face, moody as the sea
shifted with the tides
of her memory,
serene in the morning
tremulous in the afternoon.

She didn't stop weaving this basket
until it was fully formed,
desperate in its need
for things to hold.

With her hands she offered it to me
saying, this will hold a kilo of rice.
Her hands have sanctified it
and I leave it empty,
remembering the sea.

TIA

My mother's sister greets me
cradling a papaya heavier
than her wrinkled body,
fruit foretelling forgiveness.

She does not think it strange
to heave a six-pound fruit
across the South China Sea
to see us on holiday.

She does not even ask
if I like papaya
but simply says,
"This is already ripe."

She brushes away
years of my ignoring birthdays,
funerals, not visiting,
not writing about America.

She watches my daughter chase
a hermit crab, tells me I look healthy,
and tests her World War II English
on my husband.

Then she turns back,
bent under the weight of seventy years
to once again ride the outrigger boat
to tend to her other papaya.

FIRE BLOSSOM

he pilot assured them that the fluid dripping from the left wing was "of no consequence," but Christina vowed she had had enough of transporting dead bodies. There was no hiding the fact that this was a traveling funeral, with black-clad women who sobbed from San Francisco to Manila. The grieving process had actually already started in her uncle's house in Daly City, built up in momentum through the complicated task of sending a body to another country with about fifty confused relatives and hangers-on, and continued in the restricted environment of the airplane.

She was sure the other passengers felt apprehensive about the possibility of a casket on board, despite the fact that the pilot had not made any such revelation. But that seemingly innocuous announcement about the wing, combined with the presence of distraught mourners, filled the cabin air with a sense of foreboding. Christina felt it and was spooked by it, and *she* was part of the bereaved party. *She* knew what rested in the cargo hold.

More specifically, she knew *who* rested in the cargo hold. The *who* happened to be her grandmother, who stopped breathing after a lifetime of being shuffled around, from bedroom to bedroom, household to household, island to island, continent to continent, finally to return in death to the place where she had been conceived.

The flight would be fifteen hours long. Right after take-off, Christina asked her mother, "Why are we bringing *Lola* back to the Philippines if her family shoved her out of there in the first place?"

In reply, Christina got an angry shush and a reprimand, the gist of which was that *Lola*, grandma, would probably have wanted to return to the land of her birth, and was she, Christina, so Americanized that she felt no such loyalty? Christina composed a mental answer that reminded her mother that she was born in the U.S. and, further, she preferred to bury people where they dropped dead. All this long-distance corpse commuting was just not very convenient for those who had to make travel arrangements. She, herself, would prefer to be buried in that cemetery five blocks from where she lived, rather than Tulsa, Oklahoma where she was born. She would rather have her friends ride in a car instead of fly on a plane to say goodbye. It would also be nice if someone she knew kept her grave clean and placed flowers or decorations weekly and on holidays.

But she didn't say that to her mother who, since the day Clara San Juan was discovered lying face down on a fake sheepskin rug a week ago, had already taken a total of fourteen Valium pills. Christina knew because it was her secret task to count them.

Christina also did not tell her mother that she would miss her *lola*. Christina thought of her *lola* as a shadow living among them, a relic from another time and place who did not part easily with old habits. During frenetic holiday dinner preparations *Lola* would amble about, unnoticed, pouring fish sauce in the turkey gravy when nobody was looking, or picking all the raisins out of a salad and depositing them in her pocket to snack on later. Christina admired her tenacity and marveled at her inscrutable poker face. "Raisins? Me? I'm allergic to them, don't you know?"

Instead of telling her mother all that, Christina said, "Mom, I don't want to spend most of my summer vacation in the Philippines."

To which her mother replied, "You should be grateful your *lola* died in July, instead of let's say, May, when you were taking the SAT's. And it is not your entire vacation, just a month. In fact, we're practically sneaking out of this funeral. Mourning takes forty days, you know, during which the soul of the departed just hangs around, not quite knowing she's dead. That's why we pray—to gently push her on to the next life."

A month was not a day too soon for Christina. This was her first visit, and the accounts of her Filipino-American friends who had gone before were not encouraging. "Too hot, the boys are strange, don't drink the water." She did look forward to the shopping, and anticipated that funeral activities would probably take up only a few days.

She had been to one of these forty-day post-funeral stretches where people came and prayed, ate and played mah-jongg to keep the bereaved family "company." Hardly anybody actually talked about the 'departed,' except in cooking reminiscences, such as "Yah, she cooked tripe like nobody else could." She pictured the soul of her grandmother "hovering" for forty days above the din of clacking mahjongg tiles, coffee-fueled gossip, and sports TV. She would probably be admonishing them from her above-ground position with her trademark, "You're leaving me alone again?"

Christina decided to try and sleep instead of watch the remaining two in-flight movies. "For every visitor, there will be ten greeters," another friend had warned her. By her calculations, there would be one hundred thirty-five people waiting; she thought the three children traveling with them would fetch about five greeters each. She would need all her strength to just be able to stand up, literally, in such a crowd.

When Christina woke up, the airplane was already on the tarmac but not at the gate. There were no other planes waiting on the runway. Her watch, which she had adjusted mid-way, said it was almost midnight. She heard someone saying to her mother, "Vivian, this is Christina's first time, isn't it? Don't worry; she'll have fun. Maybe she'll meet a nice Filipino boy. I hear Alfonso's nephew graduated at the top of his class and is going to med school."

Christina turned toward the voice and found it to belong to the group's busybody, Auntie Fe. She wasn't even really a blood relative, just a family friend who Christina was certain decided to come along partly for the drama, partly for the highly attractive bereavement ticket price.

Christina ignored Auntie Fe and asked her mother, "What's happening? Why aren't we moving toward the gate?"

"They're towing the plane," her mother answered. "The pilot announced it's not engine failure or anything unusual. That's just what they do here, to save on fuel."

A truck drove up in front of the airplane. Great, Christina thought. That little truck is going to overshoot the terminal and crash. She imagined the cargo hold being torn open upon impact, spilling everything: suitcases, boxes, coffin.

With great precision, the truck started to pull the airplane in a huge arc, moving slowly toward the only fully-lit terminal. Christina shut her eyes and waited. The airplane eased to a halt, and after a few seconds of nothing happening she opened her eyes and looked out the window. Everything seemed to be normal. As soon as the cables were detached from the plane, all the passengers stood up and started opening overhead bins, stretching, shuffling to the aisle.

A male voice cackled over the speaker system. "May I request members of the, ah, San Juan party to allow all other passengers to leave first so that we may provide you with your, um, whatever assistance you might need."

Christina's mother pushed her toward the aisle. "We're not waiting. It will be a madhouse. We'll go ahead through customs, get our luggage, and go straight to your uncle's house. They will be waiting for us with a car, and we don't have to go with the others."

With a sigh of relief, Christina forged ahead, grateful that she didn't have to witness the unloading of cargo. Already some of her aunts were beginning to cry again, and it was just too late in the day for any serious weeping.

It did not surprise Christina that funeral preparations progressed very quickly. She assumed her grandmother's body would not last much longer, especially since she heard that air-conditioning was not reliable in many places. The day after their plane touched down in Manila, she and the "San Juan party" assembled at the funeral home for the first of many services, and reassembled at other people's homes for lunch, afternoon snack, and dinner. This itinerary was repeated the next day, and Christina felt like she belonged to a pack of animals or a traveling performing group.

At each place it was the same refrain, sung to different audiences.

"Such a shame, she had to go like that."

"I hear she left substantial property in the province."

"Which priest is doing the funeral service? Can't the Bishop come? They were childhood friends, after all."

"More than friends, some would say."

The pack prayed, talked, ate, and left.

At Dr. Ibanag's house, Christina met Mayette, who was only a year older than she was. The Ibanags had lived in the U.S. for five years, and came back to stay permanently in the Philippines. They hit it off right away.

"Let me show you our garden," Mayette said to Christina, soon after they were introduced. Christina thought the garden a strange place for a teenager to show another, but she was grateful to break away from the group.

Christina was not a plant person, but she felt like she had entered paradise. The scent of unfamiliar flowers drifted toward her, and her sight fixed on a wall that pulsed with a mass of vibrant red-orange flowers she had never seen in the U.S.

"It's beautiful here," Christina exclaimed, approaching the flower wall. She bent close to a flower to examine it, and marveled at how many intricate parts one flower could hold. "What do you call this?" she asked Mayette.

"I don't know," Mayette answered with a shrug. "Mom would know. She didn't have much of a green thumb when we were in Ohio, but here everything grows pretty much by itself. It's the humidity. I sweat so much I bet I could fill a watering can everyday."

Christina thought the petals looked like the tongues of a flame, and the bright red center looked hot to the touch. "I think I'll call it, 'fire flower, fire blossom.' Yeah, 'fire blossom.'"

Mayette looked amused. "So, you like naming things?"

"Only things that don't have a name," Christina answered, "and need one."

"Oh, you'll find that we can do even without names here. Pointing works just fine. You know, Filipinos point with their fingers and their mouths, like this." Mayette pursed her lips, first in front as if waiting for a kiss, then off to the side.

Christina found it both ludicrous and hilarious but was hesitant to laugh. After all, she had just met Mayette and wasn't sure about her sense of humor. Instead, she asked with as much seriousness as she could manage, "Why would anybody point with her mouth?"

"Because their hands are busy?"

Christina thought she detected sarcasm, and she didn't laugh at that remark, either.

They walked to the veranda chairs and sank into the plastic cushions.

"I come out here when it gets too crazy in there," Mayette said, waving her hand toward the crowd inside the house. "You know how it is in a Filipino's house—it's never empty. Sometimes, I watch my mom working in this garden from my window, watch her snip and twist and water these branches. Now it's this huge, awesome thing. I've become sort of fond of it myself. What's that they say...bloom where you are planted?"

Mayette closed her eyes and continued. "I actually like the name, fire blossom. It sounds like it belongs in another place, in legends with fairies or half-horse half-man creatures." She opened her eyes and turned to Christina, waiting for a response. "You don't know what I'm talking about, do you?"

Christina shook her head. "Mom wasn't into Filipino folk tales, just American ones."

"Ah, but Filipino folk tales are so much more disturbing, sort of ironic. Filipinos are happy on the outside and a mess inside. Ironic like your "Fire Blossom" because how can a flower be on fire? And speaking of fire," Mayette said, pulling a cigarette from a pocket, "would you like one?"

"Oh," Christina said, caught completely off-guard. She thought a conservative country like the Philippines would be strict about things like underage smoking. "Where did you get that?"

"From a store. Why, where do they sell cigarettes in San Francisco?"

"Did you buy it yourself?"

"Well, technically, it comes from my allowance, which comes from Dad, but yeah, I bought it. I don't let other people run errands for me, even though everybody has maids to do everything. Part of the kick is being able to buy it myself."

"It's legal, then?"

"Well, I've never been refused, so yeah, I guess it is. But then in the Philippines, there's really no drinking age either. Or driving age. All rules are breakable, or at least bendable."

Christina chose not to accept a cigarette, mostly because she didn't want to give her mother another reason to take more Valium. She half expected Mayette to whip out a bottle of beer, or wine, but was very relieved when that did not happen. Christina and Mayette just sat there, engulfed by the cigarette smoke, the fragrance of flowers, and the weight of the night.

On the third day, Mayette's family "officially" joined the pack of mourners, justified by the fact that they were once U.S.-based too. Along with the pack, they drove from house to house, ate lunches, afternoon snacks, dinners and after-dinners with them. At each place, Mayette would find a place to smoke in: the maid's room, a corner of the backyard, on the street. Most times, Christina kept Mayette company, always refusing to try a cigarette herself.

It didn't take long for the grieving mass of travelers to evolve into something else: a gossip club. By the fourth day, members started to venture out on their own and they began to collect news about not just long-lost relatives but also, unfortunately, present company. They were like ants who found kernels of food and brought these back to base camp. Clara San Juan's funeral, now a maintenance-free project ever since the funeral home took over, became secondary. Each succeeding gathering now buzzed with fresh talk.

"The half-brother of Rita's second cousin says Rita still owes him money."

"Apparently, Pido is with his fourth mistress. Still."

"Dr. Ibanag made a deal with Vivian's uncle to buy Clara's ancestral land in the province. Without Clara's consent..."

That last piece of news moved through the pack quickly. To her relief, Christina thought it a testament to Filipino sensitivity that the news had not reached the Ibanags immediately. However, that restraint lasted only until dessert.

Auntie Fe approached Christina's mother as the maid poured coffee.

"Vivian, I think you should confront Dr. Ibanag about why he bought Clara's land—may she rest in peace—without Clara's permission."

Christina looked around for Mayette but did not see her. Earlier, Mayette excused herself to make a phone call. Christina hoped she would not return just yet.

"But that's over and done with," someone protested. "Let's leave it alone, for Clara's sake—God rest her soul."

Auntie Fe persisted. "It is precisely because Clara is gone—may the Angels in heaven take her—that we should continue to protect her *interests*."

"Actually, it might get a lot more complicated when her will is read," someone offered. "What if she bequeaths that land to someone, not knowing it's been sold?"

"I heard she wanted to donate it to the orphanage."

"Yes, but what if..."

Christina's mother remained silent up to this point, her mouth drawn in a hard line. Watching her, Christina remembered something that happened right after her grandmother died. In one of her relaxed, probably Valium-induced moments, her mother told her that she had a copy of "some sort of a draft of a will" dictated to her by Christina's grandmother. Christina's grandmother had not wanted to go to a lawyer, saying she trusted her daughter more. She had actually forced a pen in her daughter's hand and pushed a piece of paper toward her. Christina's mother obliged, intending to see a lawyer later. "Later never came," Christina's mother told her then, with deep regret. Christina had asked if they were to receive anything, and was only told "we have everything we need."

Finally, Christina's mother spoke.

"Look at us," she said, her eyes flashing. "We are only two days away from burying my mother. I prefer to dwell on memories that I shared with her, that she shared with you, rather than who-did-what-to whom. What do you want? Do you want to drag Uncle Ernesto away from praying at his sister's casket to interrogate him?"

Christina held her breath. She didn't know what her mother would say next, if she would reveal that she had some sort of a will.

Her mother continued. "If you are up to digging up dirt, then find some other grave to desecrate. I did not travel halfway around the world to see and hear what I can see and hear in San Francisco. I came to say goodbye to my mother."

Christina could not look away from her mother. Anger transformed her face, turning her pale skin crimson. Her eyes smoldered. She had never seen her on fire like this before. She was beautiful.

"It's true." Dr. Ibanag's deep voice broke the hush that followed the outburst. He had entered the room without anybody noticing. "We made a deal with Ernesto. It was all legitimate. We both behaved honorably. That's all you need to know." He turned to his wife and took her arm. "Let's go."

Mayette was still nowhere to be seen, and Christina rushed out to look for her. She found her in the garage.

"Did you hear?" Christina asked, out of breath.

Mayette took out a new cigarette. Pointing to it, she said, "My third." She lit it, took a puff, and exhaled slowly. "Of course I heard. I was in the next room when the shouting started, but when I heard Ernesto's name I sort of hid behind a houseplant. A mob can get pretty ugly."

Christina looked at her friend, unbelieving. "So you knew?"

Mayette again took her time, this time allowing herself two puffs. "Of course I did. Nothing in this country stays secret for very long."

The cigarette smoke started to get on Christina's nerves. "Why didn't you say something to me? Your father knew my grandmother owned that land!"

"And were you hoping to inherit it?"

"No, no! I...I just don't think it's right..."

Mayette shook her head. "You are so ignorant. In this country, everybody goes to church and says their novenas and then turns around and finds a way to get what they want. Everything's up for grabs. People learn to look the other way."

"But you're family!" Christina was panting now. "How could you do this to us?"

Mayette threw her half-smoked stub on the floor and squashed it with the tip of her shoe. "You forget, Christina, we're *not* family. We're not even friends, really. We certainly wouldn't be friends stateside. Here, we're friends—hey, call me family, even—for convenience."

The bond holding the pack together tore after that incident, and the group splintered. During the two days before the funeral, the bereaved party planned their own dinners and did things they had not done previously on the trip, braving crowded flea markets, sunbathing at fancy beach resorts. They made conversation with the security guard at the mall, the fish vendor, the tricycle driver, commenting on how different things were in America. Some even changed their departure itinerary. When the time came, they went to the final wake and funeral in their own transportation, commandeering vehicles from the funeral home, rental companies, friends of friends.

Christina hardly went anywhere, choosing to hole up in her uncle's air-conditioned and spacious suburban home. She tried to log on to the computer to send messages to friends in San Francisco, but her uncle's dial-up took so long she gave up. She read, watched television, and took long walks around the subdivision to quiet her mind. On the day before the funeral, she finally relented to the gnawing feeling inside her.

Christina found her mother alone in a bedroom, stretched out on a bed and staring at the wall. Her eyes darted to the bedside table and fell upon a medicine bottle. It had two pills left.

Christina's voice wavered as she spoke to the motionless figure. "Mom, can I ask you something? Did you keep *Lola*'s will?"

In a voice heavy with fatigue, her mother answered, "*Hija*, it would do you no good to know. Look at what happened at the party, and they didn't even know a will existed."

"Existed, or exists?"

The question was met with a silent shrug.

"Don't you trust me, Mom? Do you think I'll act all crazy and upset-like them?"

Christina's mother sat up slowly, and reached out to stroke Christina's cheek. "Your *Lola* was a good mother to her kids. She was always looking out for them, even when it seemed like she was just being stubborn or difficult. When she insisted on writing a will her way, I wanted to tell her 'no lawyer, no will.' I knew it could get very complicated. But she wouldn't listen. And I knew that if I didn't do it, she would pick a stranger from the street to do it if she had to. I guess she had her reasons. She was old and fragile, but as long as this fire burned inside her, she would not give up."

Not able to contain her curiosity any longer, Christina asked, "But when she was alive, did she still have the land that Mayette's family bought? Did she think she still owned it? Was her brother a crook? Did the doctor lie to us about everything being legitimate?" Inside her head, Christina was screaming, *the Ibanags fooled everybody; Mayette's probably laughing at us now.*

Her mother started to weep. Christina knew she would not get an answer now, maybe even never. She left her mother's bedside and silently closed the door.

In her head, a plan was hatching. She would sneak into Mayette's garden tonight and destroy her "smoking place," her place of comfort. Christina didn't quite know how to do it, but she would. She would show Mayette that she could be cunning and heartless too.

While *Lola*'s mahogany casket was being lowered to the ground, mourners threw flowers after it. The kind of flowers thrown revealed where the person lived: roses from U.S.-based mourners, orchids and sampaguitas from local ones. Christina reached inside her purse and caressed a fire blossom from Mayette's garden, but did not throw it on the casket. She watched Mayette and her family arrange a big bouquet in a vase at the head of the grave where the casket now rested. Mayette threw a scornful look in her direction, and Christina met it with a steady gaze.

Yesterday, she had managed to enlist her uncle's driver to bring her to Mayette's, and the place was dark when they got there. The driver said that the family was probably out and that the maid would not let her in. Christina knew there was a way to get into the garden without going through the front gate. The driver would probably not squeal if she offered him money. What was it Mayette said, "All rules are bendable?"

The driver repeated, "Ma'm, they're not home. The Mercedes is gone. Shall we go home?"

As Christina sized him up, debating about how much money to give him, a light went on inside the foyer. The door opened, and someone in a maid's uniform peered at her from a distance. As soon as she recognized Christina, she ran to the gate and unbolted it.

"Good evening, Ma'm. They're not here, but will be soon. They called a few minutes ago to tell the cook to start dinner. Would you like to come in and wait? The cook is preparing *paella* tonight."

Another plan started to emerge, and Christina stared at the maid, the driver, then the maid again as she worked out the details. How much is too much to ask household help? How strong is their loyalty? Her gaze traveled to the side of the house where a smaller gate guarded the garden.

Her voice quivering, she asked the maid, "Would you please do me a favor and pick some flowers from the garden for me? I want to bring them to the funeral. I really like the red one, you know, from the big bush that covers the wall."

"Of course. Would you like to come in and choose it yourself?"

"No, that"s okay. I'll wait here."

The maid insisted on letting her in, so Christina took one small step inside. When it became clear to the maid that Christina would not be going any further, she hurried to the garden. She came back soon after, cradling so many flowers her thin arms could hardly hold them all. The bouquet burst with *sampaguitas*, ferns, a few orchids. and the requested red blossoms.

Christina smiled. "Thank you so much. But, you know, I just remembered, that my mother complained yesterday that there were too many flowers at the funeral home. I'll just take one flower to pin on my dress for mass." She plucked the fire blossom that had the longest stem, careful not to disturb the maid's handiwork. Not wanting to get her into trouble, Christina instructed the maid, "Tell Mayette I asked you to pick flowers for the funeral. Tell her to bring these tomorrow to the cemetery, not the funeral home. But," Christina said, smiling sweetly, "don't bring the red flowers. Just throw them away. I also just remembered it's bad luck to wear red to a funeral." Christina didn't care that she probably didn't make much sense to the maid. The deed was done.

The fire blossom felt like velvet to her touch, and she hoped that the container she prepared would not dry it out too much. When her mother announced they would leave in a few days, Christina rushed preparations for her flower's journey. She hoped the flower would make it past the immigration officials in San Francisco and not lose too many parts on the way home. Once home, she would make a cutting from the stem and try to coax some roots to grow, keeping the soil and air around the stem moist like the air in Mayette's garden. Maybe getting the plant to thrive was too much to hope for but Christina knew that in such a situation, *Lola* would have found a way to make it grow. Her *lola*, a transplant like her fire blossom, never gave up, and Christina promised to do the same. And when the first bud appears in its new home, Christina would tell her mother the name of the flower, or maybe christen it with a new one.

Almira Gilles has published in several genres of children's literature, including picture books, poetry, and short stories. For the young adult and adult market, she has written and staged short plays, published essays and a chap- book of poetry. Born and raised in the Philippines, she came to the U.S. for graduate study. After finishing her PhD, she taught graduate school in De Paul University and worked in consulting. Now she writes full-time and volunteers for UNICEF.

H. Francisco V. Peñones, Jr.

TIES THAT BIND

"Fagen was a traitor, and died a traitor's death, but he was a man, no doubt, prompted by motives to help a weaker side, and one to which he felt allied by ties that bind... He saw, it may be, the weak and the strong; he chose, and the world knows the rest."

An Indianapolis newspaper editorial on David Fagen, a regular in the U.S. Army who defected to the side of the Filipinos in the American imperialist and expansionist war in the Philippines in 1899-1901.

Crumbling bilboes bind this bas-relief of your footmen
across the Pacific a century ago with David Fagen
and my tropical islands.

Outside, a balloon string loosened and slipped
from a tiny finger, its blessed break the rupture and airiness
this hotdog-munching spring strollers have in their heads
for history. Thank Sainte-Gaudens you still have a girded
and gilded tie to the present, thank Cal his mind was right
you needn't worry about ever falling into a ditch again.
They're all here, your men, his words have all them accounted for.

At the park, the balloon-man's strings point to the direction
of dates and palms scooped by a sickled moon, farther.
A 'Nam vet reading today's paper said roped sands do not tie
the umbilicus of this country's children
to the rhetoric about the republic, not worth giving up
everything for as your men did, as David did.

Among mosquito insurrectos he bound his blood
with the pygmy arms of my fathers seeing too his skin
as kin to our sun-browned flesh and land, our
betrayed republic. No slingshot saved us
from a praying mantis, its assimilating treachery,
bound us in your language, made us like scattered beads
of a rosary, left us with taste for patties
and soda, made us borne you as an added burden.

Back in the islands, a young agriculturist
was feared to have kissed the soil
courtesy of the military,
which tied this to the war on terror,
a common vocabulary taught them
by advisers from the Pentagon.
There are no foxes in our lush
forests, but it is a howling wilderness,
with foxholes in them, nevertheless.

HOMAGE TO FRIDA
On the Centennial of her birth

Kahlo: *kaluluwa*: (n). Tagalog for soul—
O Soul of my bleeding heart pigeon-
holed in tin retablos hung in antiseptic wards
unwind your bandaged flesh and let me in
your body its plains of crumbling rocks
and howling dust is no strange country
to me. *Buko kanakong estranyo 'di*.
Back home, the land cracks and opens wide
throwing up the bodies dumped at night.
Its womb refusing now any stirring of seedling
despite so much marrows in its furrows.

O Nuestra Señora de Dolores y Tristezas[1]
wrap me in your leafy arms as you did
Diego Rivera or yourself in infant's bodies
yet with your lusting faces in a kind of *pieta*,
in a loving moment caged in the canvas.
Arog ka kanakong banwaan, (like my country)
Natusok naman ako. (I am pierced too.)
Pero en sus autoretratos por ejemplo,[2]

I am not pricked by the thorns of the cactus
which thrusts up like a pen against the sky
and my brows are as high and thick and black
as your brushes and your gaze—a doll's,
set in place and silent in a corner yet forever

1. *Our Lady of Sorrows and Sadness*
2. *But in her self-portraits for example...*

SELF-PORTENTS FROM A CRYSTAL BALL

Between the onyx equinox
and the Martian meridian
your Saturn son is on the ascendant
towards the power clique.
Rorschach stains
whirl nebulous as violet capes
worn in Salamanca:
Beware of men in ties,
they shake your hands while
coming out straight from the john.
Swirling lights tie up
the head and the tail, a circular

tale and mandala of survival and decency
you may well just be
heading for St. Francis Alley.

Acid rain dust leaks out
slimy green in brain drain canals:
invest in futures, better still
the dioroxine fuel yet to be found
and named.

Some silicone spilled semen
unearth Buddy Holly, a boozed
night out in Malate
and the apparition in the 7th Virgo
of one claiming paternity.
Raspy grains the pores of skin
up close your nose oooom
a hint of civet in heat:
go pick a lady in the primary
though you keep a red card
in your wallet for lemme see...

H. Francisco V. Peñones, Jr. is currently enrolled in the MFA Creative Writing program at San Jose State University as an International Ford Foundation Fellow from the Philippines where he is acknowledged as having started the rebirth of his native Bikol literature. He opted to write in the Bikol language in the late '70s when his contemporaries were either writing in English or in Tagalog. In 2006, he came out with his first poetry collection: *Ragang Rinaranga* [Beloved Land].

Salvage(d)*

*H*e knew it was coming. But not that soon—or that messy. He thought the whole world had collapsed when an avalanche of trash covered his shack and him inside, last night. The rain which had gone on for weeks had accumulated in the troughs dug up by government bulldozers to accommodate more trash. This loosened up the mountains of garbage piled up in this open dumpsite for the whole of Metro Manila. When they started to dig the troughs, he said he warned their village leader about the dangers it would bring to those who were living on the slopes of the hills surrounding the dumpsite. Why did they not seek some safer grounds, I asked. "When you live at the edge of a garbage dump, you do not think or talk about some safer grounds for your survival. Your survival is in being in the garbage dump itself," he explained in a voice that seemed to come from the bowels of the earth.

So despite the perils posed by the rains, he stayed on like all the hundred others who considered this dumpsite home and who depended for survival on these mountains of perpetually smoking, burning and stinking trash by picking and salvaging whatever recyclable materials there were—plastic, bottles, papers, and cardboards, which they eventually sell to scrap dealers. Because of the rains, the streets of Manila were as usual in knee-deep waters. The rains brought glee to the by-standers and the jobless. They suddenly had a new source of income—loose change really, which were payments for their pushing to the sides cars stalled by the waters. Others earned a windfall from users of the wooden planks they improvised as bridges for pedestrians who did not want to get wet. Almost always though, their money

---

* *Salvage has acquired a quaint and sinister meaning, in the kind of Filipino English, particularly during the martial law years where it refers to extra-judicial executions or killing of persons picked up usually without warrants of arrests or legal papers, either as thugs or suspected Communists; or even opposition leaders.*

all ended up at the corner store where they went for their bottle of gin and *chicharon bulaklak* or crunchy pig entrails. To "kill" the cold and the loneliness of living in the city during the monsoon they say. The students too welcomed the rains for Malacañang suspended all classes for a week. Expectedly, the media had a heyday lambasting the MMDA for its failure to collect the garbage blamed for clogging the sewers and as a consequence, the floods.

When the rain finally stopped, it gave much relief to the residents of the dumpsite from fears about the possible collapse of the smoky mountains. The rains put out the pockets of fire spread all over the place, yet it aggravated the stench of what seemed like fetid, rotten eggs and methane gas that oozed from whatever scattered, stinking things there were. It also halted the regular schedule of the dump trucks hauling the daily garbage of Metro Manila which the city mayor said was equivalent to an eight-story high building. The last fleet of trucks which came before the collapse brought with them the leftovers, mostly styropor and plastic cups bearing brands like McDonald's, KFC, Kenny Rogers, and Wendy's, from the prayer rally of charismatic religious leader, Mike Velarde, at the Luneta Park which expanse he could fill with his followers who wave their handkerchiefs while shouting, "Amen! Alleluiah!" That it takes a dozen dump trucks to haul the garbage which these prayer rallies leave behind, shows just how many believe in Bro. Mike's words. This is the reason why politicians, including the President herself, have been wooing his support in the coming elections. They always vote as one, as a bloc, much like the Iglesia ni Kristo, another sect whose spiritual head dictates for whom his flock will vote. Whomever Bro. Mike chooses then, is a surefire winner. To these thousands of believers, mostly from the provinces who come by the busloads for these prayer rallies, it is Bro. Mike who will lead them to salvation, whether from mortal sin or physical suffering.

To him, however, and the hundred others living in these smoky mountains, the garbage, like what he said, is their salvation or their sustenance for living, for their survival. He is a living proof of that. At least, as long as I can still hear his voice through this protruding PVC pipe which serves as some kind of a medium and microphone for our talk, which I presume is part of his makeshift hovel. "Are you still there?" I paused when I realized the silliness of my question. Then I pressed my ear closer to the round hole of the pipe. It was from here that I first heard his groans and him telling me eventually his story. And is it still him groaning? Or is it some water flowing? I wanted to calm myself as I rejected the thought that the garbage that is his source of life would also be his grave.

No, I shook my head. I couldn't let this one slip again this time. No, you would not be like those faces that until now kept on flashing every now and then in my mind. Ghostly visages covered with freshly-mixed cement and sand, squirming, screaming and moaning in pain, their hands outstretched, asking for help. No. Not this time.

I looked up and noticed a precariously piled debris overhead. "Hang on. We'll get you out of there in time," I assured him, as I signaled to my fellow rescue workers that I had found a survivor down where I was. Where I heard and found him was rather far from where the search and rescue was centered or going on, that is, on the upper part of the collapsed garbage heaps. It could be that his house was dragged down by the first onrush of the water and the trash. Some residents of the place whose make-shift houses stood on top of the hills adjoining the dumpsite said no one could have survived the disaster. It was as if a giant mountain of plastic bags, cans, paper, wood, broken bottles, scrap iron and dirt swallowed all the makeshift houses built on the slope of the hill, obliterating any trace of their existence, a resident told us this morning when our group answered the call for volunteer rescue workers. Indeed, what we saw was expectedly a scene in a garbage dump site. No one would think that beneath that debris were human beings. "I did not even hear cries, just a loud sudden thump like that of a sack of cement suddenly put down by its bearer because of its weight," said a resident who went home late that night after rendering overtime in his construction job. "They were living in the shadow of the mountain of garbage and it just caved in on them. I don't think there's any hope of finding anyone alive," the construction worker said.

My find turned out to be an exception. Perhaps his hut was on the lower slope of the hills, and the sheer volume of debris and water pushed his house down here below where, I didn't know why, I seemed to have been led by my feet. It might be instinctive or because of the lessons I learned in my own first experience at rescue operation.

The construction foreman told his men earlier they had to finish paving the floor within that day, so they can beat the deadline given by the contractor of the building. That was, two days from that day. It was the First Lady's order, the contractor said. And what the First Lady wants, she always gets. So, the whole building was a picture of haste.

On the western side, a group of laborers hoisted with pulleys the heavy curtain in front of a very large white screen, a size never before seen in the Philippines. At its front, another group set in place and tightened with wrenches the nuts and bolts of the upholstered chairs that would seat the hundreds of expected foreign guests. It was the planned great hall at the eastern side, where the reception and banquet would be held after the opening night, that had to be finished in the next two days, and for which the chief engineer already ordered another overtime that night—their seventh such overtime work within that week which made some of the laborers sleep for only a few hours. "We had to work till the wee hours of the morning," he said, which was then actually already a mere three hours before dawn. On the ground, several dozen peons had formed themselves in a line as they passed, mano a mano, pails containing newly mixed cement which were then poured on the floor on top of a basement. Overhead, were the scaffoldings of bamboos and iron where scores of painters were edgily guiding their long poles that hold paint rollers on the wide ceiling. Then suddenly, the crack of something that snapped. And then, the ghostly faces from being washed in freshly mixed cement. And the blood, illumined by the few fluorescent lamps thereabout, dripping from bodies skewered on the broken scaffoldings. No. I will not let you slip this time.

He said he grew up in Olongapo, near Subic which was the R&R stop for the American troops in the Philippines before they were driven home by the eruption of Mt. Pinatubo. He did not know who his parents were, but his questions about them always lead others to tease him, particularly about the color of his skin. "Your sonababitch father? Oh, why don't you look at yourself in the mirror, then you'll know," they told him. Only the Irish administrator of the orphanage where he spent his childhood had the answer. He was told he was left at the gate of the orphanage with a postcard showing a smoking, perfect-coned volcano clipped on his diaper made from used bags of wheat flour. It was that of Mayon volcano whose perfectly conical shape and violent eruptions had made it world famous. This made him think, for a time, that his mother was from the Bikol region where the volcano lords over the landscape. On the back of the postcard, however, only a terse "I'm sorry son" was written in Tagalog. Nothing more.

At 17, he left the orphanage and survived by salvaging the American discards dumped at the periphery of the barbed wire fence of the Base: used helmets, slightly damaged ceramic toilet bowls, cut-out plastic pipes, raincoats, combat boots, empty shells of missiles used in the war games of the GIs. These would eventually be big money when they brought them up for sale at the second-hand supply stores along Kalaklan. He and his fellow scavengers would then later be led to Magsaysay or Barreto where suddenly the whores would notice and invite them in the clubs that lined those streets. That would be, however, when there were no American ships docked at Subic. Otherwise, he didn't exist. Yes, in 'Gapo, he was non-existent. He was invisible. He gets to be noticed only when he figures in another drunken brawl or a rumble. The police blotter had already attached almost all of the offenses in the books to his name and for which he already got used to coming in and out of the city jail. Yet, that's the time when they remember his existence. For in 'Gapo, when you're black, and when you're in the streets, then your mother is dumb. For you're supposed to be in the States with your American father with a green card and enjoying the blessings of America, the Beautiful.

This made him dream for some time of also going to America. The America of "Hey Joe, Wanna Buy Watch?" The America of dem sailors wanting a good night fuck. The America of Sarge Willis, to whom he sold fake heroin—actually ground cassava flour—for which he avoided the streets for sometime when the enraged sergeant, now ceaselessly sneezing for weeks, threatened to skin him alive. Deep inside him, however, he developed a silent hatred against Americans, like Sarge Willis, or his father, whoever he was. His father who cared perhaps for no one or nothing but his lust. *"Come on baby, bend 'em behind me."* Then he goes, *"oomph, oomph, oomph, aaah."* And that's it. *"Here's you dolla'. Mah ship's leavin'. Bye."*

He imagined and thought if being an American was like being his father, then to hell with America. At least, he said, his mother asked for his forgiveness. This, and the memory of his friend Igoy, woke him up from this impossible American Dream. Igoy, who was also black like him, was shot dead by a white guard while they were picking the day's garbage near the fence of the Base. At the police station, the guard who was later assigned elsewhere, explained that he thought Igoy was a "scavenging wild pig," a description that would become a classic in the Philippine press.

In 1991, the American flag was lowered in Subic, signaling the end of America's almost century-long presence in the Philippines. As the last of the American soldiers ceremonially fired their guns, he remembered his other friend, Totoy, *the Small One*, whose body was shattered by an unexploded bomb used during one of those war games conducted on the premises of the Base. He also remembered Igoy. Their fate and his own led him to board a Victory Liner bus for Manila one afternoon.

At the capital, it was literally his own blood which became his source of income. He became a regular at those dingy rooms along Sta. Cruz where for a slight pinch of a needle at his wrist he could already have P500 or P1,000, depending on how many c.c. of blood was let and sold. Two *balut*, those boiled duck eggs with premature chicks in them, and a bottle of San Miguel beer would be all it took to counter the drowsiness and weakness one felt after each extraction. In time, however, his body started to give in. His face became as pale as a duck egg itself, while his eyes sunk in their hollows, deep as the troughs at the dumpsite, giving him a catatonic look. A traffic policeman, however, took him under his care until he was well enough to start peddling hand towels for the jeepney drivers, and later, cigarettes and candies, the initial capital for which was provided by the traffic cop.

Tsip was no ordinary traffic cop. He drove a stainless jeep and wears a silver Rolex watch, a large gold necklace—the kind worn by the *balikbayan*, or returning overseas contract workers from Saudi—and big gold rings on each of the fingers of his right hand. He always had two companions who seemed to always have bloodshot eyes. These were the same guys who one day handed him small packets of what reminded him of *tawas*, a white laundry bleaching granule. "Tsip wants you to make this rock into money," one of them told him. Later, he learned that in fact, it was shabu—a low kind of crack. He thought what a small and easy way to make big money. Once, he sold a hundred thousand pesos of the stuff in a day for which Tsip took him for a night-out at a girlie bar in Ermita. There, Tsip partnered him with a diminutive girl, Viktoria, whose thin pouting lips and flicking tongue would make him a regular of the place.

At this time, Manila's tabloids were replete with stories of vigilantes getting back at criminals and drug pushers like him—*tulak*, as they put it in the streets. He became Tsip's best seller. He would learn later that these were all for publicity and because of business competition. The police had to show they were doing something about drugs in the streets. They picked out for liquidation bums and incorrigible recidivists and had them photographed and written about as pushers—SALOT NG BAYAN, or dregs of society, in the press. However, he would discover, some were just bad for business. They were either standing in the way of a monopoly in the market or had problems with remitting their sales. He saw some of them done in, and in at least three instances, he became the executioner himself. Each time he pumped in that lead, he thought of his faceless father.

It was then that he decided to leave Tsip's business. He just couldn't stand more blood in his hand. He showed the postcard with the smoking, perfect-coned volcano to Viktoria and told her of his dream of leading a new life, living with her and raising their family in the shadow of the volcano. He told her of his plan of running off with the day's sale and that he would wait for her at his rented room in the evening on their trip to Bikol. She did not say a word, but her tongue flicked in the dizzying light and curling cigarette smoke.

Sure enough, she was there that evening. But as he let her in, one of Tsip's sidekicks gave him a blow in his groin, making him curl like cigarette smoke. "Ah, so you want to live in the shadow of a perfect-coned smoking volcano. We'll take you there," he heard one of them say. As he crimped in pain, he imagined the next day's tabloid headlines: BLACK VENDOR SALVAGED, VIGILANTES SCORE ANEW, *NEGRO SINALBEYDS*. He also recalled the faces and bodies of those he himself wasted on orders of the Tsip. He felt another thud on his head and all he remembered was seeing Viktoria smiling as she received a wad of peso bills from one of Tsip's bodyguards whom she kissed on the cheek with her flicking tongue, a lace of smoke coming out of her mouth into the dark.

I heard him groan once more. It was a sound that seemed to be drawn from a very deep hollow or pain. Was he perhaps thinking of that night he was thrown and left for dead in this smoking dumpsite? I moved my right arm up and down, signaling to the other rescue workers for some help. It was getting dark. If he was not hurt and the roof of his hut was protecting him, then he's got a fighting chance. Otherwise, hunger or asphyxiation could do him in. If he's hurt then that's another story. The pipe, meanwhile, was still doing fine for our conversation. I needed to make sure he was alive and give him the much needed air. The retrieval operation, however, had seemed to have stopped. I decided to go up for help.

When our rescue team arrived, we came upon the bodies of the workers covered in fresh cement and scattered all over the place. Some of them had been rendered immobile not only by the quick-drying cement but also by the weight of the scaffolding on top of them. Some of the iron scaffoldings propped either the prone body of a worker or the neck of another, their tips piercing either the belly where curlicued viscera hung like misplaced purple neckties; or, in one, the eye socket. I heard a groan, then another, then another, coming from among the rubble. I started pulling, pulling whoever's arms I could hold. I could not remember how many. I just kept on pulling the bodies I thought were still alive. Until the soldiers came. They suddenly ordered us out of the place when there were dozens more bodies still waiting to be saved.

On the ground were the recovered bodies, all wet and dirty, aligned and laid out in such a way that made the photographers busy. Some newly-arrived rushed to them then broke out crying, perhaps relatives who discovered their kin among the victims. Near them, policemen were pushing back onlookers to give way to the funerary employees who were arranging the bodies in some kind of a final inventory.

"What do you mean we're stopping the rescue work," I asked the head of the mayor's staff directing the operation while he was in the midst of what I overheard was a secret deal with the mortuary agent for a commission from the embalming of the victims. "There's a man down there and he's waiting for us to get him out of that rut," I protested. The burly mayor's man pulled me aside, his grip like an iron wrench on my arm, as he whispered that I tone down my voice.

"There's no man down there," he stressed, "but we've got a horde of media people up here. It's election time in a few months. We cannot risk the re-election chances of our boss with bad publicity about this situation," he reasoned, sounding like a political analyst which this country has plenty of, from the street thugs to TV entertainment hosts. "We'll tell the media we are through with our work. All the victims had been found and accounted for. The village chief said the number of bodies we have dug up already tallies with their census data. Besides it is already dark, we are all tired and we thank those who helped in this rescue efforts. The government will provide assistance to the families of the victims and we'll see what we'll do with this dumpsite," he promised, now sounding more like a true-blue politician as he walked towards a TV reporter who sidled up to him for a live interview. "No more bodies there," he repeated, his finger moving like a car window wiper to denote nothing. "But I had just been listening to his story," I snapped back. "He is alive," I shouted. But he's before the camera now and his face is already sporting a look that says, we're done.

"What do you mean we're stopping the rescue work? " I asked silently. It was still martial law in my country. You cannot ask why. You just have to follow. I have not seen anything. I have not heard anything. Yes sir. As you ordered sir. Hands covered in drying cement that are waving for help, faces, with only the holes in their gaped mouth visible, popping out of the mire of now drying concrete but whom I could only watch helplessly. These are the ghosts that have haunted me since then, torturing me, making me hear voices wanting to be saved from the rubble. Since the soldiers ordered us to leave those crying and moaning workers in pain. Since we saw on government TV that the First Philippine International Film Festival went on as scheduled, a week later. That was after the death of perhaps over a hundred workers whose gruesome end was never written about in the papers, and whose bodies were never recovered because the contractor was ordered just to cover them in fresh cement instead of pulling them out because Brooke Shields, Franco Nero and an Italian director were coming to town as personal guests of President Marcos and the First Lady. So, even if the contractor had to paint the brown grass green to make the front garden of the new building appear newly-landscaped under the moon, the bone-white Film Center was inaugurated with the Asian premiere of Bertolucci's *La Luna*.

"Did you say he was black and that he was dumped here?" the village chief asked. I nodded, glad that I found somebody to corroborate my story.

"Yes, yes, I know him. From stories of the early settlers of this place when this was called *Lupang Pangako*, or Promised Land, when this was planned as a relocation site for squatters of the city, when this was all *cogon* grasses and no one yet made it the biggest trash can of Metro Manila. Yes, they said there was indeed a black man whose dead body was thrown in that part where you say you heard his story. Yes, perhaps a victim of salvage. But that was perhaps, ten, fifteen years ago. His ghost could not have been among those that were buried in those tons of garbage last night," she ended in a mocking tone as she left me shaking her head.

Still baffled and shocked by what I heard, I headed back to the spot where the PVC pipe was. I suspected the village chief was instructed by the mayor's aide to help in shutting me up.

But what if what she told me was true? Who was it then or was it him that told me his own story? I felt stupid not having even asked his name. Suddenly, I felt a lump in my throat. I was certain it was a very human voice I had been talking to. There was only one way to find out, I surmised as I went back to where I found him. But the pipe was nowhere to be found. The debris I had noticed earlier must have already covered it. From where I thought it was, however, I spotted and picked a postcard, soiled and wet with cement powder. And by the soft and cold light of the rising moon, it unmistakably had a picture of a smoking, perfectly-coned volcano in the background. On its back were the words written in Tagalog: "I'm sorry son." Nothing more.

❧

Rhodora V. Peñaranda

BAMBOO LIVES

When the sun streams into the basket's hollowed
weave, you can catch the smell of bursting shoots,

the edible shoots from which weavers eat and drink
in the nodes between growths. Or sometimes,

with eyes closed, you might even hear the giant's sigh,
the tall grass bending with the wind on its woody stem,

or hear the burning sea wind into the resilience
of field lives winnowing out of their husks.

Yet only when your eyes lift to the sky
to count the intervals of lives between the nodes,

the living rings that mark themselves between
partitions — like fluvial floats parading for the sun

do they finally leaf and branch beyond the generations.
They seek the hands that shall shape them

whom they'll owe for the meaning brought to their strength,
strips furled or unfurled to carry grain or a shelter's beam.

There's the spring they add to the shaft of a cradle,
or the lilting in the pole across a peddler's back,

and there's the blunt weight of enduring feuds
in their blowgun's hollow, or spears staked to the ground.

II. COMFORT FOOD
from "Tryptich For Father"

You fork a slice from the pan
glutinous, steaming on a sheet
of banana leaf. Golden-brown, a touch
of spice and cinnamon. Your tongue
unbinds their sticky hold on your teeth.

You said it resembles rice
but is grated finer. "And squeeze out
the coconut milk as much as you can," you add.

I combine, re-combine, sift.
But I lose myself in the procedure.
Rising to the top, and thickening,
an old sadness reassembles in the heat,
my head in meaningless fog
to cook it mindfully in milk.

The pancake heaven steams,
wrapped in leaves, yucca sugar sprinkled over it--
sweetness and softness
and sunset streaming through the kitchen door.

I slice the cake in eight parts.
You count the twenty resemblances
of all my grated selves. The sweet Virginia
vanilla of your tobacco mingles
with the ferment of tea and cake. You turn
your cup, silent in the sizzle of a good burning,
patiently wait for me to pour.

III. THE PIPE HE LEAVES BEHIND
from "Tryptich For Father"

Like a photograph
or a tombstone that glows once,
then fades, bends
with the discoloration of light,
here it lies up close on my palm,
suddenly, unexpectedly small.

Heirloom whose stain and chip and crack
will never be touched for its power
to turn back time.

Inside the empty grainy bowl,
through the downward pine shank
and black lucite upcurve stem, across
the continents and distance of nights
and sighs, it carries yet the spiced flavors,
the thousand different odors
of snapshots. Sweet cherry blends

and mellow honey nights, cool smoky
vanilla evenings after work. The long narrow
ribbons of slow burning leaf,
rings of smoke curling up
to mornings already ancient, as a house
no longer surrounded by shadows,
still hides the echoes of our encounters.

A cake of ash on the mouthpiece—
Molecules of raisin or fig,
or a dried yolk of your lingering being?
I leave it alone, leave it
to cling thickly, visibly, on the grain.

GREAT EXPECTATION

The light goes off in this town of rationed power.
Brief dark shadows up and down the road.

A village dog picks up her scent and begins to bark.
Out of the sky, a flood of darkness with invisible beasts

bounding over the street and wedging into the heart.
She comes home, and out of the steaming dark,

her little brother, the boy like a cat waiting all night
purring for a rubbing on his back, leaps to his feet,

begging her to stay. She flicks her fan to spread the coolness,
and he gropes for the arts of her comfort, the tucking

into the soft bed, rocking him to the wind's mothering.
But she is hurrying. She does not feel the present under her feet.

She does not know the future. She does not have the past.
She passes through the rooms and gathers only tedium's grief,

the unwashed growth of things crowded with details, details
accelerating with the pressure of wars around her, so she leaves

in the veiled cold of the room,
                              the soft gestures curled inside the glass
of a burning lamp. Leaves him instead the words that order him

to face it like a man leaving him alone on a night like this where only
the dead walk, to conjure the man he has yet to be.

MIDNIGHT CHILDREN

"My children, my children, where are my children?"
—*La Llorona, the ghostly Weeping Woman,*
seen wandering along the banks of rivers and streams.

Do they see you standing there
suddenly alone, deserted along the winding
passage into the night, the unfamiliar streets
the crumbling houses and silent edges,
the descending groundlessness
and the thieving, beginning your wearying separation
from the small lives who wait long
in the vast, emptying room?

Do they see you hurrying
from the wind of a complicated origin, your nightdress
flailing where the moon writhes out its beast,
hunting, weaving sluggish in the air, where flame-red
scarab eyes close in on your silent howl,
where the stranger crouching
on the stone beside you, hides you
where his gaze sink into a slender coil
where his teeth swirl in the swell
of your heart?

Call up your children
your pixies, your beasts, they sit shimmering
at your side and weave the endless
threads of your dreams, little stitches
little steps, one step in one step out—where the serpent bird goes,
a god precedes. They skip once inwards and once outwards,
slithering, sliding, joining one world and another.

Call up your daughters,
your sirens, your witches, they drive

the blue ripples from your pebble
through the orb of the earth
like echoes rising on the wings of rain;

They sit at the cradle like nursemaids
anxious to heave your child to the world,
like titans bursting the bounds
of your venerated peaks.

What trenches did you find
that have stopped your course
and enchained your paths? The anguish of returning,
walking towards the place from which you started,
walking toward a stairway of thresholds,
repeating themselves, seeking the hour, the month, the moment
to shift a word or path, seeking the corner suspended
between water and earth, planet or star,
 when the umbilical ties strain you and tie you
but to the one you loved, seeking his children,
his parting gift of betrayal that you cast blindly
upon the waves.

And do they see you,
your streaming hair in the moonlight
sweeping the uneasy breast
of the river, calling, calling,
your feet floundering
on rotting wounds and accumulated tears?
Your ears press close to the mud,
and with a kiss, wait with your watchful
sleeplessness for the cancellation of debts,
for the voices of your midnight children
who will speak to you again
of love.

La Llorona, like the Euripedes' Greek tragedy, Medea, has come to symbolize the archetypal character of a distraught woman who loses or kills her children, for different reasons: to keep the love of a man, to take revenge for his illicit loves, or in the psychic sense, to make sense of one's own inability to sustain or nurture one's creative birthings.

In the Shadow of a Palm Leaf

You, with the blank stare in the streaming shade,
will you come along with me? Will you ride
with me to the distant capitals that have receded
From you, the tides that have moved with you?

Your tiny foot knits my name in the sand,
Waiting for release from the burning sea,
knocking at my splintered door, circling the blue
shade of my human outline—darkened

twin to your face lit by flies. Listen: a bird
of omen strums in the breeze. We'll ride
past the clouds with their theater lights on.

We will sweep up and down
your heartstrings and pluck the stars in them.
Beneath the sun's gold, I will show you
the pathless places where feet

could not take you, the spectacles that will not
repeat themselves. And before the clouds slip,
I will show you what will suffice.

Selected poems are from
Touchstone
by Rhodora Peñaranda (Menagerie Arts, 2007).

DADO'S FOOT

*O*f Jacqueline, her mother had said that she always looked for things in the wrong places. It seemed to her mother that all her daughter's decisions became suspect the moment she chose to abandon commerce for art. Not that it mattered, but she gloated over the idea that she was soon to prove her mother wrong—alas, God had relented, her prayers were answered. At twenty, not only did she find a mentor who would show her the ways to wield her paints, but also got herself a husband for a muse.

Anthony, genius anarchist artist, could very well have snared a foothold for her in the mystery of their art; he loomed among his peers though he had little to do with their club. He thrived on the difficult, the contradictory, the unusual. His opinions fascinated her. His luminous mind and high taste and manners in all pleasures sensual awed her. In those starry young eyes, Jacqueline believed she could not have found a more perfect man.

And as all perfect unions go, a child was born of the two. The boy had his father's intensity and a dogged curiosity foisted on objects and the physical secrets they held. To his mother's breathless anxiety, little Dado had this hawkish fascination with anything he could lay his hands on; he would slam an object against a wall or floor until it broke or cracked open, then let his eyes skulk around and little hands fumble inside it. He did not wait for answers; he took things apart and wrested their spirit. His father recognized his own genius in the boy and often looked proudly on his son. To the boy, toys were inferior gadgets to machines and he had little patience with the former. Over broken objects, Jacqueline pronounced her son utterly destructive and quaked at the imagined savage deeds of his future, but Anthony simply dismissed her. "Just you wait and see," he said. "This boy will have you pouring your lifeblood on your parched sketches!—Savage little genius, what wily gift the gods left you in your cradle!"

After five years with Anthony, however, Jacqueline had yet to learn to see, to look; how to liberate form, liberate the singular, inspired creation on canvas. Cooking, feeding, folding, washing—the mundane rooted her, and disabled her for flight. Then there was the matter of material insecurity. Since Anthony wouldn't take odd jobs when commissions ran out as he had nothing but scorn for so-called ordinary work, she had no choice but find work. He made it clear that he would rather die with his reputation as a genius intact than wear the clothes of the masses.

Jacqueline began to doubt her ability to create. She could no longer be sure if she could ever paint in the right spirit, engage herself in the passionate affair of the eye, to see with the sense behind the senses, as she intuited great artists do. But the day came when Jacqueline finally resolved she would rather tempt the fates than continue slaving under illusions she no longer shared. She left Anthony, took a new job in a town off Manila Bay, and rented a modest studio that stood sloppily among narrow rows of low-roofed dwellings. The passageways opened up to heavy traffic on one end, and the coastal sea on the other. The sea had, over time, carved estuaries of alleyways inland whose inhabitants eked out their livelihood through fishing, salt making, and raising livestock along the back shore. Having lived in the city for years, Jacqueline realized how the gravity of city living jaded her, now that it seemed this new landscape was like drink to her withering soul, in need of some buoyancy. She'd become like a fledgling bird soaking up the sound of the town's church bells, the playful breaking of the waves, and the wind-borne scent of kelp, sand, tree, and earth—all beckoning with the promise of renewal. Anthony seemed rather indifferent to this turn of events, and it wasn't long before he himself had a revelation of some sort and set himself loose on some exotic hamlet in faraway Indonesia, never to be heard of again.

*M*other and son managed along quite well for a while, but normalcy was not to be their lot. Once again, fate weighed down on Jacqueline when one sweltering night, Dado awoke howling and screaming, his hands gripping his left foot. His screams ruffled neighbors from their sleep that they came knocking gingerly at her door. Each one took turns with his foot, turned it around this way and that, and pronounced their own theories: vertigo, diabetes, the evil eye, voodoo, rats. The weepy wound that began as a pestilent itch two weeks before had rebelled, mutated itself from a timid eye to a spreading sea of blisters frothing with blood yolk. She held in one hand his head—a crown of rippling, sea-dyed curls, fine and fragrant—while her other hand held Dado's foot, billowing in the swell of a creeping dementia. She debated in her mind whether to take him to a doctor or wait till the morning.

As the night wore on with everyone frayed from exhaustion, the neighbors left one by one until Jacqueline was all alone to reckon with Dado's foot. Dawn soon shed the harrowing night and the boy —wound down and cooled by the passing breeze from the window— finally fell asleep. But with the silence, Jacqueline was seized less by sleep than by shadowy forebodings. She pondered what bizarre fate had been unleashed on her life that it should hound her like a creature from a distant past just when the sun was coming up for her.

There was never enough money for doctors and it simply came to pass that the pain in Dado's foot seemed to have diminished and everyone in the neighborhood, including Dado himself, got used to the way he walked. After all, he could, even on stilts, outsprint any one of the neighborhood boys on sand or gravel, and with his easy talent for anything, could command the approval of the older folk with his outlandish sandcastles that stood three feet high, royally decked with turrets and cannons and windows and passage doors made dark and deep that passersby couldn't resist a peek into them.

The young and the old—grandfathers who sunned themselves by their front doors—the men and women walking to and from their offices, and even the street bums who momentarily shed their swagger to puzzle over Dado's Brueghlian sketches, marveled at the boy's uncanny gift for drawing. Whether he built kites whose tracery recalled the cathedrals of Intramuros in Old Manila, or sketched intricate space stations richly rendered with tactile values and movement—to his neighbors, it did not matter that Dado cut an isolated figure with a reckless energy that spun on a hobbled leg. For though it seemed he unraveled in order to build, from the disorder he created images of untapped realities that jolted them and compelled them to see through his gifts rather than his curse. In the eyes of others thus, Dado's foot was but a mere outcropping scar, a big wayward mole, a mocking kiss of creation that dangled like a bow behind serpent limbs, coiled and set to lunge at every goal his wild mind seized on.

But to Jacqueline, though she worried less and less about doctors, Dado's foot swelled daily in her life like an unholy blister; it had a riveting yellow eye, a wicked incandescence that seemed to grow on her and strike her numb, leaving her with a deep sense of something that had yet to take form.

Insight was the one thing that eluded her. She had hoped her intimacy with Anthony would count for something, like his vision rubbing off on her, some grasp of proportioning, a way with lines, with forms, with colors that would draw into the flatness more than a third dimension, more than a rhythm, a way with seeing or feeling that could sight a mysterious fourth so that all else dissolved but the insight that found itself stirring among the heap.

She took up work as a framer at Uy's Art and Frame Shop because it was the only job that came remotely close to painting. Though she spent most of the day measuring and fitting, cutting and slicing, and securing the paints for Samuel Uy, the respected mural artist—for her it was enough that she was associated in any way with him. It offered her a spark of hope that Sam Uy might yet take her as an apprentice in his art, and with that thought, roused her into believing she can yet expect to come fully alive into her own.

Mang Uy, as everyone called him, was already a big name in the business; word was out that he was up—one of five—for the National Artist award. He disdained hefty commissions that dictated the terms, but he had a practical side that allowed him to engage in business where he could make money; one could even say he had no compunction about self-promotion, cashing in on his name to boost his frame and art business. And Jacqueline was not above using people like Mang Uy who had both artistic gift and material resourcefulness, a time for everything and a knack for finishing; or like Mamang who was more than pleased to keep Dado in her home while she was away at work; people like them who had the power of their skill and control over their lives, power that only filled Jacqueline's empty cup from which she drank every morning over her tortured sketches of tedium.

Mamang had been widowed early on and had grown children who lived away. She had an insistent maternal presence about her that drew the restless of spirit and blabbermouths alike. In going about her daily chores, Mamang invariably evoked mother earth who managed her multitude of cares with instinctual economy and infinite resource, something Jacqueline could only envy and admire, aware that she was of the age gap between her and this older woman who had more energy than a mother could ever give, who had great reservoir from which she lavished attention tirelessly on the rambunctious Dado. Mamang, it seemed, was built for ten tasks all at once and it did not escape Jacqueline how the only singular task that she hoped to manage evaded her. For herself, she had nothing to show but the endless striving to make the leap from sketches to full-blown paintings. Between preoccupations that her better works were yet to come, and the feeling that she was instead receding on a deserted narrowing tract, she struggled dimly with the sense that her caring was reaching its limit, so that even her own son appeared to her as little more than an urchin who had invaded her shore.

In the office, Jacqueline found that she could navigate the most mundane task. To her surprise, she managed to filch yet some passion from her torpid blood. She did not only pour ready-made paints for Mang Uy; she gave it concentrated thought as a general poring over maps and plans. She experimented with color pigments and made notes about their peculiar subtleties, neatly labeling each with recommendations of use. She was a tough customer to suppliers, meticulous specs of frame sizes and designs, and had become quite unpopular with them for rejecting deliveries that did not meet up to her standards. To each one's satisfaction, Mang Uy and Jacqueline found each other indispensable. He marveled at her color novelties and inventiveness, though he himself would caution some restraint.

"Ay, Jacqueline, I don't need too many of these brilliants. There is room for the flats and the graves too, you know." He squeezed out and mixed the flat colors on his palette along with the bright reds and greens that Jacqueline had mixed.

"The brilliants on the graves and flats," he said with a dab of highlights on the moonlight, a splash of the bold on a flat pond. "But it's the graves," — the gesture of his arms sweeping grandly across the canvas — "these undefinable, mysterious graves — these open up dimensions!"

And she saw the moon, the moon that was no moon but a queen that commanded the night; and the lilies, no longer crouched in secret corners, but boldly ascending, watching blue shadows beneath a canopy of fronds.

Mamang kept a thriving corner store and took care of Dado at the shop. There seemed to be no happier arrangement for the two women. With Dado, Mamang felt giddy with abundance, ensconced in her nurturing role. At home with his mother, Dado would disappear into his own sacred space with his objects; between mother and son, there were no ripples of affection. It was as if Mamang had cast her own huge shadow on them, for neither one could move beyond each other's intensity, content as they were within the familiar grip of their isolation. Jacqueline watched Dado in a drowsy stupor, while he constantly pined for the proximity of Mamang as though he had suckled at the old woman's breasts from his first day. And yet on some nights, in the glow of soft evening, she would watch the little boy's eyes close and her heart would stir as though catching the throb of a song coming, or a wave sweeping up, striking scorched stones.

Time came when the set rhythm of such days would again pass. News came to Jacqueline that Mamang was struck with an agonizing muscle pain on her shoulders, a warning symptom of bursitis according to the doctor. Though the old woman insisted she was well enough to continue, she had to confine her boundless energies to the couch to relieve the spasms, a condition indeed that threatened to end the happy arrangement with Dado.

Fate, as it turned out, had hatched such a plan, for shortly afterwards, as Mamang fell asleep one hot afternoon, Dado was seized by the firelight at the altar. Fire, the element that had always piqued him—that lean fluttering glow dancer that even now made his cold naked blistered foot palpitate as though the sun itself promised new life into it. Drawn to the flame's call, Dado took Mamang's stepladder to the saint-laden altar, clambered to the top, and reached out for a votive candle and match beside it. Soon the boy was delighting himself with flashing phantoms, completely oblivious of the ensuing moment when, upon striking another, a tiny renegade spark escaped and landed on the rug. The spark grew and gathered strength, sensing within its own seed-light the future power of conflagration. What it could devour, it crunched, and inside the store where things—food, drinks and dreams—were stacked in rows, and with Mamang asleep, there was plenty to burn unhindered. Mamang awoke as the burning tongue licked her leg, gave out a piercing cry, and in one big leap scooped up the startled boy and flashed out of the room.

At the hospital, Mamang's look was punishing. Jacqueline felt the woman's silence as a struggle to devise blame that she put squarely on her shoulders.

"I will work nights to pay for your loss," Jacqueline assured her, without really thinking how it would work out. Mamang kept silent. She said she would work nights while Aling Pat, a widow in the neighborhood on the side of the coast, would stay home with Dado.

"You dare not give the boy to that senile, toothless woman!" She broke her silence, offended by the suggestion.

But Jacqueline took it as the woman's abiding affection for the boy. "God bless your warm heart," she said.

"I only worry that he might succeed the second time around and burn the whole neighborhood! What will you do then?" Jacqueline held her silence, humiliated.

"How can you repay the losses with your wage?" Mamang asked, finding her words being shaped by the wretchedness of her greater loss that was Dado. Her children, she said, had asked her to live with them, one daughter at a time, while they rebuilt the store. But it was clear between them that she could not keep Dado. She sighed, and then spoke, this time as though accusing her. "You have lost far more that cannot be repaid, not even with a king's crown. There—there's a burning bush you can't put out."

The fire shored up Jacqueline's determination to relate with her son; albeit, how to sail this silent strength made her more anxious than she had ever been. She made herself, by fits and starts, accountable and let an openness of feeling coax her into enacting nightly rituals of bathing him, reading to him, and tucking him to bed. But Dado's foot, the distempered foot—oh, there was too much to deal with all at once! In her heart she had always known where her true creation lay, but it was not ever willing to be born, not yet, not with her. But the one already created, the one already born—irony of ironies—what of his destiny now, she asked herself. So imperfectly conceived, undisciplined in form. Nevertheless, the resolve that had fused itself in the wake of the blaze had struck root, creating new opportunities that might yet blossom for them...or die.

The evening air pulsed with the rhythmic hum of the waves, bearing upon their folds the sighs and laughter between leaves, the perfume of promise in the wind. Tonight, she was expecting Vincent.

She had met Vincent at the shop. He came in one morning looking for Samuel Uy. He wanted some paintings for his law office. The artist was away, but what stroke of luck it turned out for him for he had not left empty-handed after all. He had made her promise to meet with him again.

She knew his steps on the pavement for it was unlike any other:

sure, lordly, worldly. The beam of the harsh fluorescent on the porch did not diffuse his features nor flatten them; on the contrary in such light he stood, breathing power. For the last time, Jacqueline ordered the old woman to keep the boy locked inside his room until they had left. But then no sooner had the young man stepped into the house and settled himself on the couch when the door to Dado's room flew open and the boy came bounding out in a seething rage. He lunged at his mother's neck and would not let go of his fingers around it, bawling yet demanding nothing in particular; in dejected horror Jacqueline saw that her son chose this moment of moments to run riot with his mood. The man evinced an old look that Jacqueline knew all too well, an awkward half smile, tentative, groping, and altogether visibly shocked. After several moments, it became apparent to both of them that neither could console Dado into silence. To leave the boy behind in a mad tempest didn't seem quite right, not in any case something their conscience could handle while they treaded through the evening on their first date.

At the dinner table, all three—mother, son and old woman—silently faced their late supper. Jacqueline nibbled, a pendulum of emotions riling the acids in her empty stomach. And while Dado chomped like a wolf, Aling Pat masticated hers, toothless and dimly comprehending the burning brooding presence at the head of the table, oblivious of the wild throbbing in the young woman's head, the impulse to implode in the deepest hollow of being even as her body held up, head propped high in the stiff dignity of surrender.

In the weeks not long after that night, Dado fell ill. His deliriums filled Jacqueline with her own cabal of ghosts crawling out of her murky, swept-under emotions. She nursed him through four mosquito-plagued nights, giving him the care and attention she had otherwise devoted to her paints and work. On the fourth night, Dado eased into a peaceful sleep for the first time. The grace of relief and sleep triggered something in her she was not accustomed to—a simple passing joy that sounded its exhaustions, and having sounded its pointlessness, had suddenly ceased.

Vincent had sent her a gift—a purple-splashed muslin shawl, light as air. On her shoulders, it felt like wings, and this she put around Dado, which amused him, and titillated his imagination of himself —bird, angel, king, Arab, Hindu, Superboy. Jacqueline made the appointment for Vincent with Samuel Uy. But nothing more was to happen between them, save a card of thanks she sent out without delay.

Dado had barely been out of the woods, when one early afternoon, Jacqueline came home with neither boy nor the maid in the house. Her undergarments were scattered over, her dresser-drawer and vanity case riffled through. She knocked on every door in the alley, fanned out to the coastal bank, but couldn't find anyone who knew where Dado was. She crouched and peeked through doorways like a mad, snapping dog. Then, beyond the gate of the school, she saw him.

There he was in the middle of a crowd, in his mother's long, wavy, auburn-tinted wig, wearing her gold-embroidered vest, and on his good short leg, her black fishnet stocking fallen and gathered in a heap around the foot. Stretched flat on the stone bench for all to see, as though *HE* wanted them to see, was his bloated, florid, deranged foot, indifferent to the stares and dread and protests of the crowd, yet abominable as it was, presented itself quite calmly reposed.

On his eyelids, blue shadows glared like sunrays, while splotches of brilliant pink ringed his mouth. His mother's purple muslin scarf lay crumpled on the ground.

Blood boiled over, a heart's fist poised solely on the creature of he whose hobbled rhythm and hideous foot animated all the mortifying failures of her fate. His utter neutrality merely amplified in her the cruel obstructions that one's own could wreak, the divided one that allied itself with the shadowy menace. Her mind shone coldly on her fortunes, which dragged the painful secrets out into the open.

But, slowly, through the trembling rage, and startling her, she felt herself being hurled and knocked about, thrown back as against a wall, yet devoid of any concern. It seemed that there appeared no more corner to turn, and the weight on one's back, an albatross of ancient expectations, had finally broken ground. Fate, once so shifty and sinister, had pulled down its parapets.

So there he was, smiling openly as she approached him, the boy wearing the finery of her make-up and mask, sheen wrappings ripping from his legs, and on his face, a theater of sorts. She pushed her way through the crowd, and the blast that so fevered her all but flickered dead as though it had nothing more to run on. The sun shifted on his face, shade and light changing places, and the eye, now focused, seeing what it had missed: the moss on the gray wall, the wind circling a pile of yellowing leaves, the bluish shroud on a still canal. Dado dashed out of the inner gate toward her, a hobble attached to his one leg. In the lilt of his hindered gallop, Jacqueline caught a rhythm that alone played to the accent of his perfect joy.

She picked up the scarf and wiped the paint off his face. She lifted him up and carried him out the gate and threaded through the traffic. People stared, the children laughed, the market crowd gossiped, the beggars gawked, the cars honked, the deepening dusk around them shattered into a thousand brilliant red suns before caving in. Dado's naked, blighted foot—calloused, corpulent, glowingly severe—lay in the concave of her hand against her breast, digging deep within and beyond the defiance, piercing through bone, into the seeing heart.

Rhodora V. Peñaranda is the author of two poetry books, *Touchstone* (Menagerie Arts, 2007), and *Unmasking Medusa* (Menagerie Arts, 2008). She lives in upstate New York with her husband, the composer Bayani Mendoza de Leon, and their three children. She works independently for a textbook publishing firm.

Marianne Villanueva

Isa

Daughter, our islands are disappearing. Once, there were two: two proud pieces of rock rearing high above the waves. Our islands had always existed: they were the two arms of Laon, who slumbered in the caldera beneath us. Around us were rings of hard and soft corals, and in the cave-like spaces of these corals lived an abundance of animals: snakes and eels and starfish and seahorses and clams. Surrounded by such abundance, we seldom knew hunger, or sickness. You and your sisters were born on these islands; until today, no one had ever left.

But you don't care anymore; your eyes look only to the silver bird that will bear you far away.

Remember, your island is Isa. Isa, the first, the mother of all. Remember your mother, Raymunda, she who was the only person brave enough to swim underneath the blue water we call Pangarap, the only one to see the bowl of the volcano Laon that lies deep beneath the water, the volcano that birthed us all..

Remember the names of the fishes and birds. Remember the beings of the sea, the beings of the air. Remember how you fell asleep each night, listening to your mother's crooning and to the sound of the waves.

Five families lived on Isa. At first, there was a way to walk on the ground between the houses. But gradually the water rose and that was when we began to use the rope bridges.

We wondered, occasionally, about other beings, the ones we guessed must inhabit the world. The world that was so far away we couldn't smell or taste it. Because we couldn't imagine that other world, we decided to think only about things we could smell or taste or hear ourselves. Smells like what was cooking in each other's houses. Tastes like the opaque, soft, peppery insides of mollusks and snails, or the juice we sucked from the bones of fish.

We knew how to pray.

Every year, the storms came. We shut our windows and waited. During one storm, the one we called Insiang, the house at the opposite end of Isa was swept away. That was the house of Ligaya and her five sisters. When the wind died down and we opened our windows, we didn't recognize the world. And gradually we realized it was because a house was missing. Far away, we saw a pointed shape, bobbing on the waves. A few of the men took out boats and rowed to the wreckage. When they reached it, they saw Ligaya's body, floating on its back, her face already purple and swollen. They knew her because of the scar above her right eyebrow; we all remembered the day, 10 years earlier, when she had been clambering over the slippery rocks and fell. Hers was the only body to be recovered.

Your mother said it was Urdo's fault. He should have built a stronger house, one that could withstand the lash of wind and waves. He was the father; he should have known. In a house with six women, the men grow weak, your mother said.

Your mother's voice grew rough and hard, and you and your sisters stopped listening to her. One day we discovered that she had shouted herself out of her body. She was sitting at the kitchen table, as always, but we could tell it was merely the shape of her that remained. Her soul had escaped to somewhere far beyond our reach.

Naturally, we looked high and low: under the eaves of all the houses, in the storage rooms and even in the caves beneath the rocks. But her soul was truly gone. Behind your mother's eyes now was a still darkness, and her skin became soft and papery.

Once we caught you jabbing at her forearm with the serrated edge of a clam shell. Tears were running down your face. Insistently you called out to her, demanded a response. That was when I took your mother's form and put her in the wooden box that I had kept in readiness all these years. Once she was in it, it floated gently on the waves. I pushed it as hard as I could, and the current bore it away. You remained watching the sea for hours.

The other island, just over the horizon, was called Dalawa. It was almost exactly the same size as ours, but for whatever reason the families on Dalawa had many more children: there were almost ten houses clinging to their rock.

One day the people on Dalawa sent word. They said that either Pangarap was rising, or their island was sinking, they couldn't tell which. They had started building a wall out of coral. They hoped it would protect them.

One day, we realized it had been almost a year since we had had any visitors from the other island. The men took out the boats. They sailed for many days. They kept telling one another, It must be only a little farther, only a little farther. On the third day, it dawned on them what must have happened and they were seized with panic. They set the boats straight for home and from far away we could hear their shouts, like the shouts of madmen. Get ready, they shouted. Prepare!

We realized that we had seen it happening but in our fear had refused to believe it. Pangarap was indeed rising. As children we had felt the water lapping at our toes. Now, it washed around our ankles. And strange things were being borne in by the tides: strange glinting things that broke if one pressed too hard; and pieces of clothing that might have belonged to a woman, so delicate was the stitching on the waists and hems.

Once, the sea brought a man. He was naked, and his sex was swollen to an extreme size. For hours we gathered round, studying the form of this strange being. We saw the scars on his shoulders, and the gaping wound on his right thigh. His earlobes were rimmed with silver studs, and his fingernails were long and curved and reminded us of talons. We could not tell whether he was old or young, but he seemed to have died in some fierce confrontation. His open mouth was twisted in a grimace. We anointed his body with oils and then sent him back to his home.

Perhaps it was a year or two later that the man we called Kawayan came. He stepped out from the belly of a huge silver bird that landed in the water a few meters from our house. How we shrieked when we saw the bird loom over the horizon. Impossible to describe our fear at the deafening noise it made, or the enormity of its wings. The bird landed gently on a swell and remained rocking there for agonizing minutes. Then a hole opened in its side and from the darkness within a man emerged.

He was only the first.

He told us—in a language that sounded much like our own, but with a different, harsher, staccato inflection—that there were other islands like ours, scattered all across Pangarap. Most were so far away that it had taken many men's lifetimes to create birds large enough to reach them. And the news made us happy and afraid at the same time, and for many many nights we did not know sleep. Happiness was replaced by apprehension. Premonitions crowded our dreams.

Each of us now felt a new host of ever-changing sensations. Some described it as a tickling of the arms. Some called it a restlessness of the feet. Those of us afflicted could not lie down, for the sensation made us want to get up, no matter how exhausted we were.

Others heard voices, which mingled with their fears.

There was a new feeling now, a feeling we didn't yet know how to name. There was a name for the time before the arrival of the silver birds, and there was the present time. Our memories, which we had relied on for so many years, now became imprecise, unfocused. We forgot things. Only with great effort could we pinpoint events of the past, or what was now the past.

The men who came in the silver birds had a favorite word: "Explain." They wrote down our words and hid their thoughts from us. Soon, several of us fell prey to a strange sickness. The first victim was Vina, who was only 15. She was forever staring at the silver bird men, and at one in particular whose hair was burnished and light, the color of the sun. We had lived with each other so long that any emotional disturbance suffered by one of us infected the whole. Everyone in the four remaining houses on Isa had heard the quickening of Vina's breath at each approach of the light-haired stranger. Each of us knew what caused her heart to begin its strange staccato melody.

The sickness affected the sight. One day we heard Vina's mother utter a terrifying scream. When we all came running, we learned that, a few minutes earlier, Vina's mother had found Vina naked and sobbing on the floor next to her bed. Her eyes had developed milky cataracts in place of the pupils which had been brown only yesterday. Vina's mother had fallen backwards, clutching her heart. Her father, too, had come running. Now they were inconsolable, both of them wailing with grief.

Someone suggested throwing a net to prevent Vina's soul from escaping. And so Vina lived from that day on underneath a weaving of hemp. Everyday the milky whiteness of her eyes became more terrifying, and her sobs became more heartrending.

I saw the way you looked at Vina, and I knew that you had made up your mind to leave.

Take care. Keep this amulet around your neck at all times. If you return to us with love, your voice will be high and pure. If you return to us with hatred and repugnance, your voice will be like those of all the other children whose souls were stolen by the men in the silver birds.

Love us, always. Tell yourself everyday, upon first waking, who you are and where you come from. You are our daughter, our life.

Marianne Villanueva has Masters degrees in East Asian Studies and English (with a concentration in Creative Writing) from Stanford University. She is the author of the short story collections *Mayor of the Roses* (Miami University Press, 2005) and *Ginseng and Other Tales from Manila* (Calyx Books, 1991), as well as the co-editor, with poet Virginia Cerenio, of an anthology of Filipino women's writings, *Going Home to a Landscape* (Calyx Books, 2003).

Leny Mendoza Strobel

LANGUAGE IS MY ANCHOR

What remains of the languages we no longer speak?
or speak very little of?

i speak Pampango and Pilipino with declining fluency for lack of practice. my son, 1.5 generation, understands both languages but can't speak except for a few vocabulary words. my grandson, Noah, will probably never know either except for the funny words we've taught him like *kili-kili*[1] and *buldit*.[2]

even so, Noah knows that when he hears these words, they refer to his Dad and Lola who are Filipinos. he looks at me and looks at himself in the mirror and says "I am Filipino!" he looked at the checker at WalGreens and asked her: Are you Filipino? and when she answered affirmatively, Noah said: I am Filipino, too!.

or when I play the Pilipino audibles on yahoo messenger, Noah is tickled by the different sounds and he giggles and with sparkling eyes he knows that this is his language, too. he couldn't speak the words, and he doesn't understand the meaning but he recognizes the lilt, the intonation, the pronunciation—they belong to him because he hears me speak in the same voice. *Okey ka lang?*

Lola, sing to me—he asks of me at bedtime...and he knows I will sing "Ugoy ng Duyan" and the lullaby calms him and sends him off to dreamland.

so what remains of the languages that we no longer speak in words... but yet the language lives on in our voices, in our songs, in our touch, in our eyes?...Noah will always know.

1. *armpit*   2. *buttocks*

READ ME

Read me between the lines of my reverie.
Read me between the lines of my laughter.
Read me between the lines of my sighs.
Read me between the lines of my
Read me between the lines of
Read me between the lines
Read me between the
Read me between
Read me
Dear

Leny Mendoza Strobel is the author of *Coming Full Circle: The Process of Decolonization Among Post 1965-Filipino Americans* and *A Book of Her Own: Words and Images to Honor the Babaylan,* as well as numerous journal articles, book chapters, online essays. She is Associate Professor in the American Multicultural Studies Department at Sonoma State University.

Alex G. Paman

KAMPANA

My fondest childhood memories have always revolved around Sunday morning. I can remember waking to church bells clanging beautifully on the hour, resonating over our small community and reminding us to attend our weekly obligation. Time always slowed to a crawl when the Sunday sun came up, where the normally bustling streets were empty and quiet, and even the sunlight itself seemed brighter than usual. A wonderful, deafening hush had swallowed the world, and the only thing that mattered was that you arrive at mass before the priest's procession began their walk towards the altar.

I admit I wasn't the most punctual person, but I wasn't the only one, and I really did try. It all depended on who was ready for the next convenient mass; sometimes we came together as a family, and other times I came with different siblings and relatives. It seemed we could never really get there early enough, and in more times than not, we ended up just sitting outside and watching the mass through the front entrance doors. But this had its advantages too, allowing us to leave early before the massive congregation could filter out during communion.

On the times we were able to find seats, I sometimes paid more attention to my surroundings than the sermon. I knew the routine of sitting, standing, kneeling, and bowing perfectly by heart, so I was able to hide my lack of attention successfully. I even made it game sometimes by being the first to make the motion or gesture before anyone else. One of the easy thrills of being a child, I suppose.

I was always fascinated by the birds flying in and out the bay windows, chirping as they alighted on steep ledges that framed the altar. They were God's creatures too, after all, and their presence seemed natural and almost divine. I must admit, however, that those saint statues that towered over the congregation used to scare me, and it wasn't until I met them in person that I realized that it was just the lighting that created that illusion. Tall oscillating fans whirred around us from different corners, their flickering ribbons helping to circulate the air streaming in from the outside. Veiled grandmothers held paper fans in their hands, flapping their wrists vigorously for relief against the claustrophobic heat.

Don't get me wrong now, but my favorite part of mass was always when it ended. This wasn't because I found the entire ritual boring or uninteresting; I was born a devout Catholic and I died as one, too. It was my favorite, because we were greeted by rows upon rows of vendors the moment we dipped our fingers in the holy water and exited out the door. Weaving between balloon salesmen and *sampaguita* lei stands, my dad bought me *barquillos*, sweet pastry tubes that came in packs. As much a social scene as it was one of prayer, my parents often stayed well after mass and mingled with their friends and acquaintances. This afforded my siblings and I quality playing time with the other children, often ending with a stern lecture about soiling our bright Sunday clothes.

The meal after mass was a treat too, something to complement the solemnity of the day. TV shows were all religious anyway, and didn't get interesting until the night-time variety shows came on after the evening news.

And it all started with hearing the *kampana* or church bells early in the morning. I can honestly say that those were the most beautiful times of my short life, and I try to relive them through the parishioners whenever I can. One Sunday morning, I crossed the street without looking and was run over by a horse carriage. As painful a death as that was, it pained me even more to see my entire family grieving on the roadside, at the hospital, and at my funeral. I now visit our church once a year, on the anniversary of my passing, and I say a prayer for my family in return. I sit next to my Mom on the bench, and although they can't see me, I know they can sense that I'm there.

I hope they think of this church not as a place of tragedy, but one of peace and beauty. They should see the mass through our eyes, with all the angels and saints looking down. We participate in the mass as much as the parishioners do, believe it or not. And up to now, I still don't have the words to describe the color of candlelight after it's been lit with a prayer.

The church bells are still enchanting to my ears, and you really should take time to listen to them. You never know who they're calling home, even if it's just for a nostalgic visit.

Alex G. Paman began writing shortly after graduating from California State University, Sacramento, majoring in Fine Arts with an emphasis on graphic design and journalism. He covered the entertainment beat for the *Philippine Review* and Philippine Fiesta community newspapers, interviewing major Filipino musical acts that toured Sacramento, Stockton and San Francisco. His work has also appeared in the popular *YOLK!* Asian-American magazine. Although the bulk of his writing involved Pinoy pop media, he also wrote pieces on native folklore and mythology, his personal areas of interest.

Although not writing for any specific newspaper, he is currently working on several projects that he hopes will promote native Filipino culture to the mainstream American media, particularly in the areas of science fiction, fantasy and horror. He can be reached at manilacoast@aol.com.

Janice De Jesus

ISLAND TULIP

*F*lowers are very much like us, none more so than the tulip. Tulips smile at you, talk to you, let you know when they need water, have too much light; and before they die, they are at their most serenely beautiful, stems flagging as if reaching out for a final embrace, the folding petals expressing in their contortions every imaginable emotion.

—*Mireille Guilliano*

As soon as the dainty, white, star-shaped blossoms open at night, Milo hovers slightly above them, marveling at their sight.

He knows that once they blossom, they will wilt in less than a day. This is why he insists on eating his supper before sunset, as he does not dare to miss the miracle he has witnessed since he first visited the botanical garden 10 years ago.

Bending over, Milo buries his face in a few of the flowers and inhales the blossoms' sweet fragrance and out of all the domestic species of jasmine, the sampaguita is his favorite.

Garden visits at night have been ideal as Milo avoids the crowds as best he can. Daylight becomes his enemy as visitors staying at the nearby Batangas beach resort who flock to the garden tend to view Milo as a rare specimen, often regarded with more scrutiny than the flower species themselves.

The essence of Milo shocks the average person at best. From a distance, one gathers that he is a small child wandering around the garden. But close inspection reveals otherwise.

As he turns, people gasp at the ghastly, wrinkled brown face inhabiting his large head. Black marble eyes protrude and with no eyebrows and eyelashes to frame them, the eyes just seem to suspend themselves from the hollow of his skull.

People continue to stare as Milo holds the plastic watering can over his precious flower charges. Milo hunches over pretending not to be affected by their intense scrutiny. He just wishes they would either turn their attention to the flowers or leave.

It's at night when he's most peaceful at the garden where the flowers are the only living beings in the world he cares to be with.

It's a different story during the day, especially at breakfast as Tita Diwata waits on him diligently.

If it were not for the humid conditions in the Philippines, a daily bath wouldn't be necessary. Not only has it become a necessity, it's become an inconvenience as Milo ages, his range of motion lessens.

A bath has become a daily torture session as Diwata strips him of his clothes and along with that, his dignity. In the cold cement floor of the combination outhouse and bathhouse, Diwata scrubs Milo's scaly skin until he begs her to stop.

There's no need for shampoo for his bald head.

Breakfast, lunch, every meal for that matter, year after year has been added torture for what is the use of eating healthy greens grown fresh from Diwata's garden if Milo is not destined to be a growing boy?

What is the use indeed? Milo asks himself day after distressing day.

After breakfast, it's off to the garden again where Milo decided four years ago he was the happiest. There would be no more school for him and, what a shame, as Milo loved to learn. He loved books and exploring the world outside his cocoon that was the small barrio in the province.

He remembers the day as if it was only yesterday. The day he learned he was different than other children his age.

The day that he learned that, as soon as he was born, he was marked for death.

"Progeria," was the word his Tita Bianca used.

A foreign word—as foreign as she was. Tita Bianca, Diwata's youngest sister, who left the Philippines years ago to study medicine in the United States, often sent money back home for Diwata and Milo.

She was nurturing, Bianca was, nurturing from afar, unlike Diwata who hovered from day to day relentlessly. Surely, his aunt could see how her mothering was emasculating.

Bianca often wrote home about her tales and mishaps abroad. About the time she kept referring to men and women as "sir" and "ma'am" and how they bristled at her use of formality—a custom she was raised to uphold.

"Apparently, I shouldn't address young people as 'sir' and 'ma'am' in the States," Bianca wrote. "I have to be American since I live in America now."

"Mind your manners," Diwata wrote back. "Don't you ever forget where you came from."

And she never did. Even before Bianca became a full-fledged doctor, she sent money or *pasalubong*, American novelty items for her sister and Milo.

Milo sensed that Bianca felt she had to make up for Nimfa's absence. In fact he knew that.

"Nimfa failed us, Diwata, and she failed her son when she abandoned him," Milo overheard Bianca tell Diwata in the living room of the family home during one of Bianca's visits. "We can't fail our nephew. He needs us, more than ever, he needs us."

He barely remembers his mother, the middle child, the prodigal daughter. She left when he was three and she was barely twenty, a young mother, who was barely a mother even before she decided she didn't want to be one.

Or maybe his disease sent her away. All these years, Milo couldn't help but think maybe he was the reason Nimfa left. His father, whom Diwata never mentions, isn't worth a thought.

She was young, frail, skinny, soft-spoken. Her only gift to him was his name. Milo. After her favorite Nestle milk beverage, Diwata told him.

How he barely remembers her now.

"*Tingnan n'yo si Tanda!*"
"Look at the old man!"
"*Tandang Milo! Tandang Milo! Tandang Milo!*"
"Old Milo! Old Milo! Old Milo!"

What Milo does remember was the way the kids at school used to tie him to a coconut tree as they circled around him chanting.

He was the butt of jokes and the children kept hurling ridicule after ridicule, regardless of constant reprimanding from teachers.

But the teachers themselves didn't quite know how to approach Milo, so he was often ignored and misunderstood.

That was when Diwata finally decided to take him out of school.

"I should have done this a long time ago," she told Milo apologetically as she rubbed the essential oil of ylang-ylang on his back, arms and legs.

As the only faith healer in the village, Diwata relentlessly applied various potions and oils — a mixture of scents, herbs and herbal blends to see if she could cure Milo of his progressive aging disorder.

"Did you know that ylang-ylang comes from the Tagalog word *ilang* which means wilderness?" his aunt asked as she continued to massage his frail limbs. "The word *ilang-ilang* means rare and its scent is the most delicate of all. You are an ylang-ylang to me, Milo. You're a rare flower in this wilderness."

To Milo, what his aunt said didn't seem like a compliment.

"Is that your way of saying in a nice way that I'm different, Tita? I know I'm different!"

Diwata sighed as she got up to pour some herbal tea made from *Gumamela* leaves, Milo's usual beverage since he was three-years-old.

"Drink this," she commanded.

And he did, allowing the hot, soothing, fragrant liquid to open up the clogged passages of his body and soul. Funny, he thinks to himself, he remembers reading that *Gumamela*, or Hibiscus, is associated with longevity. How ironic.

Diwata sat on the floor and resumed her massage this time concentrating on Milo's feet. He cringed a little in his chair as he held the hot tea. The tickling sensation was the only thing that really made him laugh in his life.

*H*er name's Tala.

Tala, means "bright star." Milo looked it up as soon as he met her.

Tala, was fifteen, a year younger than Milo, but bright, like her name. She appeared one day, like a dream, at the garden.

Her bronze skin shone in the sunlight, her black eyes luminous and shiny black hair all caused a sensation Milo had never felt before.

Tala, the niece of the botanical garden director, was helping out at the garden during the summer.

Milo admires Tala from a distance, afraid to approach her lest she disappear as suddenly as she appeared. And so he quietly watches her as she hums a sweet tune, a smile on her pink lips, as she showers the sampaguitas, her bare arms flexing as she holds up the watering can.

Every day he notices she wears different clothing, sometimes bright, sometimes pastels, always in a very modest skirt. One day, she shows up wearing a plaid, pink, full skirt, another day, a red and orange striped one.

The sleeveless blouses, with its fitted bodices, boast her sensuous, nubile chest. Somehow, Milo doesn't remember noticing the chests of Diwata or Bianca or the other women in the village.

One day, as Tala's movements mesmerize him, the flowers seem to spin all around him as he realizes he's losing his balance. He holds onto a vine to keep himself from falling.

His near mishap distract's Tala as she looks up from watering the flowers and Milo curses himself for his clumsiness.

She leans her head forward, revealing her lovely, swan-like neck, richly exposed with her hair swept up in a ponytail.

"Is someone there?" she calls out, her voice mellifluous.

Milo continues to hide behind some shrubs and branches and stands completely still, afraid to breathe.

The next thing he knows, a delicate hand draws the branches separating him from the desired.

Black eyes meet and lock—one pair captivated, the other drenched in fear.

Tala stares in morbid fascination. She wants to look away, yet something in his eyes entrances her.

"Bright star," he says, breaking the silence.

The fear in her eyes turns to puzzlement then to sorrow as she viscerally examines Milo's face.

"There's nothing to be afraid of, Bright Star," he says tenderly.

She puts down her watering can, the muscles of her face relax a bit.

"How do you know the meaning of my name?"

Milo strokes the petals of a sampaguita, his eyes never leaving her face.

"I looked it up. Just like I looked up the meaning of my Tita's name, Diwata," he tells her.

"Goddess." They both say it at the same time and look at each other, pleasantly surprised.

"Do you believe in goddesses?" Tala asked, looking at Milo through long, thick eyelashes.

"Goddesses rule the earth," he says, picking the *sampaguita* and handing it to her.

Tala lowers her eyes and raises them only slightly as they meet with Milo's again.

She slowly reaches her right arm across to take the flower.

Voices break their interlude as a group approaches the garden. Tala turns to look at the visitors—two serious-looking young men wearing glasses and khaki pants, scientists perhaps, perhaps professors.

Perhaps just ordinary men, Milo thought.

Tala hurries to greet them as Milo watches helplessly, hopelessly besotted.

And so a secret friendship ensues.

Tala and Milo spend nearly every day quietly watering plants and flowers, sweeping the floor of the nursery, talking about the essence of propagation and the wonders of the natural world.

She wants to become a botanist, she says, that's why she's helping out and plans to continue to do so until she goes to college.

This is when Milo's face collapses. Tala notices the sullen look on his face.

"College," he says softly, a word he can barely utter. Any word that speaks about the future he deems unbearable.

"Yes, college," she perks up at the prospect. "I can hardly wait. You get to choose your own instructors, your own classes. You have the freedom to choose what you want to be."

Nodding, Milo feels squeamish. He finds not being able to face the future nauseating, as this is the sad fact of his life. His unfortunate, wretched life.

She never asks about his condition and he never talks about it. As far as he knows, Tala never seems to mind his strange looks.

Milo invites her to lunch at home a few times and Diwata is curious, thrilled, cautious, suspicious, but curious. Especially curious because she's never seen Milo connect so intimately with another human being before besides herself. Curious because she longs to find out what Tala thinks of her nephew. Curious to see where this friendship will lead to.

Evidence that Tala is every bit the city girl oozes out of her every pore as her eyes absorb everything archaic and unusual that is Milo's milieu. The dirty kitchen, an extension to the real kitchen outside the house, that really isn't dirty, it's just called that because homeowners want to preserve the real kitchen to show off when entertaining guests.

The outhouse/bathhouse where large pails sit side by side and one pumps his or her own water as they continually dump it for their baths and fills it up as a courtesy to the next user. Large tumbler cups are dipped into the pails and water splashed onto the skin for a shocking cold bath. A smooth, oval stone sits near two bars of soap and Tala at least knows that the stone is used to scrub the skin, raw at times.

Tala observes the toilet does not flush. A person has to pump yet more water in pail and dumps it directly into the toilet and with force or else it won't flush right, Milo informs her.

She notes a pile of folded mosquito nets in the corner of one room—Bianca's room when she's visiting.

"How old is your Tita Diwata?" Tala asks as she looks at a picture of Diwata taken years ago at her high school graduation.

"She's in her late thirties. She keeps people guessing," Milo says as he walks towards Tala standing next to a bookshelf filled with family photos.

"She's never been married?" Tala asks as she scans an array of photos of three sisters, an older couple, and some individual photos of Diwata and Bianca. For someone in her late thirties, Diwata looks older, with her sagging eyebags and salt and pepper hair, Tala thinks to herself. She's had a hard life.

Milos shakes his head. "She's too busy healing people, healing me."

Tala notices there are no pictures of Milo and wonders why.

"I'm not a picture person," he says brusquely and she doesn't pursue the issue.

Days later, Milo insists he bathe himself.

"Nonsense! You're not strong enough to pump water and carry all those pails of water by yourself and still have the energy to scrub your body," Diwata argues, pumping water with frenzy. Milo notices how his aunt has developed muscles after years of pumping water not just for her baths but also for his.

"Binata na ako!"

"I'm a grown man!" He yells, raising his voice over the gushing water.

Diwata continues to pump and when the pail is full she walks over to add more water to the larger pails waiting to be used for the bath.

Milo used to think his life had no meaning until he met Tala.

"Our last name is Dimayuga, meaning unshakable," Milo shouted. "I can beat this disease, Tita, I know I can! I am unshakable and unstoppable!"

He says this with conviction now. During his many moments of depression, he used to call himself Milo Dimasalang, meaning untouchable. That's what he used to feel like. An untouchable. Someone lower than the lowest caste on earth.

"Tita, do you hear me?"

"*Basta!*"

"Enough!" she says, waving her hand, dismissing him, keeping him from gripping the pump's handle.

And so Milo grudgingly allows his aunt to scrape his skin clean once more.

Diwata is a lot gentler with her hands for their usual massage session after his bath.

"Did you know that the essential oil of ylang-ylang helps to relieve high blood pressure, normalize sebum secretion for skin problems, and is considered to be an aphrodisiac?" she asks.

Milo blushes. He knows about aphrodisiac. That's the result of having a debilitating disease—you have too much time on your hands so all you do is read.

Suddenly, he thinks of Tala and blushes even more.

Diwata scans her nephew's face, looking for a sign, any sign.

Her lips form a straight line.

Tears well in Milo's eyes as he turns the page of his glossy, new, hardbound book—the book that Tala gives to him on his seventeenth birthday.

It is a miracle he has lived as long as he has, but he knows he hasn't much time on this earth. But on second thought, he reminds himself, no one does. Only, he's been living his life fast forward.

Tala's eyes start to moisten as well as she tries to keep from crying. She marvels at the wonder that is Milo, her dear friend, her soulmate that was not meant to be.

Tala notices how much Milo has aged in nearly a year since she's known him.

It is a book of tulips, she says proudly, as his eyes devour every colorful page after page of luscious flower photography.

"Unfortunately, tulips can't grow in the open in tropical climates. A cold winter season is required to grow them successfully," Tala says sitting down in the rattan chair across from Milo on the terrace of

Diwata's house. "A tulip won't thrive in our climate."

She continues to watch him as he turns each page, careful not to get any creases on the corners.

As the tears come close to falling and he could barely see the tulips on the pages, Milo thinks back to the time when Tita Bianca used to call Milo, her little tulip, as he described to him all the beautiful tulips she'd see blossom in the spring in the land of the free.

He knows he's the island tulip, something beautiful, but rare in the islands and not meant to thrive or survive in the tropics.

He thinks of Tala, who will be college-bound soon and how he will never go to college. He thinks about Tala, and how she will graduate, with honors, he presumes and get a coveted career in botany. He thinks of Tala and how she will go on to meet a gentleman, perhaps a professor, perhaps a scientist and they will marry and have beautiful children together and perhaps go on vacations and see lots of tulips.

He thinks of Diwata and how sad she will be without him.

And he thinks back at the tulips he will never see and the places he will never visit, the space between breasts he'll never bury his face into, the groan of sheer pleasure he'll never utter, the children he'll never have.

He dreams of a world he will never see, a flower he will never hold, a spring season he will never experience.

And no matter how careful he is in handling his new book, the tears eventually tumble onto a page of bulbous tulips, so vibrant, so alive.

And Tala kisses him softly on the lips and all is well in his world.

❦

Progeria results in rapid aging of a child, beginning with growth failure in the first year of life. This results in a disproportionately small body given the size of the head. Progeria children (male and female) are thin and balding, with wizened narrow faces and old-appearing skin.

Janice De Jesus was born in Portsmouth, Virginia and raised in Louisiana and in the San Francisco Bay Area. She lived and studied in the Philippines for six years. She is a featured reporter for *Contra Costa Times* in Walnut Creek and is currently a Master of Fine Arts in Creative Writing candidate at Mills College in Oakland. An animal lover, she spends time fostering orphaned kittens. She lives in Hercules and is the foster mother of an adorable black and white kitten named Domino.

Janet C. Mendoza Stickmon

A BLOSSOMING HYACINTH

"*I* always look forward to meeting Larkin," Hyacinth thought to herself as she drove to his office. She stops at an intersection and reminisces silently, "I remember the time when we sat in my car, enjoying the view of the East Bay from the top of the Oakland hills. We talked for hours as we waited for sunset. We spoke about every topic imaginable. If I had something to say that I couldn't quite articulate, he patiently waited. He always waits. His complete attention anticipates a beauty in what I have yet to express. His patience coaxes the words from me with ease. I can't help but be completely transparent before him. Because I have his patience, I have no need to hide anything; my faults are not made beautiful; instead, they are left alone—accepted and held. I am not beautiful because of what his eyes see; I am beautiful because of what his eyes allow me to be. His vision dares not dictate the form my beauty takes. This beauty defies the curves and shades of his imagination. He knows that it is boundless and beyond his comprehension. So he cannot help but bow before it and let that beauty breathe. I never thought a man's patience could be so arousing. Now I know nothing sexier than this virtue."

She finally arrives. She knocks and peaks around the side of the door. Sitting behind his desk, Larkin motions her in as he finishes a phone call. Hyacinth walks into his office and sits across from him, looking at the bookshelf as she waits.

"Uh, huh, uh huh, I know exactly what you mean," he says, half-interested in the phone conversation.

Every few seconds, he steals quick glances of Hyacinth. She is wearing a lavender turtleneck and jeans, sitting with her legs crossed. At second glance, he sees her pull her sepia braids over one shoulder as she bends down to see a book low on the shelf. She turns his way and he quickly averts his gaze, looking as if he'd been honing in on some random spot on his desk. The snapshots he took with his eyes made him curious enough to stare, but wise enough not to. With the phone still in his hand, he walks to the shelf, remembering a book that might interest Hyacinth. He leans over her, reaching for the book. She's not sure if this is deliberate, but she feels the warmth of his body close to hers and it makes her uncomfortable, and yet excited. Sitting perfectly still, she waits, wondering how much longer it will take.

Larkin is stalling. He smells gardenias and cocoa butter. The scent rises off Hyacinth's copper skin. He stops to breathe her in. Larkin doesn't want to move, but he also fears arousing her suspicion. When Larkin finds the book, he slowly hands it to her with a seductive look of invitation, and within the same instant quickly snatches back his provocative energy. Covering the receiver, he whispers, "I think you'll like this."

"Thank you," she says, smiling. As she peaks at the book, Larkin takes a step back, brushing back his long bangs with his fingers, lightly biting his bottom lip searching for a way to prevent his hormone buzz from becoming transparent.

"Is he flirting?" she wondered. She quickly dismissed the idea, forcing herself to believe she imagined it. However, the more she resisted the thought, the more she hoped it was more than her imagination. She doubts she should be feeling this way, especially toward a priest.

Janet Stickmon is a teacher, writer, and performer who holds a Master's of the Arts Degree in Religion and Society from the Graduate Theological Union in Berkeley and a Bachelor's of Science Degree in Civil Engineering from the University of California, Irvine. In her performances and literature, she explores issues of life in the context of her identity as an African-Filipino-American woman. She is the author of *Unfragmented*, a book of poetry, a spoken word CD entitled, *Visible*, and her memoir, *Crushing Soft Rubies* (Broken Shackle Publishing, Intl., 2003).

Maria Teresa Mendiola Crescini

TWILIGHT AT EL DORADO DRIVE-IN

"Vic, you didn't tell me we're going to a drive-in. I thought you told my parents we're going downtown." Rosario protested gently, trying not to sound ungrateful.

"Yeah, I did. What difference does it make? The drive-in's better. No crowds." He grinned at her, small and even white teeth showing, lighting up his dark brown face.

"Well, it's not really what I had in mind." Rosario looked at her hands. She bit the hangnail off her right index finger.

Since her parents did not usually allow her to go out on dates, she felt Lady Luck was with her when Vic Hayupan, her father's friend, offered to take her out to the movies. She watched Vic's Dodge Charger make its way through the rows of speaker stands.

Pigeons scattered across the islands of broken heaters and speakers as Vic's red and white Charger cruised for a place to park. The sun disappeared behind floating clouds. Rosario brooded. The shadows of the heater and speaker stands sprawled on the ground like grotesque black crosses.

"Next time, we'll go downtown, okay?" He slowed down for a speed bump and looked at her. "Don't frown, it makes you look terrible. Anyway, if we went downtown we would have to stand in line." His dark, brown eyes scanned the evenly spaced rows of artificial meadows and hills in the parking lot of El Dorado Drive-In. "The Godfather's a hit, you know. Everybody and their brother want to see it. We're here, so smile." Vic smiled at her, and then parked the car at the back center facing the screen. He rolled down his window, propped the speaker against his window, and then rolled it back up to secure the speaker against the glass.

After what seemed a long silence to Rosario, Vic placed his hand on hers and said, "So how do you like your senior year at Edison High?"

"I hate it. It's boring." She scrunched her nose making a face of someone who might have just smelled something rotten. "Stockton's nothing more than a barrio." A light breeze drifted in. The odor of manure assaulted her nose. "It stinks here. I wish I lived in San Francisco." She stared at the white screen and at the slow descent of darkness.

"Well, I happen to like it here. Lots of Filipinos, not too much traffic. All the free fruits and veges we can stand, fresh from our farmer friends. Give it a little time; you'll like it here, too." He patted her hand and continued, "Listen, I'm going to get us something to eat before it gets dark." Vic opened the door and strode towards the snack bar.

As soon as she was left alone, Rosario relaxed and sighed softly. "You'll like it here, too," she mimicked Vic as soon as he was out of earshot. "Yeah, right. And end up like the rest of the folks around here, breaking their backs harvesting fruits and vegetables for minimum wages. No thank you. I didn't come halfway around the world to exist like that. Give me San Francisco. The tall beautiful buildings of the Financial District. I can see myself working there. Nobody's written a song like "I left my heart in Stockton." She wanted to have said all that to Vic, but being polite was drilled in her head and she figured he didn't want to hear her opinion about this town.

The sun's descent turned the sky tomato red amidst the telephone poles, electric wires, and billboard ads. A lone star appeared distant in the sky and she wondered if it was Mercury or Venus. The air writhed with heat and the sky grew gray like a sac of darkness that was ready to burst open.

She daydreamed of another time, of sitting on the stone wall of Manila Bay watching the sun disappear into the horizon and how the brilliant gold, red, and purple lights bounced off the rolling tide, bathing her with dancing colors. The dialogue of the rocks with the breakers, an endless conversation. Like a hermit crab stranded in a tide pool, she awaited the sea water to enter, to take her to the wondrous ocean. She took a deep breath and the suffocating heat and stale air of Stockton brought her back.

Vic arrived with a cardboard tray full of drinks, popcorn, and hot dogs. His black shoulder-length hair that flipped at the ends made him look feminine, yet dark and menacing. Tall for a Filipino, he looked older than his twenty-three years. He motioned Rosario to open the door of the back seat.

"There's more room in the back," he said. His smile showed black gums sprouting small evenly spaced white teeth.

Rosario tried to smile back. Instead, she grimaced, her stomach suddenly feeling queasy.

"Here, have a hot dog."

"I don't really like hot dogs. They taste like chemicals." Rosario looked at the soggy bun smothered with catsup.

"It's actually pretty good, once you get used to the taste. Americans eat them all the time. Try it." Vic shoved the hot dog to Rosario's mouth and she took a small bite and quickly washed it down with Coke.

"I love this country. Doesn't this make you feel American?"

"What? Eating a hot dog?" She looked at him to see if he was kidding her.

"Yeah! Eating a hot dog, drinking Coke, watching a movie inside a car." Vic relished his American food and burped after a long swallow of soda.

Rosario rolled down her window, quite sure that there wouldn't be a second date with this guy. Darkness swallowed the small crack of light in the clouds and the movie began. Flickers of light brought faces of characters on the screen one thousand times their life size. The speaker crackled sound in time with the actors' mouth.

A close-up of an Italian man with a receding hairline talking to someone began, "I believe in America. America's made my fortune. And I raised my daughter in American fashion. I gave her freedom, but I taught her never to dishonor her family. She found a boyfriend, not an Italian..."

Vic sipped the last few drops of his soda, slurping air and liquid through the straw. He lit a cigarette and blew smoke out the window. "Your Papa told me you're a quarter Italian. He's pretty proud of that," he spoke without looking at her. One of his eyes closed when the smoke floated up near it.

Irritated that he was talking while the movie went on, she said, "I don't know why he likes telling people that. Isn't our family name obvious enough? I mean how many Filipinos do you know with the last name, Francini? Anyway, it's not like our last name ever got us anything."

"It made your skin light. That's something." He stroked her cheek gently.

She flinched in response. She kept her eyes on the screen, on the men and women dancing a traditional Italian folk song. Mama Corleone stood on the stage singing. Don Corleone continued to grant favors to the men requesting them.

Vic touched Rosario's hair. She tried not to move away this time. Without taking her eyes off the screen, she asked, "What about you? I heard your family owns a coconut plantation. And that you went to La Salle Seminary. Were you really studying to be a priest?" She gathered her long black hair to the side opposite Vic.

"Yeah, it was my mother's idea. She wanted to lock me up there. I guess she heard some rumors that a girl was after me." He scratched like a comb his newly grown mustache with his fingernails.

"Really? What do you mean *after you?*"

"Well, she was spreading gossip that I got her pregnant. My Papa said she's just trying to get into our family. She's dark like an *ita*, an aborigine, with black coarse hair. Papa thought she's more suited to be my housemaid. So he sent me here to live with my aunt and uncle before she gets any grandiose ideas." He blew circles of smoke out the window.

"How do you feel about that?" Rosario looked into his eyes that were brown as cold coffee.

"I don't know. She was alright. I only know she's not as pretty as you." He stroked her face with the back of his hand.

She sat still and silent. The full moon slid under thick clouds. Flickering lights cast a few straws of light through the darkness. Rosario has heard before that her light skin made her look special, a *mestiza*.

"Yeah, I think you're beautiful." He glanced at Rosario who stared at the screen. She watched Johnny Fontane sing a ballad which made the girls swoon. Sonny Corleone, the oldest son of Don Corleone, whispered something in one of the bridesmaids' ear. Sonny's wife was demonstrating the size of something which impressed the other women. The bridesmaid lifted her pink gown off the floor and ran up the stairs. Michael Corleone, the youngest son, explained to his girl-friend, Kay, how his father helped Johnny's career.

Vic tossed the lit cigarette butt out the window and moved his body forward to watch the next scene. Sonny Corleone lifted the brides-maid's gown, his hand between her legs. She put her arms around his neck and hung there as he opened his trousers. Then he placed both hands beneath her bare buttocks and lifted her up. His body moved up and down against her.

As if getting instructions from the movie, Vic moved closer to Ro-sario and placed his hands on her bare knees. She grabbed his hand which was trailing up her thighs. He moved even closer and put his hand around her shoulders.

"You know, I love it when you're angry. You scrunch your nose and your lips like they want to be kissed." He attempted to kiss her, but Rosario turned her face away from him. He squeezed himself closer and held her head tight, cramming her against the car door.

"You're hurting me. Please move." She pushed him gently.

His hand traveled to her breast, cupping it with the palm of his hand, kneading it like fresh dough.

"Stop. Please don't." Rosario removed his hand from her breast. Her skin felt sticky with perspiration.

"Just relax. I won't hurt you." But, he did not let her go. Grabbing the back of her neck with one hand and her face with the other hand, she felt his mouth on hers, tasting of burnt tobacco, bitter. Rosario tried to free herself. Her long straight hair tangled in the door handle. She pushed him away with one hand while she tried to free her hair. He kept on kissing her neck and it sent conflicting signals through her body. Electrifying goose bumps traveled through her skin. Her cheeks blushed. He put his hand back on her thigh.

"No, Vic. Please stop." Her hand grabbed his, not wanting to be touched this way by this stranger who knew nothing and cared less about getting to know her first. She felt the flex of his arm before he touched her breasts.

"Vic, please stop. I don't want to do this. Not yet." Rosario's voice quivered like a little girl, pushing him away with no success.

"Oh yes, you do. You smell so good" He moved as if he believed in taking what was his, including the moon, the air, the space in the car. The shadow of his head and arms loomed large. His hand reached underneath her skirt and tore away the flimsy underwear. The speed of his movement froze her. She struggled to free herself but his weight pinned her down. The struggle drove him in frenzy. While holding her down, he unzipped his pants. She felt something burning pass between her legs.

"No! Vic," she heard her voice small as if her throat had been cut with a sharp razor. Something ripped inside her. Her body received lightning-like jolts, innumerable, painful. A giddy, sick sensation rippled in her stomach, and then she felt nothing for what seemed an eternity. She watched his eyes grow narrow and glisten, felt his hands full of desire, but the fear in her voice seemed to please him best. Vic released a groan and relaxed his grip on her. She felt his hardness break and then a crawly fluid oozed down her thighs.

"You're delicious," he said, out of breath, sweating, sitting with legs apart on a slump. Slowly, he took a white handkerchief from his shirt pocket and wiped the blood off Rosario's crotch. While she laid limp and blank, her body bruised, her lips pulpy and tender, her legs trembling.

Inspecting the handkerchief in the screen's flickering light, he said, "I didn't know you're a virgin. I thought you were just playing hard to get." He sniffed the blood stained handkerchief and folded it neatly, as if a ruby was wrapped in it. "Well, I guess, this means we're engaged." He wore a wide grin-his face like a winner in a cockfight. "I'd like to see the faces of my friends who told me there's no way I could get a mestiza. Yup, Papa's gonna be proud." He smiled at her.

Rosario stared vacantly at the film, her eyes unable to focus. Tears streaked her cheeks. She bowed her head. The heat and friction between her legs left her raw, trashed. She closed her slick, greased thighs.

"Rosie, I'm sorry." He removed her loose hair from her face, but she pushed his hand away, violently. Silent tears and clear liquid running from eyes and nose flowed together. She wiped them off with the sleeves of her dress.

"Come on, it wasn't that bad. I'll be gentle next time." He smiled at her again.

She looked at him in disbelief. "I want to go home now," was all she said. She noticed for the first time her body's stench, sour like vinegar, mixed with the acrid smell of blood and semen. The windows of the car fogged.

"We can't do that. The show's not over yet. I'm sorry, okay. I don't know what else to say." He moved away from her and looked at her. She hugged her legs and placed her face against her knees, rocking herself lightly. Wiping the tears from her face, she watched the moon move into the thick clouds. She sat in darkness.

"Gimme a break. I just felt so horny. You looked so good. Besides, I know you want me too. Remember that time I was helping your Papa rototill his garden? I had my shirt off. I saw you peeking through the window curtains, and then you came out with a pitcher of lemonade. You touched my hand when you handed me the glass. Remember that?"

"Why, why didn't you stop when I asked you?" Rosie's voice trembled with anger.

"Oh, Rosie, I know you liked it too. Admit it. I couldn't help myself. I just had to do it. To save us some time, you know." Vic cracked the window open, allowing the still, night air to come in.

"To save us some time?" Her words filtered between gritted teeth.

"Your parents approve of me. They told my aunt that if they could arrange your marriage like the old days, they'd pick me." He thumped his chest. "They know I'm your suitor. They haven't let you go out with anybody else, have they?

It dawned on Rosario that the boxes of grapes, asparagus, and to-matoes given to her family by Vic were not just leftover fruits and vegetables from the field's harvest. The helping hand extended to them had a price. Rosario moved to open the door, but Vic pushed her down.

"Listen, you're not a virgin anymore. You know what that means, right?" The volume of his voice threatened her silent. "No man's gon-na want to...come after me." He let out a laugh. "Get it? Come after me." He gestured an up and down movement with his hips.

She cut a glance his way, wishing she had a knife. She knew exactly where she would slice him.

"You know, you could wind up pregnant from this. I was so hard, I could have busted a coconut open with it." He giggled.

A wave of nausea rippled through her. She cranked the window all the way down and dry heaved sour spit at the ground. Clear liquid ran out of her nose and eyes.

"You're lucky I'm nice. I'm offering to marry you. I like your pretty white face. You'll give me handsome sons. I'm not a bad guy, you'll see." He shook a cigarette out of the pack. He kept running his fingers through his hair. Only the small speaker responded to his conversation.

Crackling through the speaker, the voice of Tom Hagen, the God-father's *consigliore*, was making an offer. The movie director character was showing Tom his prize stud, a $600,000 pure bred horse. He ex-plained to Tom that he wanted Johnny Fontane run out of town for screwing the best piece of ass he's ever had. Tom left.

Vic blew circles of smoke at the warm summer air. The sound of his own voice underscored her silence. "If a cholo fucked you first, you'd end up a whore. Your Papa told me about your cousin and her Mexican boyfriend. Did he marry her? No. Where is your cousin now? Work-ing to support him, right?" He looked at her. She held her mouth with her left hand.

"You don't want to end up like that. Your parents don't want you to wind up in the same boat." He grabbed her face toward his. "Listen to me. The first time is always the worst," his voice almost soft and tender. "I want you. I'll take care of you. I know you're mad at me right now, but you'll get over it one day. You'll grow to love me. Your parents already do. So stop crying now."

Rosario curled up in the corner and hugged herself tight. She flinched at the movie scene where the dead horse's head laid in the yellow satin sheets of the movie director's bed. He screamed and screamed at the sight. An offer he should not have refused.

For a moment, the moon slid out from behind the clouds. Rosario dried her eyes and asked his permission to clean herself in the bathroom before she opened the door to the leaden evening. As if sleepwalking under the mercurial moon, she felt abandoned by all the people she loved, her parents and even by Jesus and Mary at whose stony feet she offered flowers and prayers in exchange for blessings. A quickening raged through her veins, she felt dangerous, with nothing left to lose.

She felt free.

✻

Maria Teresa Mendiola Crescini is a survivor of domestic abuse; a woman who broke the shackles of cruelty to become a successful businesswoman, author, mother and "Lola." Born into poverty in Pasay City, she came to the U.S. with her father at the age of 13, leaving behind her mother and six siblings.

She graduated with distinction from San Jose State University with a Bachelor of Arts in English. Her first fiction short story, "Pinay from Pasay," was published in the anthology of *Philippine American Short Stories*.

Today, Tess has success in the real estate industry. She is the president and owner of Enervenge Solutions International, Inc. and serves on the national Board of Directors for the Asian Real Estate Association of America.

As a member of the Filipina Women's Network, she recently performed in an all Filipina benefit production of Eve Ensler's *The Vagina Monologues* and *Usaping Puki* as a part of the V-Day worldwide campaign to end violence against women and girls.

Oscar Peñaranda

PRELUDE TO A GIG

In San Francisco, everyone's favorite city, the city that knows how, cosmopolitan city by the bay, one grew up with musicians and artists and writers walking its steep and windy streets in almost every neighborhood. This is a story of two artists, one very famous and one quite obscure.

Charles Mingus, the legendary jazz bassist and composer, came in from the San Francisco autumn mist for a game of pool because he had a couple of hours to kill before his performance at the Keystone Korner near Chinatown and Manilatown. Big droplets of slanted rain shone in cars' headlights as they maneuvered the arduous streets on this particular night during the era of the fifties merging and forging into the sixties. The Mabuhay Restaurant was one of the favorite hangouts of Filipinos. It was owned by the Brotherhood and Sisterhood of the Dimasalang, one of the largest and influential Filipino organizations at the time, and it is said that writers such as Carlos Bulosan, P. C. Morrante, Stanley Garibay and many others, hung out there during their stay in San Francisco when they wrote pieces for the local Filipino papers and journals.

The Mabuhay had a mid-size counter and several tables for eating. In the back, where happens the real action, as in this case, behind a flimsy faded curtain that split in half, were three pool tables, a big brass spitoon on the floor, hat racks and coat racks, benches that lined the walls, tin-can ashtrays spaced evenly over another counter, and a light bulb above each table. In the pool hall, smoke from cigars and cigarettes floated lazily up becoming distinct shapes where the shafts of light pierced the room.

That game of pool was Mr. Mingus' undoing. Mingus wanted to wait out the hard part of the rain before his gig (he had a couple of hours) when he saw the sign "Mabuhay Restaurant Food and Pool." It would be a perfect combination for his wait in the rain before his gig up the street at the Keystone Korner. But as it turned out, like most seemingly perfect beginnings, it was a disaster. For at the pool hall of the Mabuhay Restaurant, he had the misfortune of playing Yaw-Yaw, the Pinoy hustler from Mindanao.

Charles Mingus was a large black man, and Yaw-yaw slightly smaller than a medium Filipino. Charles Mingus put his big instrument case down beside the door as he checked out the place, seeming to take a liking to it right away. He flicked off beads of raindrops from his long black woolen coat as he took it off and hung it on the rack sticking out of a cement wall.

"Hi. How you all doin'?" he smiled. After a while he said, "The sign outside said food and pool. I see only food tables. Where are the other tables?"

"They're right behind that curtain, in the back," Manong Al, an old timer who was not that old and who himself dabbled with the jazz piano, volunteered a reply. "Are you gonna eat first? You know Filipino food?"

"I love that stuff," he said. "Can't get enough of it." He lifted his scarf off his neck and hung that with his coat. "But I never eat before I play," he said, opening up his hands, palms up, like a preacher blessing his congregation.

Manong Al meanwhile seemed to be in a state of restrained euphoria. He did not know what to do with himself, as if holding his pee in some discomfort or in delight.

"Anyone for a game of eight ball, nine ball, rotation...whatever?" Charles Mingus ambled towards the curtain and parted it, ducking his head in, the footsteps of his big smile still on his face.

It was a friendly smile. Manong Al sidled over to answer the stranger "Why, sure. What you wanna play?" And he followed Mingus inside the curtains.

"Well, whatever you want."

"No, no, not me. I retired. I just bullshit now. Maybe you play Yaw ober der. Hey, Yaw-yaw. Come on ober here. Play some pool with this gentleman." This back room was a little darker, and the light was not as uniform as it was in the restaurant. Their brightest spots were of course the light bulbs directly over the pool tables.

"Yeah. Just trying to kill some time before my gig up the hill," he said, his voice deep-sounding, like his instrument might be.

From the smoke-filled room emerged a brown Asian figure, pool stick in hand, tapping the floor with the handle end and chalking the tip, cocksure and five foot five. "Sure ting," said Yaw-yaw. He had on a crumpled floppy-brimmed hat. "Who's your friend, Manong Al?"

Manong Al turned to Mingus and, gesturing towards the newcomer, said, "this is Yaw-yaw." The old timer then whispered in Yaw-Yaw's ear, "this is Charlie Mingus," and added with restraint fury, "you dumb ignorant shit!" Yaw-Yaw looked Chinese in Chinatown and looked Japanese in Japantown and looked Pinoy in Manilatown. Because of this, he frequented these neighborhoods' pool halls and felt at home there, including George's Pool Hall on Buchanan Street in Japantown, where every game was only a dime and one can buy just up the street, a good Chinese meal for seventy five cents from Soo Chow's, who were Korean. The family son who did the serving was a boy of about 15. Saving up for when he goes to college, he would say. But Yaw-yaw is Pinoy. He got his name for pretty obvious reasons: he talks a lot when he plays. *Yawyaw ng yawyaw.* "What's your pleasure?" he asked the big man.

"Let's do some eight ball."

"Sounds good to me."

Charles Mingus was a large, black man, not only in status, as in the field of jazz, but also in plain physical stature. He was quite massive. And his huge case for his string bass did not diminish his stature. Yaw-yaw said, "I break." And they played.

To make a long story shorter, Mingus lost big. In fact, he lost more than he could pay. The more he lost, it seemed, the more he got into the game. Yaw-yaw always trapped Mingus into dropping all his own balls too quickly in the game of eight ball. Yaw yaw would still have a lot of his own balls left before having a shot at the eight ball, but those same balls serve as obstacles to Mingus' path of shooting. Those balls would always "hook" Mingus so that he would have no clear shot whatsoever. Then he would have a lot of Yaw-yaw's balls to block his shots every time. And when Yaw-yaw would see an opportune moment, he would shoot straight and true. He would run two or three or four balls at a time, talking and yaw-yawing all the while, and then, at the end, take the game. Mingus could not resist shooting his balls into pockets every time he had the opportunity. He did not know that patience was a virtue even in pool. He did not plan ahead like Yaw-yaw did. Now he was paying for it. Well, not really, as it seemed to be turning out. The question of paying became the problem.

The big black man's head was turning every which way and saying something about him being short of the money he had just lost to Yaw-yaw. "Well, like I said, I don't think I can cover ALL of it, but I got to go to my gig now or I'll be late, see. But I'm coming right back to cover the rest, okay, brother? I mean I'll be just be up the street. That's where I'll get the rest of the dough, see."

Yaw-yaw, small as he was, lunged at Mingus. The big man seemed to have almost laughed in astonishment. But Yaw-yaw was not going after the big man, and that laugh provided the gap of distraction for Yaw-yaw to snatch the big cased instrument of Mingus, almost ripping it from the latter's loose grip as he held the case on top by his left hand. As Mingus' head snapped left and right for some explanation, from someone, anyone, Yaw-yaw quickly swept the instrument away, like a newly-wed bride, to the toilet. Everyone heard the lock click from the inside. "You give me my goddam money, I give you your instrument." He shouted from inside the toilet.

"I got a gig in half an hour, Joe."

"Das your problem. Your word is as good as cash you said. And my name aint Joe, Joe."

"Name's Charles. My name aint Joe, either. I'll get the cash for you. Right after the gig. C'mon man. I'm only short 25 dollars. I'll give you the 25 plus another 25 after the gig. Come to the show. Bring whoever you like. I'll give it to you right there."

"He doesn't know you, Mr. Mingus", said Manong Al turning to the musician, trying to explain.

Yaw-yaw true to his name shouted from the toilet: "I know him. He gambles without any money! He's gotta pay before he plays"

"He had the money, Yaw-yaw. It ran out. Just like everything else."

"Yeah? Why did he keep playing, then?"

"Because he's a stupid gambler like you. I seen you do it lots of times."

For a while there was dead silence. "Do I have to pay?" came the voice weakly from inside the toilet.

"Pay for what?" Asked Manong Al.

"For the show up the street."

"Of course not. I'll take you in myself," Mingus interrupted.

"Nah, you don' need to do that," came Yaw-yaw's quick reply, his tone slightly softening. "I'll be there, though. I wanna hear you play dat ting. Al says you're good. He's the one who knows music. Hear him play the piano. It'll make you cry." Though not loud, Yaw yaw's voice rang clear in that toilet acoustic. He opened the toilet door just a wee bit, ever so slowly, and asked, "You really want to go, huh, Manong?"

"Yeah, he's good, Yaw-yaw."

"I hope he's not good like the way he shoots pool."

"He's good, believe me. Angels will be singing to you, youngblood. And you'll remember your first kiss, man." Manong Al said.

"First kiss? First kiss my fist!" Yaw-yaw snaked his way out the toilet and appeared tightly hugging the instrument and added: "you sure he's good? I play, too, you know."

"I know. I know you play, youngblood. I heard you pluck that guitar."

"Come with me, then."

"You bet I will."

The two Pinoys turned to Mingus. "Take it." said Yaw-yaw. "Go on. I'll just go across the street to the International Hotel and clean up a bit, then we'll be at the joint."

"I'll be waiting. My word is cash."

"You said that before. We'll see," said Yaw-yaw.

"Do you guys do 'Prelude to a Kiss'?" asked Manong Al. "I like dat."

"You just show up, baby. We'll do it for you."

Yaw-yaw handed Mingus his enormous instrument case until the big man got complete hold of it. "Here," said Yaw-yaw curtly. Mingus grabbed the case and quickly turned to go. Without smiling or saying a word, he lumbered up Kearny street, then Columbus Avenue, then he was gone.

Beside the famous Hungry-I nightclub, across the street in his room at the International Hotel, as he was quickly getting ready, Yaw-yaw thought of his own guitar playing days as a youth among the vast plantation fields of Dole in Mindanao. Yaw-yaw was a guitar player himself who had a makeshift band in his hometown in the Visayas. It was a rag-tag type of a band with a one-string bass grounded on an upside down washbasin, a wash board for some fancy percussion, a guitar and/or a ukelele, and for vocals, whoever was drinking and/or handy at the time. He played guitar with a lot of spontaneity (they way he played pool) all his life so he could be considered a jazzman, only his text was Filipino music with some contemporary mainstream U.S.A. music around the Second World War era. But this Charles Mingus fellow he had never heard of before. He put on a fresh dip of his Three Flowers Brillantine pomade then put on his floppy-brimmed hat. He was ready to step out.

He met Manong Al waiting at the lobby and started walking towards the Keystone Korner. Manong Al, unlike most of the manongs here in Manilatown, was born and raised in the City. Never been to the Philippines. Manong Al was ten years senior to Yaw-yaw, but they always talked like peers. Just as they were passing the police station about a block away from the joint, Yaw-yaw asked.

"Are you sure about this Mingus cat, Manong?"

"He's the real Mccoy, youngblood. Aint you heard of Charlie Mingus, man? That's him," said Manong Al.

"Mingus my ass," said Yaw-yaw. "He owes me money and he's gotta pay."

"I told you he's the fucking legendary jazz musician, you idiot."

"Mingus cunnilingus my ass," Yaw-yaw said.

"What kind of a musician are you? You don't even know the masters of your trade."

"The kind who can play pool."

When they turned the corner, they saw a line at the ticket booth hidden under the awning, folks smoking and making small talk, their collars turned up against the wind and misty rain. The gig was about to start but there was some commotion at the bar inside. Yaw-yaw spotted Charles Mingus through a crowd of people and he in turn saw Yaw-yaw. Mingus waved and smiled and immediately talked to someone near him, gesturing towards Yaw-yaw near the ticket booth. Before Yaw-Yaw and Manong Al got to their turn on the line at the ticket booth, someone from the joint came up to them and whispered something in their ears whisking them away to a choice seat, front and center.

Then the show began. Mingus, when the music started, seemed to have forgotten about Yaw-yaw altogether. He never looked at him once. First, the notes started hovering around Yaw-yaw's sentimental rememberings. He recognized some of the tunes but it was the notes themselves and their sounds that took Yaw-yaw away. Each note rang crystal clear and the tone that came out of the trumpet player resonated in his brain even when he was not playing anymore. The musicians played independent of, yet essential to, each other. Like smoke from the pool hall lazily drifting into the night, the saxophone came in as subtle as the rain. He was not familiar with any of the players, but Yaw-yaw loved the sounds they orchestrated. The saxophone's silky maneuverings took him away, past remembering, and behind it all persisited the pulse of Mingus's bass. Somewhere, somehow he heard the *rondallas* of his hometown in the Philippines. Then they played "Prelude to a Kiss" for Manong Al and they called and mentioned his name and told the audience that he too played some and if he would like to dabble with the piano and play along with them.

"Hell yah, das my paborit." Al said and he jumped up on stage leveraged by his arm. He played and they all played along with him and Yaw-yaw was carried away into the well-deep days of his childhood in the Visayas and wandering days in Mindanao.

After the show, Mingus came up to Yaw-yaw and paid off the twenty five plus twenty five—fifty bucks. "Here," said Mingus. "I got the man to give me the night's pay in advance." This time it was Yaw-yaw who did not look at Mingus. Or the money. He just quickly took it and walked up to the tip jar by the edge of the raised stage area and said to Al, "Godammit," and dropped twenty five dollars in the jar. "You're right. He's good." Then he turned and walked away without saying anything to Mingus.

Walking back to Manilatown in the steady rain that night, Yaw-yaw told Manong Al, "I didn't know music could be played like that."

"This, I think, I have been telling you for years."

"Take you from sad to glad in just seconds. And for real, too! Real sad and real joy, you know. I saw the notes hovering like in the *rondallas* before when I was young in the Philippines, you know. You tell that Mingus, Manong Al, that next time he comes to town, drop by and get a good ol' fashioned Filipino meal from the Mabuhay Restaurant. My treat. I robbed him of his dinner tonight."

That's Yaw-yaw. Still talking.

Oscar Peñaranda left the Philippines at the age of 12. He spent his adolescent years in Vancouver, Canada and then moved to San Francisco at the age of 17. His stories and poems and essays have been anthologized both nationally and internationally. In 1980, his play *Followers of the Seasons* was performed by the Asian American Theater Company in San Francisco. He is the author of *Full Deck, Jokers Playing* (Tiboli, 2004) and *Seasons by the Bay,* (T'boli, 2004). *Seasons By the Bay* won the best fiction category for 2004 in the Global Filipino Literary Award, a literary organization based in Singapore, Paris, and Washington, D.C. It also won an award for fiction for PAWA (Philippine American Writers and Writers) for 2005 and *Full Deck* won the poetry category. The following story belongs to a work in progress, a collection of stories set only in San Francisco and the surrounding Bay Area.

Edgar Poma

THE SUFFER BROTHERS

*H*e would say quite objectively that, at the moment, the two most revered local boys who made good, both in their forties, were Barack Obama, the presidential candidate, and himself, president and publisher of his own imprint, Marcus Vest Books, the most profitable and successful division of a prestigious publishing house in New York.

What the two had in common besides their international fame was that they were men of color: Barack was *hapa*, while Marcus [in Hawaii, he allowed people to call him Marc] was Filipino-American. Also, they lived on the Mainland and were Punahou grads. What they didn't have in common was that Marc was a member of the club called *Mahu*, or gay. He was also, unlike Barack, single. But as he said in interviews with island media when the subject came up, he thought that Barack, in spite of his heterosexuality, was a good guy still yet.

Marc did not know how frequently Barack returned to Honolulu —apparently, according to the magazines, he enjoyed bodysurfing and sashimi in his old haunts—but Marc knew that his own schedule was so busy that he could only go once a year if he was lucky. This present trip, a little more than one week, was to accommodate a series of marathon meetings with publishing magnates from Japan and other Asian countries determined to make deals. He promised to listen carefully to their proposals, but he mandated that all discussions end by 7:30 p.m. every night, ostensibly because he remained on East Coast time and needed the rest.

What he actually did was load up on bentos from the hospitality suite of their Waikiki meeting rooms, then race home. Then he tore off his suit and laid out dinner and got beer from the fridge and watched Korean soap operas, because they had hooked him consummately from the first night, even though he had arrived in the middle of their plotlines. (He also thought that the young Korean actors were extremely hunky.)

Although he had little time for anything else, his cousin Bernadette, whom he had enlisted to look after his luxury condo on a regular basis while he was away, persuaded him to attend her son's school event on a Saturday morning, at which they were putting together a 1,148-pound ice cream sandwich that would earn a listing in the Guinness Book of Records.

After the record was made official, all the kids and their guests fervently attacked their creation with spoons, or chipped out wedges to drop into coolers to take home. After a few spoonfuls, Marc thought, nuff already! He thought the whole thing was gross, especially when folks around him, in their feeding frenzy, had jammed their mouths up against the giant slab, drilling scary pukas, or holes, through it.

Marc said to his cousin, "You dragged me from my schedule of meetings for this termite convention?"

"Like I had to twist your arm. You're Filipino like I am: you'll go anywhere for free food."

"Not."

"Everyone knows you're tight. Even your mom and dad tell everyone in the family they don't know where you got that 'cause they're so generous."

"Nice, yeah? I'm being disavowed by my own parents." He shrugged. "Anyway, I don't know why you're talking stink at me all of a sudden."

"It's 'cause you make me so mad. I heard you tell that little girl next to you that if she didn't get her head out of the ice cream, she'd get frostbite and the emergency room at Straub would have to cut off her face."

"But she was elbowing me out of the way!"

"But she's only five years old."

"She's Samoan—she looks my age."

"Oh, please."

"I give to charities, you know."

"Maybe ten dollars to a few every year—and they have to divide that up."

"Are you opening my mail at the condo or what? I do things for people. Didn't I send you that box of books?"

"Yeah, but you publish those books, they don't cost you nothing. And you're not paying me for looking after your place. You don't seem to do anything, like, out of the goodness of your heart. Everything is measured out with you. By the way, you got ice cream sandwich on your neck."

"I better wipe it off before someone comes over and tries to eat it."

"This is supposed to be good fun, you know, so lighten up for once."

"What, being eaten alive is good fun?"

"If you could think about something other than business and making money for once, you might appreciate the fact that the school made it into the record books, yeah?"

It was not easy for him to concentrate on anything other than business transactions. Even with the Korean soap operas, he was toying with the idea of authorizing novelizations of the best of them, partnering with a Korean company of course. Besides, he was hot and sticky and wanted nothing more than to leave. But then he was distracted by an unsettling, nostalgic thought, and when Bernadette saw the grin on his face, she demanded to know what he was thinking about. "Nothing," he said.

"Come on, Marc, I like know."

It was *pilau*, or nasty, but he told her anyway. When he was in high school, he had a classmate, Travis, who was a 3-sport athlete. He was spectacularly handsome, and his six-foot-two-inch body seemed to be carved out of stone. Also, as witnessed in the locker room by many, including Marc himself, though briefly, a half-second at the most, so impressively endowed that folks began to refer to it as "Travis's brother." Then a group of girls started calling Travis and his appendage the "Suffer Brothers" not because his last name was Sufferices but because, they speculated, when you're with the brothers, they make you suffa' so good! In school, Travis had to suffer through all this; every now and then someone would threaten to report him to Guinness or

Ripley's.

"Sufferices, Portagee," Bernadette said. Portuguese. "So what do you expect? Everyone knows they have big ones. Duhhh."

"All these years have gone by and I've never forgotten him."

"Him or his brother?"

"I always wanted to know what became of him."

"He probably got old and fat."

"But some of us haven't. Look at me. I've kept fit."

"But you're *mahu*, honey. If he's straight, he let himself go. Look at my husband."

"We weren't friends, I just heard things about how rough his life was. His parents were older than the other parents. They were different: they were into acting. His dad was in Hollywood for a very long time, trying to make it as an actor. His mom had acting gigs in Honolulu. Shortly after Travis's first birthday luau, she played Peter Pan in a community production and she died when the flying apparatus got all busted up and she went flying smack dab into a wall."

"Oh, gods," Bernadette said grimly. But she had trouble containing her laughter.

"Travis's father came back to Honolulu and had to raise his boy. Five years later, he got really sick. He was a huge man."

"What, you folks saw him in the locker room too?"

"Oh shuddup. He was huge solid, not huge fat—I heard this from a classmate whose family knew their family. But then he got cancer. Travis had to take care of him. He had to cook and clean, plus he had school to go to. He had all these responsibilities forced on him, and he was only a *keiki*—a kid."

Bernadette said, "He coulda asked his brother to *kokua*," which meant, to help out.

"The classmate said she used to see him patiently walk his dad around the block for the dad's exercise. They were so close. Travis was eleven when the dad passed on. The couple who owned the house they rented took him in as their *hanai* kid—they adopted him—because he didn't have any relatives who could take him, and later this couple sent him to Punahou, because they were well-off. But the classmate who knew him when he was younger said she could tell he missed his dad a lot by the sadness in his eyes."

"Sadness? It was probably pain from lugging his brother all over the damn place."

"I sensed later that part of the sadness was due to him being *mahu*."

"Hah?"

"No, for real. Here was this jock, the most popular guy in the class, with this secret he couldn't tell anyone about. Like I said, I didn't know him, and there wasn't talk that he was, but one day I happened to walk by him at Punahou's Carnival in our senior year. And he looked at me. And I looked at him. Being so close to him, in his face, even though he was taller than me, gave me chicken skin, gooseflesh, goose pimples. And my gaydar just went off. And it's always accurate. I could never ask him directly or follow-up on it, because I was never around him that close again."

"No, you just didn't want to be beat up."

"I thought about him a lot, though. When I was going to college in the Mainland, I wanted to contact him, but I never got around to it."

It was Travis that supplanted Marc's obsession with the Korean soaps in the evenings: Marc simply could not stop thinking about him. When he decided to look him up, he did so for fetishistic reasons. But when his overpowering lust was *pau*, done with, he was left with a feeling of romantic hopefulness and longing. Maybe, if Marc's instincts were right and Travis was playing for the same team, and available, maybe they were meant to be together. And maybe, after that...they would hold onto Marc's condo for when they were out late in town and didn't want to drive to their real home, which would be somewhere off Haiku Road in Kaneohe, where Marc had always wanted to live permanently, not in Manhattan. He had traveled all over the world but had encountered nothing more magnificent than the sight of the Pali, the Koolau Mountains, upon exiting the Wilson Tunnel.

In deference to the Alumni Office at Punahou, he did not turn to them as though they were Dial-a-Date; instead, he hired a private investigator, Kauahi Mantovicci, to do "his stuffs." Within twenty four hours, Kauahi produced a confidential file. All Marc was interested in was Travis's phone number, and he fastidiously ignored the rest, perhaps so he would not be disappointed off the bat, if there was anything to be disappointed about. When he phoned, and Travis answered, he was so nervous that he asked how Travis was doing and then he asked how his brother was. Thankfully, Travis did not seem to hear that last part, or pretended not to have heard it.

They talked story for the first ten minutes, as if they were old friends, though clearly Travis had the advantage of having read over the years about Marc's meteoric rise to the top of the publishing world. Marc said, "You don't seem all that surprised hearing from me."

"I guess I should be, not hearing from you after years of writing and calling you, but I guess I hoped you'd call someday and you did."

"You've been writing and calling?"

"Yeah. You didn't know?"

"No. I get so many letters and calls—you probably got screened out." Marc got all nervous again. Nervous and hopeful. It was so ridiculous to feel that way, he knew that. It was delusional. It was *pupule*. Crazy. Yet his gaydar was never wrong, and his gaydar was going off again while he had Travis on the phone—in fact it was shrieking. So maybe there was a chance. Maybe Travis wanted to say after all these years that he had seen Marc at the Carnival that day twenty-six or so years ago and that he had not stopped thinking about him since.

"What was it you wanted to tell me?"

"Well, we needed your help badly and that's why we were contacting you. I thought that's why you were calling me now, to say that you could help us out."

"Wait. Who is we?"

"My partner Damien and me."

"Your partner Damien and you."

"Yes. You might remember him from high school. We hooked up after graduation. Anyway, we read in the gay magazines over the years that you were, you know, like us, yeah? And so we thought you might do a favor for your brothers, yeah?"

Oh, brother, Marc thought. He couldn't believe the irony. His gaydar was correct, and it had taken all these years for a confirmation, and he wanted Travis and his brother badly, because he was ready to settle down with someone, he was ready to retire in a few years and return to the island of his birth. But Travis already had someone with a grip on him and his brother, someone who went to Punahou with them, and now they wanted Marc's help on something because they were all gay brothers. Marc said, with attitude, "What was it you folks wanted me to help you with?"

Travis hesitated, probably taken aback by his change in tone. "Awkward, yeah, to tell you now."

"Well, I think you better, 'cause, given my schedule, we may not talk again after this, yeah?" Marc didn't want to sound rude. No, he wanted to sound rude. He was irritable now. Angry. In fact, he wanted to make an excuse and hang up, or just hang up without one. But he was curious about what Travis and Damien wanted from him. He remembered Damien now. Damien Wong. Good-looking *pake* dude, Chinese. An athlete too, though not 3-sport. He and Marc were in the same Advanced English Literature class. Thinking about him with Travis and his brother made Mark angrier.

Travis said that while he was at work several years ago, he happened to get a call from someone who knew his father when they were both looking for work in Hollywood in the early 1950s. He said that they got a break and were hired to record their "local boy big-mouth laughs" for a canned track to be used for television shows at the time. "Of course, he was the one with the bigger laugh because he was bigger than me," the friend said. "I had a *menehune* laugh [a small laugh, like that of a dwarf] even when I strained, but your dad had the laugh of twelve people, and so I rode on his coattails." Unfortunately, he said he had done extensive research just for the hell of it, and learned that all the shows with their laughter in the background were all lost, except for one episode of an obscure comedy that was locked away in an air-conditioned vault awaiting massive kinescope restoration by a private foundation in New York.

"I just had to get my hands on it," Travis said to Marc. "I just needed to hear his laugh again. Just one more time." He contacted the foundation, but they had a backlog of kinescopes to preserve and they could not estimate when they could get to the one Travis was interested in. All they told him was that it was in bad shape and probably even too fragile to rescue. Travis said that he and Damien spent the next few years begging and pleading with the foundation to give them access to the kinescope. Just the audio part even would do! The foundation said no way. They asked people in power, like their political representatives in D.C., for their intervention, but nothing came of it, although attempts were made. That was when Travis and Damien began to contact Marc repeatedly, but got no response from him.

"I just miss him so much," Travis said. "The folks who rented the house on Wilder where we used to live said that it was haunted and they used to hear a man's loud laugh. They let me stay overnight many, many times so I could hear it, but I never did. I wanted to so much." He paused. "You're not saying anything—you must think I'm *pupule*."

"No, I don't." Marc was struggling to sound a little sympathetic. By this time, with cell phone in hand, he had descended the swooping staircase of koa wood and silvered bronze that connected the two floors of his Kakaako penthouse. And he had turned on the t.v. to the Korean channel, sound low. "We all get sentimental for certain things at one time or another. You just wanna hear your dad's laugh—nothing wrong with that."

"Humbug when folks ask you for things, though, yeah?" Travis said.

It's fricken *maha'oi*, Marc thought. Nervy.

"I guess when you want something so badly," Travis said, "you find the courage to ask."

"Well, you asked. And I can look into it for you folks, I guess. Doesn't mean I can make your dream come true."

"Actually, I have another favor to ask, since I have you on the line. Damien doesn't know about this. I just thought I'd ask for him—no, for us."

Marc couldn't believe the balls of this man. On second thought, he could believe it.

"Since you're a publishing executive, and I read that you also edit and acquire books personally sometimes, when you have the time, I was hoping you might take a look at Damien's novel manuscript. He's been working on it for many years. It took him awhile to finish because he has a full-time job, and he also wanted to get it right. It's great timing that you called, because he just finished it a few months ago. Not even that, it was like five weeks ago. He hasn't submitted it anywhere yet. I think he sent out some query letters to some publishers and agents. He hasn't gotten any response from them, so it would be fair game if you took a look at it...besides doing the kinescope thing."

By this time, Marc had turned the sound up and had gotten absorbed in whatever domestic travails were unfolding in Seoul. "Excuse me, but you can't possibly expect me to help you folks with both things?" he said, his eyes fixed on his big-screen t.v. "I mean, it's not like I don't have other things to do."

"Oh, I know you're very busy. It's just that...these would mean a lot if you maybe had some time..."

"I can only help you with one of the two things. You just have to decide which."

Travis said, "I'm sorry. I understand." He paused. He seemed torn, at first. "Can you read Damien's manuscript then, please?"

Marc could not distinguish between the heartbreak from the soap opera and the heartbreak from the other end of the line. He said to Travis, "Fine. I'm leaving soon, so bring the manuscript to my condo. You can leave it with the lobby guard later today." He gave Travis the address, and then he said aloha to him, goodbye. But it was a goodbye goodbye, and not goodbye until we meet again. He promised himself that that he would not think of the Suffer Brothers ever again.

But that night, when he got up from bed and turned on the light because he couldn't sleep, he looked over the contents of the file that Kauahi had assembled for him. He learned that Travis ran a non-profit in Ewa Beach that quietly found housing for poor families. Damien was a teacher at Robert Louis Stevenson Elementary in town.

Marc wanted to skip the photos, toss everything out, but he couldn't do it. Travis had thinner brown hair, and the beginnings of a gut, but otherwise looked the same, still quite attractive. Damien was still very trim, and younger-looking than his years. It did not seem fair to Marc that Damien was, possibly, a gifted writer who had the discipline to complete a novel, besides being the brother's keeper. Marc was more wistful now, not angry.

In the morning, he picked up Damien's manuscript from the lobby guard and packed it safely in his briefcase—he would read it as soon as possible and give the work a fair shake. He also went to his laptop and sent an email to one of his "people" in New York.

This one email would trigger a series of events. The private foundation that had given Travis and Damien such a hard time would change their tune and fast-track the preservation of the kinescope that the couple had first inquired about years ago. The preserved film would be dispatched to Honolulu to caretakers at the Academy of Arts, which would arrange a private screening for Travis and Damien. The black-and-white picture would be blurry, the sound gritty, but within the first five seconds they would hear the one booming laugh that gave them chicken skin. "That's him!" Travis would say, all choked up. And they would weep with unremitting joy.

Edgar Poma was born in the Sacramento Valley and graduated from the University of California at Berkeley. His writing has appeared in various Filipino and Filipino-American fiction and poetry anthologies. He lives and works in San Francisco.

Anthem Salgado

CONGERS

Spiritual Quest

*B*ushido the Warrior. Are you serious? John adopts "Bushido the Warrior" as his name. I am ten. Every Saturday afternoon, we watch the martial arts movie marathon on Channel 5. But my cousin, he takes it to that next questionable level. I ride with Bushido, each of us fighting for breath on our single gear bicycles, peddling urgently towards Saint Paul's Church on Lake Road. This is Congers, New York, one town over from Nyack where I go to school. The sun, the asphalt, everything, Africa-hot. Sweat salts my eyes. I raise my forearm to wipe my brows and set my palm again on the cushion of my newly fitted Mushroom Grips, a recently adopted first-world status symbol that magnificently bless each end of my ride's handlebars, a pair of super soft rubber pieces textured like the fanned underbelly of a mushroom.

A few years earlier in Kuala Lumpur, I saw my friends trade Rubix Cube secrets at the park near my house. No one cared about mint bike accessories like mushroom grips. Instead, there was a high premium on intelligence in Malaysia and these kids had pull. This was a place where fistfights rarely happened and physical domination was mostly demonstrated at the tetherball court. The television set technologically had up to nine channels but the government allowed only two to transmit. And even then, programming was regularly interrupted, five times a day, by a photo montage of mosques and the echo of *Salah*, the ritual prayer to Allah.

At the church, we throw our bikes on the grass, run towards the rectory, and soon as we knock on the door, Bushido double-checks our plan, "So... We're just going to tell the truth. Right?"

"What else? Of course."

Bushido's ear turns to the door, "Someone's coming."

The door opens and I force serenity, even happiness, on my face, "Father Dan!"

Father Dan's head tilts with a warm smile, "Hello gentlemen."

We had hoped for Father Dan. After years of the old Monsignor and his cohorts' dry monotone sermons, Father Dan's transfer to Saint Paul's Church promised fresh air. He was young and cool and everyone really liked his sporty black Dodge Charger, which a fortunate few got the chance to cruise around in. Today, we join that elite, though our visit is more about spiritual quest than it is about joy ride.

"Look, we need to talk to you. There's a big problem."

Sensing our worry, his expression changes to concern and he invites us in.

Sylvia

Congers is not a town I visit unless I have to. At fourteen years old, somehow, I'm overdue for my Catholic rites of passage, a sacrament known as Confirmation. And because I'm too old to take classes with the other kids, I am to visit the living room of Sylvia for private tutelage in the virtues of our faith, after wrestling practice one evening a week for many weeks over the course of a school year. Sylvia is old-world Congers, a living textbook. She says things like "Stay a while, will ya," if she wants you to hang your coat up; "Sit down, you're making me nervous," if you stand about and fidget; and "Would you look at that! You must have young blood," if she catches you not wearing any socks. Every now and then, a thick glob of spit jumps out of the side of her mouth and slaps dead on her chin, which I am too Asian to point out so I leave it be. She lives alone. And has the posture of a question mark. Her fingers are knotty branches quivering in the cold wind of time. A delicate swell of Sylvia's skin is floodwater that swallows the modest circle that vows "Till death do us part" even as it sinks beyond view. She blinks constantly to moisten her eyes that look at me lovingly through the yellowed lenses of her beat up glasses. By day, Sylvia is a janitor at Clarkstown North High School.

"For as long as I've worked at the school there, I've come to recognize many faces especially the black children since there are so few. One day, I was dragging a wet mop to the supply closet. I turned the corner of the hallway and the fire alarm started to ring. And there, in that empty hall, I looked and he looked at me, this young black boy with his hand still on the alarm lever. He stood perfectly still. I studied him. He was cute like a little lumberjack with his red plaid shirt neatly tucked into his blue jeans. His laces were too long for his gym shoes. They tied in huge ribbons with the frayed ends dragging, dirty and flattened. Then, I suppose another alarm must have gone off... in his head, because from standing there like a painting, in a flash he took off like a bat out of h–... like a bat out of nowhere."

Sylvia turns her head left and right and goes on, "Of course now, people climbed out into the hall and the teachers saw me standing there not too far from the pulled alarm. So when the police arrived, they interviewed me about what I saw. I didn't understand really. I've seen that young man many times in the past. Seemed like a good kid, decent and polite, quiet but friendly. Nice smile. Real nice smile"

Sylvia casts her eyes to the ground in worry and says, "That boy's future was in danger."

"So, you turned him in?"

"I said it was a black kid, but I couldn't tell who because they all look the same to me. Years pass without another incident from this child, nothing I know about anyway. He carries on like the bright young man I took him for. He's graduated since, you know."

Sylvia looks up at the ceiling. Her vision seems to breach the roof of the house and carries through the dark of the evening sky. With her eyes staring deep into the glittering universe, she draws a napkin neatly from her pocket, wipes her lip clean, and predicts with a smile, "Probably a doctor by now."

In meeting the Confirmation requirements, a candidate must be in a state of grace. I am to:

•*have perfect attendance to my preparation classes*

•*study the Catholic faith: the commandments, the sacraments, the sins*
•*pray and bear witness to Christ*
•*adopt a Saint's name and write a paper on that Saint*
•*perform services to the community*

I complete most of them, however minimally. Wrestling practice is wearing me down, with all the required weight loss on my already bony frame on top of the extreme cardio and strength conditioning. So I don't get to a single minute of my community service. That's the "my dog ate my homework" explanation I gave to Sylvia anyway. I don't tell her that wrestling is actually my vacation from a pain-in-the-ass home life which is the true reason for all my exhaustion and lack of concentration.

She assures me, "No matter, young man. I'm really proud of you. You've done so well," and with a bright grin and wink, she signs the form declaring the completion of my obligations as a candidate for Confirmation. "I am confident that you will satisfy this task of service to the community in the future."

Congers

A heart like Sylvia's is atypical of Congers. Look it up in the dictionary and you'll find this:

> con·ger (*knggr*)
> *n. Any of various large scaleless marine eels of the family Congridae, especially Conger oceanicus,* native to Atlantic waters.

This is a working class town that manufactures mean stares and crass jokes, gargantuan steak-and-potatoes adolescents and date rapists, all under the veil of suburban normalcy. A fist to the chin happens fast in these parts. Grudges can go on between crews well into adulthood. You can win a fight square, and then get jumped by some fellas a week later. A month after that, you spend a night cruising town with your boys to lay down some payback. Years can pass when you think it's all blown over, and then someone cracks you over the head with a pool stick when you're not looking, just having a beer with your lady. The only way to break the cycle is to suffer a defeat and accept the humiliation.

The same summer that Bushido and I bike at top speed to Saint Paul's, there is a street rumble. The pecking order in the neighborhood is a constant work in progress and anything can serve as a trigger. Ethnic slurs are a classic. Mick. Wop. Spic. And your ensuing response or lack thereof to such a call determines your fate and the respect of your family in these small towns. All is peace until someone says, "Chink."

Everyone ritualistically drops their bicycles and selects their respective fight partner. I'm paired up with the younger of the O'Conner boys; light eyes, dark hair, and so many freckles, you'd think someone pitched a slop of crap at his face through a screen door. I march right up to him with my arms long at my sides and hands balled up tight like dumb bells. In a traditional display of confidence and fight-speak, I park my feet close enough to slow dance, narrow my eyes, clench my jaw, and slam my shoulder into his. Years of Saturday afternoon kung fu flicks have prepared me for this moment. It's very cinematic though not at all practical. In the next second, I thump flat on my back, hands over my face, the only thing I can do to deflect the forceful downpour of knuckles. After the punch-out, my cousin pulls me up to my feet and I'm crying. But also, I become the title holder of a payback voucher, redeemable at anytime and no expiration date. The loser in a fight is given the awesome power of tension making, holding both allies and enemies in nervous anticipation of when the next bell will ring. The O'Conner kid and I look at each other screw face for many seasons, well into our high school years.

The way I remember, beef like this didn't happen in Kuala Lumpur. Was it because we as children in the third world understood clearly the devastation of unchecked tribal warfare? A lifetime ago when I was a single cell, just a lone ovary, cozy in the nest of my mother's fallopian tubes, interviewing millions of sperm for a qualified suitor, there was a man representing an ethnic minority who ran for government office in Malaysia and won in a political upset. In disbelief and fury, a horde of men drew their blades, similar to the machete, and slaughtered whole families and villages. No one was spared, elders nor babies. Once articulate arms and legs suddenly lay still, severed and mute. There was no Rubix Cube secret for the puzzled face that screamed wide open for its missing jaw.

PIST

Father Dan's Charger motors back to Bushido's place after we throw down our story:

It all started with the Domino's pizza that we ate in the garage while working on our bikes. After the last slice, we flattened the box and Sharpie'd the alphabet on it, then the numbers one through nine, and the word 'yes' on one side, 'no' on the other. We didn't think it would work but just to see, we overturned an empty glass on the cardboard and rested our fingertips on it. Bushido chanted, "Ooooh, great spirits, if you are heeeeere, enter this glaaaaass and talk to uuuusss."

It can be frustrating trying to connect with otherworldly beings with your cousin hell-bent on bringing his theatrically corny mumbo jumbo into the experiment.

"Hey, can you cut that out?"

"What, it's moving by itself!"

"You're moving it! Quit messin' around or it's not gonna work."

He finally admitted to wobbling the glass and promised not to do it again. But still, we argued back and forth like that before we realized that the glass was moving by some other force, at first hesitantly, and then after a minute or so, smooth like a practiced ice skater across Twin Ponds.

"No way!"

"Well, ask it something."

And like overzealous reporters, we fired a rapid succession of questions, faster than any living human being could answer, let alone a deceased person communicating through a marked up pizza box and an upside down drinking receptacle. The glass began to circle erratically, moving faster and faster, and with intense accuracy, landed decisively on the letter "P" which stared at us as if through a magnifying lens. It looped again rapidly and then stopped on the number "1", continued wildly and hit "S", and then "T".

"Holy shit, it's pissed!" I pulled my hands away quickly but the glass spun out with a sharp ting, toppled at high speed over the cement floor, and then rolled with a low growl into a dark corner.

This is the era of the Amityville Horror film series—based on a true story—and its stranglehold on American cinemas and television documentaries. "Father," we explain, "we're worried the ghost escaped from the glass and will curse the house."

He says, "Boys, I understand. And I do believe these things can cause harm."

At the house, we warn Father Dan that Bushido's parents are home but he assures us he's good at keeping secrets. We begin in the garage with the verbal blessing. And as if we had invisibility cloaks on, we walk right past Bushido's parents who are too busy with chores and the noise of a blaring television to notice that a priest is visiting and very slyly throwing holy water with the finesse of a basketball pass. Bounce, look-away, and behind the back.

GILCHREST

The summer following my Confirmation, I learn to be Zen with a pool cue, schooling kids on the table at Gilchrest; or officially, Congers Lake Memorial Park on Gilchrest Road. Wish I could say that I was as sick with my hoop ability but I still throw myself into a pick-up game here and there. I walk toward the black-top one afternoon and there are some dudes I know and some I don't know about to launch a four-on-four bout. They yell from across the way, "We're short one guy! Jump in."

Soon as I run over, I notice that freckle-face bastard from back in the day. And he's on my team. We fire each other a look but the game begins quickly so I focus my aggression on my driving technique and superior ball handling skills. Mad assists, a couple impossible lay-ups, and a three-pointer to command respect and sure enough, the

O'Connor kid has to give me dap. We slaughter the other team and by the end, we're laughing like old buddies. I have to admit, even then, there was a small part of me that wanted to sucker-punch him in the teeth, just to do it. But never mind. I think of Sylvia, something about forgiveness, and everything goes calm.

Sweaty and tired, we all sit around trading jokes and stories when the O'Conner kid tells his latest. "So get this. We're at this kegger a couple weeks ago, all hammered..."

And with a squinty-eyed cackle, he talks about pulling some girl's pants down, some girl who's passed out. He's so drunk he doesn't know what hole he's putting his fingers into. Everyone falls down laughing. Me, I smile. Scared. Like I could feel his skin split open under my fingernails if I were to follow my gut and yoke this rat fuck by his throat. I could pin him flat and squeeze. Well, I owe him one, don't I? But this is some weird hick culture. So weird. And now I'm not sure what the rules are or if the few guys that I do know would back me up. It's funny. All this laughter. I get up. Scan the group. Stretch. "Hey!" They all look at me. "Good game, guys. I gotta go home for dinner," I cough up hard and shoot one to the ground, "So, I'll see ya later."

I heave up my bike and push, in the New York swelter, riding through the swarm of summertime bugs.

Anthem Salgado is a seasoned multi-disciplinary creator: visual artist, poet, and actor. He is a graduate of the historical San Francisco Art Institute and his spoken word has been presented throughout New York, San Francisco, Honolulu, and Manila. Additionally, Salgado's original solo theater works have appeared on the stages of the San Francisco Asian Art Museum, Yerba Buena Center for the Arts, and Intersection for the Arts. "Congers" was inspired by his work with Sons Project mentors Alleluia Panis, Jaime Jacinto, and Joel Tan.

Maureen Roble

Seeds of Change

"I've decided I'm on in this quest to find myself."

"Oookay," my friend April replies as we stroll through the park one afternoon. Her tone is pseudo-psychologist. She's trying to be serious, but her voice is teasing.

"No seriously. I've been thinking about it for awhile. I'm 25 years old. I work nine-to-five, I live with my parents. But what does it all add up to? Why am I doing any of this? Who am I really?"

"That's what all the experimental drinking in college was supposed to tell you," April jokes.

"Hm..." I pluck a dandelion from the side of the path. "Can you tell me?" I ask it, lost in thought.

"Well, when you find yourself, let me know. I'll meet your spiritually transformed alter-ego in the car. It's getting cold." She jogs ahead to the parking lot.

I toss the dandelion onto the grass and chase after April. Not like flowers can talk anyway.

But I was wrong. Plants can and do talk, especially to women. Consider first love blooming with the scent of a velvety rose, or the innocuous pink of a carnation on Mother's Day. For me, however, the song of my life was not sung by flowers or plants, but by their seeds.

I remember the sting of salt on the tip of my tongue, then the short crackle against my cheek as I popped open sunflower seeds on spring afternoons. My parents were fairly strict, not really allowing me to roam as little ones imagine they can. So whenever I got the chance to accompany my sister to her softball games, I was a ball of excitement.

There was an entire ritual associated with the event. After school, I would carefully place a bag of seeds and a quarter on top of Mr. Kim's counter at the convenience store. He would smile at me and tell me to be a good girl. Then, I, the littlest mascot, would sit in the dugout and enjoy my bird food. Go team.

"So, did you find yourself yet?" April asks me over fancy lattes.

"Nah, still looking. Quarter life crises are tough."

"You're making 50 grand a year as an accountant, woman. Why not buy yourself an identity?"

"Done!" I shout, clapping my hands. "I wanna be Batman."

"That's more like it."

"How's school?"

"Boring as usual. To top it off, I have to pick a major soon. I don't want it to be nursing, but I know it's going to be."

I nod sympathetically. Looks like I'm not the only one who needs to find herself.

I met April in the fourth grade. I just moved into town, and April lived across the street from me. We were in the same class, the same age, and were both Filipino. Naturally, our parents thought we should be friends. We've been inseparable ever since.

The population of the town I grew up in was predominantly people of Irish, Italian, and Polish descent. My sister and I were the only Filipinos in the whole school. When I moved to April's town, every other person was Filipino. There were Filipino convenience stores on every corner. It was no wonder then that April's house was a Filipino snack fairy land. Her parents always kept the pantry stocked with treats like ChocNut, Pocky, and Clover Chips, the calories shiny in the purple and orange plastic.

Despite their lack of glitter, my favorite snack was watermelon seeds. In my nine-year-old imagination, the black seeds with their brown centers resembled eyes. That made them mysterious and magical. They didn't sell these at Mr. Kim's store.Unlike sunflower seeds whose taste was nutty, bright, and straightforward, watermelon seeds tasted like the earth-woodsy, deep, and somehow oblique. Every time I ate watermelon seeds, I was more Filipino than Filipino. I was a *duwende*, taking repast in a shady dell covered with indigo flowers, feasting on watermelon seeds and washing them down with clean, sparkling water from a gurgling brook.

I finished college on time and at the top of my class. April, weighed down by family problems, took three semesters off and started working at the Fancy Coffee House. By the time I graduated, April quit her job at Fancy Coffee and returned to her former occupation of disgruntled student.

The two of us make it a point to hang out at least once a week, usually at Fancy Coffee. Although April is no longer an employee there, the owners have a soft spot for her. As a result of their weakness, April and I take advantage of heavily discounted gourmet coffee and pastries. Today April appears deep in concentration, a pink highlighter balanced in her right hand, a triple choco-mocha iced coffee in the left, and her anatomy and physiology notes and book are spread out on the table.

She looks up when I sit down across from her. "Yo."

"Looks like fun", I say, motioning to her pile.

"I'd rather be drinking."

"I have a surprise for you."

"Is it tequila?" April sounds hopeful.

"Nooo. But close. It will help you study." I place the small, plastic container in front of her.

She arches a brow. "Tamarind candy?"

Of all the seeds, none were sexier than the tamarind. Housed in a clear plastic box, the sugar-coated candies resembled perfect brown jewels. I used to suck the slightly sweet, slightly tart flesh to keep me alert while studying. As soon as the flesh was gone, I was left with the dark as chocolate seed that still carried some of the fruity essence.

Like a tiny, polished stone, the seed was a pleasure on its own. When the seed, too, was bereft of its flavor, I piled the seeds on a corner of my desk, hoping one day I could use their beauty for something.

As I walked across campus, I imagined that by eating the tamarind, I absorbed some of its power. I rejoiced after winning an argument in class. I laughed flirtatiously at James's dinner invite. Tart. Sweet. Confident. Irresistible.

When James leaned in for a kiss at the candle lit table, I added "juicy" to the list.

"You're not eating your *ampalaya,** Christine" my aunt points her lips at the heap of ampalaya on my plate. True, I ate the eggplant, pork, and green beans in my pinakbet, but the lonesome ampalaya sits untouched.

"I don't really like ampalaya, Tita. It's too bitter."

She winks at me. "You know, when you eat ampalaya, then you'll know you're a true Filipino."

"And it's nutritious, too," my mom cuts in, "lots of iron."

"Your cousin loves ampalaya," my Tita continues mercilessly.

I push the bumpy vegetable around with my fork, pretending to eat it, but not before pausing to make a face at my cousin across the dinner table. It doesn't matter that we're both in our mid-twenties. He sticks his tongue out at me.

"I planted fifty ampalaya seeds this year. I'll be lucky if ten sprout and survive," my father says popping an ampalaya spear into his mouth. My father raises many plants in his backyard garden, but the ampalaya is his obsession. I'm glad that the conversation has moved away from me and my ampalaya-hate.

"Why is ampalaya so hard to grow anyway?" I ask, genuinely curious.

My father grows passionate. He almost seems to rise out of his chair as he's explaining. "Because, *hija*, the ampalaya is a tropical plant. When we try to grow it here, we're trying to make it grow in a place where it doesn't belong. Sometimes, it doesn't do so well. But when it thrives..." he pauses dramatically, "we all reap the benefits."

"Like *pinakbet*" says my Tita.

"That it why we have to try to grow it anyway, even if we fail." He jabs his pointer in the air for emphasis. He floats back to his seat with the end of his speech.

The conversation moves on to other things. Alvin's grades this semester, my grandmother's upcoming birthday party and which hall Tito Ben is going to rent for it. I alone sit digesting what my father just said. Who knew? There is a seed, correction, a vegetable for the quarter-life crisis after all.

"Mom, Dad, I'm moving out."

I finish every last piece of ampalaya on my plate.

*ampalaya = bitter melon

Maureen Roble considers herself from everywhere and nowhere. She was born in Virginia Beach, VA, and after a brief stint in Queens, NY, grew up (for the most part) in Jersey City, NJ. As a high school student, she spent a semester in Japan which changed her entire world view. Maureen attended Mount Holyoke College in South Hadley, MA and graduated with a bachelor's degree in International Relations. Currently she is writing for a Jersey City-based Filipino newspaper. "Seeds of Change" is her first stab at fiction, but hopefully not her last.

Tony Robles

The Pilipino I Want to Be Like

He didn't talk
Much

He said 3 words
Mostly

...Have you eaten?

He would stand over
The stove cooking
His *adobo* and rice
sweating

I'd watch him and
I would talk
And talk

I'd talk about how
Our people had been
Oppressed for
Hundreds of years

By the white
man

And the rice boiled
And he sweated
With a smile on his
Face

And I'd talk about
Politics and oppression
While sitting on my non-
Oppressed brown butt

When the rice
Was done he
Put some on my plate

He sat and looked
At me and said,

There are only
2 kinds of people
in this world

those who know
good adobo...
and those who don't

I shut up
And ate

The *adobo*
Was good

An Alibata* Lesson ⌐

Alibata tattoos
On arms legs
Armpits
Eyelids

Wiggly symbols
And lines that
Resemble waves

What wave
Are you?

Grandpa used to say
That the way to
Tell if spaghetti is
Properly cooked

Is to take
A single noodle and
Toss it on the
Ceiling

If it sticks,
It's done

Grandpa is
Long gone

*A pre-Hispanic Philippine writing system,
more commonly know as "baybayin."

I looked up
At the ceiling
One day

A noodle
Was stuck
Up there

Probably there
For 50
Years

It looked like
An Alibata
Tattoo

A wiggly
Line which
Means

"I'm still
here with
you"

no
translation
needed

Non-Returnable

Only met
Grandpa
Once

He gave me
3 tootsie rolls
and a wink

2 weeks
later he
died

he came from
the Philippines
as a young man

met my Grandma
in America in
1920 something

only hear
bits and pieces
about him

Heard he snuck
Over to America on
A ship inside a crate
That read

Non-returnable

Must have
Been his
Destiny

He never did
Return to
The Philippines

Neither did
His children

He was buried
In a box

I assume it too
Read *non-returnable*
As well

But he breaks
Free like the
Wind that brought him
Here

From time to
time

And returns
In a
Poem

THE REAL ANTHONY

*L*et me tell you about the real Anthony. The real Anthony doesn't have a job. The real Anthony is too fearless for that. The real Anthony has a conga drum held hostage awaiting freedom from the pawn shop. The real Anthony has music in his blood and bones, and his walk is a dance. His words are poetry and sometimes he taps rhythm on a garbage can, bringing to life all the things that go wasted and unnoticed. The real Anthony is my uncle Anthony.

Uncle Anthony is my father's younger brother. In many ways, my uncle Anthony provided me with things my father couldn't. Uncle Anthony provided laughter when my father provided anger. While my father ridiculed me and convinced me that I would be (and I was) awkward with women and incapable of acquiring a minimal amount of pussy, my uncle spent time convincing me that I was handsome, had a dynamic hairstyle, and would, upon reaching legal age, get laid with regularity. He would sit me down in a chair and douse my hair with an array of African-American hair products. He would use a large afro comb and would spend a great deal of time "picking out my mop". He had me looking like a wild man and, at other times, the child lead singer of a rhythm and blues group. He would stand me up and walk me to the mirror.

"You're the prettiest brown boy in town," he'd say as we stared at our likeness in that antique mirror. He'd then spend time admiring himself. He'd fix his hair and strike several well-rehearsed poses. He'd conduct imaginary conversations with women.

"Excuse me Miss, I don't mean to be rude but you're very pretty," and "You know, if pretty was a minute...you'd be an hour," and so on. I stood watching, receiving my real education. He'd take me out for walks in the park or in the neighborhood. It seemed every time we walked together he would get into a conversation with a woman. It seemed he knew every woman in the world—black ones, white ones, Chinese ones, and ones whose nationality I couldn't make out. He would introduce me as his nephew and the women would lean over and pat me on the head while my uncle would talk about how well-behaved I was, and that I was well-trained, like an obedient puppy, by none other than him. He would then dismiss me.

"Why don't you go over there and play?" he'd say.

I would look around and all I'd see was cement.

"Where do I play?" I'd ask. At that point, Uncle Anthony would have his arm around the young woman.

"Here" he'd say, reaching into his pants pocket, "Go buy an ice cream."

This was code for "Get lost." I'd take the dime or quarter and walk to the corner store where I'd stick my head into the freezer in search of a Popsicle or Eskimo pie. I would start working on my ice cream, the chocolate melting into my lips and cheeks. When I returned, my uncle would be kissing the girl and upon seeing me, would separate from the woman like a boxer pulled apart from an opponent by a referee. He would straighten his hair and the woman would fix her hair. He would ask for the woman's phone number and that would be that. I recall this happening on 4 separate occasions in the course of one outing. I didn't realize the significance of all this at the time—that I was basically part of the bait my uncle used for attractive females. All I was concerned about was my ice cream.

I was named after my uncle Anthony. Relatives called us "Big Ant" and "Little Ant" for short. Uncle Anthony wasn't a big guy—I'd say about 5 foot 7, 145 pounds or so. When I was young, I'd rummage through boxes in a storage closet at the end of a long hallway near my grandmothers' room. I'd sneak past her door as she knelt down in prayer. She had an altar with flickering candles. On the wall was a painting of Jesus: thorns pushed into his head dripping blood. I was terrified of Jesus because of that picture and I never went near that altar. I opened the door and got lost among the boxes and trunks. One particular box was torn and gnawed. It stored the family photo albums. I wasn't supposed to be in the storage room, but that gave me all the reason to be there. I noticed a tin jar on the floor. I removed the lid and saw candy in bright wrappers that looked like diamonds. I don't know how long the candy had been in the jar, but I grabbed a piece and wrestled off the wrapper. I popped the candy into my mouth—it burned the taste of cinnamon into my tongue. I noticed a photo album that was leather and shaped like a pig. I opened it and saw an old black and white photo with torn brown edges. My fingers seemed to attract dust like a magnet as I turned the pages. There were pictures of men in suits standing next to cars. Each page I lifted revealed faces, both familiar and unfamiliar. I came to a photo of a group of children standing side by side in front of a house. I looked at the faces—5 girls and 5 boys. The girls had pigtails and dresses while the boys wore duplicate pants, plaid shirts, and sported "rice bowl" haircuts. I realized that these children were my aunts and uncles as kids. One of the children stood off to the side, his arm cocked as if he were flexing his bicep. His face had all the forced toughness a 7 year old could muster. It was my uncle Anthony. I turned the pages of that photo album looking for Uncle Anthony in each snapshot. One by one he appeared, biceps flexed and armed cocked as if ready for battle. I laughed at those pictures.

I thought about the things I had heard about my uncle Anthony on the streets. I'd heard he was the nicest, most courteous guy you could ever meet. I also heard that he could knock you out with either hand. I'd heard he had been involved with streets gangs—blacks and Pilipinos—in the 50's and 60's. I'd heard he would fight anybody, no matter how big they were. I'd heard he'd knocked out a Samoan 100 pounds heavier than he at a community luau feast. I would ask him about fighting when we were alone. I wanted to know whom he knocked out and why; and what punch did the job.

"Was it a left hook or a straight right cross, Uncle Anthony?" Uncle Anthony would just smile and tell me to forget fighting and to read books and study hard. I read my books and did my lessons, but compared to my uncle Anthony, those things were boring and dead. I took a picture from the album. It was a lone picture of Uncle Anthony, but this picture showed him without his arm flexed. It was taken in front of a car that appeared to be from the 1950's or early 60's. I put the picture in my shirt pocket and snuck past my praying grandmother back to my room.

Today I am an adult. I have been busy trying to figure out the meaning of life and I keep hitting my head on the same brick wall with the words, *it's meaningless*, spray painted on it. I watched my uncle Anthony go from full time janitor at Children's Hospital to unemployed. There always seemed to be a supervisor at the hospital that Uncle Anthony would have a dispute with. They were always bigger and required not only work, but that the worker accept humiliation, often times public, with a smile on their face. Uncle Anthony was not the kind to do this. I managed to attend City College of San Francisco and a couple of years at San Francisco State University. He was always a bit taken by my schooling. He never went to college nor did he finish high school. Uncle Anthony and many of his generation—at least the one's I have seen in San Francisco, and by that I mean men of color—became janitors, it seemed. All of his friends and my father's friends earned a living doing janitorial work. Occasionally they'd reflect on their schooling, saying that the schools or church didn't care for poor kids like themselves and just allowed them to fall through the cracks. Who knows what they might have become had they had life's advantages?

But Uncle Anthony had the one quality that you can't learn in a classroom—laughter. He always had a smile on his face, even when his luck had run out the back door. He had truth in laughter and truth in emotion. Not for one second in my life have I ever doubted his love for me. He always looked for the truth in an experience. He was the kind that couldn't fake a laugh or smile or handshake. He's gone through numerous ups and downs—divorce, loss of jobs, issues with substance abuse and so on; but despite this, Uncle Anthony always looked for a bigger meaning in his life.

Nearly a decade ago Uncle Anthony lost the two people that were closest to him: my grandmother and cousin David. The passing of

Grandma and Cousin David hit Uncle Anthony the hardest in our family and he sank into the shadows of his room, the bed sheets soaking in the icy sweats and tears that he felt would drown him. I remember the times I'd visit Grandma. She and Uncle Anthony lived on opposite ends of a squeaky hallway with a hardwood floor. Uncle Anthony and Grandma would spend time teasing each other.

Grandma would tease Uncle Anthony about his long hair. She said that he looked like a wild man from some remote jungle and that he probably had lice or other creatures crawling in his hair. She'd also make fun of his flashy clothes. On one occasion, Uncle Anthony walked into the kitchen sporting a strut and a pair of cherry red platform shoes.

Grandma laughed and said, "You wear those loud colors all the time. What are you, a flag or a fire engine?"

Uncle Anthony would laugh and say, "That's a cold shot ma, but I love you anyway". He would then start teasing Grandma about her Pilipino nose.

He'd say, "You know ma, I love you and your Pilipino-African nose. You are my little Pilipino woman straight from the heart of deepest darkest Africa".

Grandma would then tell Uncle Anthony to shut up and Uncle Anthony would try to explain to her that Africa was the cradle of civilization. Grandma would end up waving Uncle Anthony away as if shooing away a swarm of flies. Uncle Anthony would shoo her back and leave in a huff. He'd return to grandma's room an hour later and kiss her on the forehead. Grandma couldn't stay angry with her youngest boy for long.

My cousin David was the same age as Uncle Anthony. When I was a child they would come and visit me. They would spend time in the mirror combing their hair. They loved the music of Smokey Robinson and would spend hours fixing their hair like Smokey's and playing records, hitting the high notes and moving their legs and arms and sliding across the hardwood floor like the Motown groups of the day. I would sit and watch with my mouth ajar. Uncle Anthony would take my hand and show me the steps: One-two-three, and over again. It would take a little time, but I was finally able to get into step with them with my short legs. Then my father would walk in. "Hey, go to your room" he'd say. Uncle Anthony would protest. "Aw, come on Jim, let him trip with us for a while." But my father didn't hear the words. He would push me through the old-fashioned sliding door and I would sit on my bed. I listened as they sung to the records spinning on my father's record player. I could hear their feet executing moves on the floor. I heard their muffled voices. Their bursts of crisp laughter seemed to kick open that closed door and hit me in the chest. I sat and wanted to be older like them, I wanted to be them but I was trapped in a 7 year-old body. I can't forget the music from that room. Those songs play over and over in my mind and in my Uncle Anthony's mind too.

Cousin David passed away after a long battle with brain cancer, followed by Grandma shortly after. Losing the 2 people closest to him was devastating to Uncle Anthony. I watched Uncle Anthony go through depression. He slipped into things that he warned me about. I wanted to help him, but felt helpless myself. Had I been the one in Uncle Anthony's shoes, he would have found a way to reach me. How I wish I could love the way he does. But despite the loss in his life, he was able to find meaning and walk the streets and reach out to those who suffer. "I'm working for the lord now", he says, handing out religious tracts. I sometimes walk alongside him in my fancy office attire. Some folks ignore him and his tracts. "God bless you, brother," he says, moving forward.

I worked at an insurance brokerage for a number of years in San Francisco. I was one of those guys who wore slacks and a tie and looked like I had my "shit together." Uncle Anthony saw the slacks and tie and the fact that I worked behind a desk typing numbers into a lifeless computer and thought I was some sort of executive. He said I had an educated way of speaking—which was true—I did sound white when I spoke. But in reality, I was a customer service rep doing a job that anyone with an ounce (or even less) of common sense could do. I would try to convince Uncle Anthony that I was an underling, a mere cog in a controlled, florescent environment.

"Uncle, it's not what you think. I just sit at a desk and answer phones..."

"No, no, no," my uncle would reply, "the guy who answers the phone is important, right?"

"I guess so."

"You damn right he is. You think those rich folks who own that insurance company are gonna have any bozo off the street answering their phones, talking to their important clients?"

He would tell me that I was smart. I had to be smart. Working at a desk and not as a janitor cleaning toilets was proof of that. It was all logical to my uncle.

He saw me as educated and successful, but it is actually Uncle Anthony that's done more to form my way of thinking than any job or classroom could ever do. He was a man who could sing in public. I remember him breaking into song as we walked downtown or in a particular neighborhood. It would always embarrassed me and my uncle, sensing this, would sing louder. It made me want to slip into a crack in the street but those cracks and fissures were filled with the songs and lives of men like Uncle Anthony—I just didn't know it at the time. I wish I had the freedom—no, I wish I had the guts to sing in front of strangers, to share my voice freely without fear or embarrassment. My Uncle Anthony's song, words and life are a part of me. My life is better because of him. It is an honor to have his name. He is the real *Anthony Robles*.

❧

Tony Robles—San Francisco native. Father of Lakas and son of Jimmy and Florence. Learned to write while mopping and sweeping floors for the "Pilipino Building Maintenance Company." Writing poems on napkins in Chinese restaurants —going on 25 years.

Gayle Romasanta

THE BRIDGE

*I*t was on the day of our Lord, a Sunday, after church. Bright and gleaming in our best, me, ma, dad and my younger sister Lanie walked to a farmer's market called, *Ilalim ng Tulay.* In English it meant, "Under the Bridge." It should have been called "Under the Freeway," since after all it was sitting under the 205 in downtown Stockton. Today ma was on the look out for okra, Chinese long beans and a chicken. She bet us as we walked that she wouldn't spend more than $5. We believed her. She was the best haggler we knew.

Ilalim ng Tulay wasn't the kind of Market like the ones on the north side that sold art and crafts, or pretty Zucchini with their tops cut off just right. No, these farmers had no time for woodcarvings or bow-tied sachets. Some of the produce were left overs from the season, or irregular and bruised fruit and vegetables. Most of it was fresh and surprisingly organic. The kind of stuff that health food gurus pushed on their well-to-do clients: hard to find, but abundant under the bridge, like muddy Bok Choi, Chinese broccoli, sweet potato leaves and squash flowers. Sold for under 50 cents a bag. Some people also sold soft and hard-shelled turtles, salamanders, live crabs, clams and chickens (like my Tito Boy). Not for pets, but for food.

Under the bridge it smelled like dirt and the waters of the Delta. It was the smell of freshly watered soil, the first 30 minutes of a rain shower. There was also no lighting, just whatever sunlight that draped on both sides of the highway. The cars roared above us, but the sound was never an issue. Everyone was loud. The people who came in after church would get the scraps of what everyone picked through. The market started as early as 6:30 in the morning. By one in the afternoon it was just a space under a freeway. The homeless could settle in once again after the crowds and the last truckload of produce left.

I could see Ilalim ng Tulay, fifty years from now in some history class:

"Ilalim ng Tulay — the Filipinos fondly called it. It was a gathering place for the large immigrant community of Filipinos in Stockton, as well as an outdoor market. This was a renowned meeting place that nursed the labor movement which included Philip Vera Cruz, Cesar Chavez and Esperanza Makulit."

I was Esperanza Makulit, not yet in the history books, but I imagined I would be. I just had to finish high school. Mr. Price, my English teacher, busted his ass to get me enrolled at Tokay High, where there was more "opportunity." Of course opportunity meant probation for the first semester. No fights, no cutting, no gum chewing, no cussing. If I was to stay at Tokay I had to agree that for the first semester I would be the best little girl I could ever imagine. Never mind that I wanted to kick someone's ass every time the bus passed through Morada on the outskirts of Stockton, where houses had columns instead of black iron grills, mile-long front yards instead of drug dealer infested public parks, and perfectly painted cream fences, with no chicken wire anywhere. And never mind that my classmates had names like Alyssa Napoli, whose family owned Napoli's Sunflower Seeds; Dana Kraft, her father was the vice president of Swiss Pharmaceuticals; and Colin Loeb, whose father owned all the Baskin Robbins stores in Lodi, Stockton and Modesto.

"Yeah, never mind Espe," ma said when she heard the news that I received 148 on my IQ test. The test was administered, free of charge, to kids who scored in the top one percentile of the California Achievement Test. "You are still you. Still *Locaretta*. Crazy." Never mind.

By nature I wasn't crazy—Locaretta. In places that I could call my own I was calm and never thought about hurting anyone. Like St. Anne's was mine; I grew up sleeping through Father Andres's sermons there. Ilalim ng Tulay was mine too. The beggars, buyers, sellers, the salty smell of urine escaping from the sidewalk cracks. I walked this place in my sleep. Even Mariani's store had my name on it; all the men out front with their dirt crusted boots, waiting in long lines to get paychecks cashed, or to buy Levi's and cowboy hats. This was my "queendom." I acted the part, serene and calm. Locaretta behavior was left for school and stupid girls who giggled behind me in the lunch line whispering, "Shhhhhh. Doesn't Espe get free lunch tickets?" Only then did I imagine beating the living shit out of anyone who would cross me.

"I'll pay $2.50 for that chicken!" Ma yelled over the noise to Tito Boy, my fake uncle and part time chicken salesman. He was chewing tobacco and wearing a green beanie that read, "Cock Fight." Tito Boy wasn't technically my uncle, just a close family friend, but Filipinos thought every other Filipino was their relative. That way we could all treat each other like family, which also made it easier to treat each other like shit. Like the time Tito Boy told me, "Espe, you're getting fat! Smart and fat is not a good combination. Smart and skinny will find you a boyfriend!"

Tito boy was such a jackass sometimes. Yet I liked him nonetheless. He gave money to all the cousins as Christmas and birthday presents. He also let me interview him for my social science report, the History of the Filipino American Labor Movement. He told me about the big farm he lived on with the other migrant farm workers and the small barrack-like living quarters they shared. The quarters weren't insulated, so in the winter he and his friends would be too cold to sleep through the night. But they would still get up the next morning to pick tomatoes for 20 cents an hour. He couldn't marry his white girlfriend because of the laws at the time, so he stayed a bachelor. But the lucky few who could, married Mexicans and younger Filipinas.

Since he was too old now to work the fields he sold chickens under the bridge from the back of his pick up truck on the weekends. He had wire cages stacked on top of each other, cramped with chickens, clucking and sticking their heads out. On the weekdays he worked with my dad. They worked graveyard shift together, Monday through Friday, pulling Mylar coating off computer boards that would one day live in pacemakers, electric wheelchairs and walkie talkies.

"Mare, how about if Espe just helps me until 1:30 with the chickens? I'll give you one free," Tito Boy bartered. Ma smiled when she heard this. A free chicken. Of course she'd let me go. She gave us kids a look that said, "I told you so," and said yes. She, Lanie and dad would come back in two hours.

"You know how to hold chickens?" Tito Boy asked when they left.

"By the neck." I answered.

"No, like this." Tito boy opened the door to a wire cage and gently lifted a white hen and held her in his arms. He stroked the hen's feathers.

"See?" He asked.

I nodded and he motioned for me to pick her up. I held the chicken like a baby, her legs kicking in the air. I flipped her right side up and her wings flapped uselessly against me. I looked at her closely and noticed she was missing an eyeball; one eye socket was crusted and empty. I cringed and put her back in the cage.

Out of the corner of my eye I could see Tito Boy shaking his head. I challenged him with a look that said, "what?" as a customer approached us and Tito Boy greeted him at the front end of the truck.

I chewed on a hangnail until a line formed and I had to help customers. One old woman wanted me to kill the chicken for her. I politely told her no. Another man wanted a discount because I gave him the chicken with one eye. I politely told him no, and reasoned he wouldn't have eaten the eyes anyway. When the line dwindled, I heard a boy's voice call me.

"Esperanza?"

My head snapped up. It was someone I recognized all too well, with two girls standing behind him. It was Colin Loeb. He was in my Gifted And Talented Education program, which meant we had every class together. He was the smug, good-looking type: chlorine bleached, sandy brown, hair, 6'3." He was the best water polo player Tokay High had, and off-season, he was the swim team's number one breast stroker. He was built long and lean. One day I spied him wearing his speedo, getting ready to jump into the gym pool. Time stood still.

Colin was the only boy I thought was my mental equal. In Geometry he finished English homework. In English he finished Social

Science work, and so on for the rest of our classes. Yet he answered questions in class with ease and managed to undermine our teachers' intelligence by asking them questions they couldn't answer.

However, physically, he was the complete opposite to my chubby, straight haired self. Only my grandma thought I was good looking. I knew this because I wasn't Mestiza, half white, half Filipino, and my nose was too flat for anyone to notice my good attributes: almond eyes, thick lips and high IQ. Colin and I only talked to each other if he needed me to move or vice versa. If I saw him walking in the hallways alone I would nod in his direction and he would smile in recognition.

With Colin's popularity came the blonde girls. They were behind him now: Brittany Digert and Jenny David. They were popular because they were rich. Other than that, I thought they were just plain dumb. Their matching outfits proved it. They both wore silk, polka dotted, ruffled shirts and short shorts. I had seen similar outfits at the yuppy store, Campbells, in the Lincoln Center.

It was just my luck. The three of them together, like their own little gang, walking on my side of town.

"Hi," Colin grinned. I wanted to shrink and crawl underneath a small, small rock. But I said hello back and nodded to the girls.

I looked over to Tito Boy, who was now spitting in a rusty coffee can he kept for when he chewed tobacco. Oh God no, I thought.

"Is that your boyfriend?" Tito boy asked in Ilocano, my mother's dialect. His customer, who I presumed was more of a friend than a buyer, laughed.

"You should shut up," I answered back in English.

"Is that your dad?" Jenny asked. She asked the question like she was afraid of the answer.

"No," I said to Brittany. "What are you doing here?" I asked Colin.

"My dad's buying a store down the street. He's gonna turn it into a Baskin Robbins. You eat ice cream, don't you?"

I wasn't sure if this was a genuine question or a sarcastic quip. I decided to answer as if it was the former.

"Yes. I like Vanilla ice cream," I said in a monotone voice. I looked for an excuse to end our conversation. But Tito Boy was laughing with his friend and there were no customers to tend to. Instead I found passerbys staring at Colin and the girls. Light skin and eyes, anyone would have haggled for that.

"You live around here? You go to Tokay. How does that work?" Colin prodded.

"They let me in because of GATE, but you know that," I said, not sure if he really did and stood up. "Excuse me, I need to get back to work," I said. I rolled my eyes. Colin leaned in closer to me.

"Don't get mad. I was just walking around. I saw you, I decided to say hi. I really liked the report you read in class," he said in a loud whisper, enough for the girls to hear.

"The one I did last week?" I asked him in a lower whisper.

"Yeah. That was really cool. I didn't know Filipinos had to fight for their rights and stuff. Crazy. You had a lot of footnotes."

I beamed. No one listened when I read the report in class. At one point Mrs. Kazan had to remind the class that I had "the conch" and everyone had to listen. I read that day sick to my stomach, because my report meant so much to me and I knew everybody could care less. Why should they care? They didn't know anybody who worked the fields. They only saw the farm workers who picked the "Tokay" grape fields that surrounded our school. Our school was named after the grapes, but no one knew who made the grapes possible. But if Colin heard what I said, then maybe others did too.

"Maybe we could work on homework together. I could use extra help. I should call you," Colin said, in front of the girls.

Unexpectedly I smiled. I had no friends at Tokay. Colin would be my first. Unfortunately, this made the girls smirk and give each other knowing glances. Jenny playfully swatted Colin on the arm.

I thought about bashing the girls' heads together, like in the action movies I saw on TV. They would crack upon impact, and instantly the girls would fall to the floor, unconscious.

"You did not just say that." Brittany said. "Colin you're so rude, don't be so sarcastic all the time." She turned her attention to me. "It's just that he's never been to this neighborhood. I'm Brittany." She gave me a flat smile and held out her hand. I felt confused. Was Colin being mean? Or was Brittany? I counted to ten to calm down and hesitantly shook her hand. At the same time Tito Boy started to laugh hysterically and started to cough into his coffee can.

"Espe, why don't you introduce us to your friends?" he said in Ilocano.

Brittany and Jenny locked eyes for a brief moment. They didn't laugh or smirk. They just knew. And I knew from what they knew, that I wanted to rip their eyeballs out. Breaking the moment, Brittany started to cough. She composed herself.

"Does he know how to speak English?" She asked and pointed to Tito Boy.

Obviously, Colin didn't tell Brittany about my report. Even if he did she would still think that all farm workers were inarticulate and illiterate. However, Tito Boy was not. He had been in this country for longer than she had been alive. Brittany was one person out of many who would never get it. I hated her.

The world turned into a slow motion reel. I took hold of Brittany's hair and shook her head like a rag doll. I wanted her to shut up forever. FOREVER. Tito Boy ran towards me. No one made a sound. I only heard the shuffling of feet on loose gravel and my own voice.

"He Knows How To Speak Fucking English! F—ing English! Do You Understand?" I yelled.

Tito Boy tried to hold me back, but I held on. I wanted to rip the hair out of her head and balled my hands into a fist to make sure I could. With one hand on her head, my other hand reached over to cup her eye. I forgot to breathe. I forgot I was alive. I fingered an eye socket and felt a tender lid between my thumb and forefinger. It felt like velvet. Suddenly, Tito Boy placed me in a headlock. He tightened his grip.

"Are you crazy? Stop this!" He grunted in English. I could see a police officer walking up the dirt aisle towards us. Another officer followed close behind holding a walkie-talkie.

"My uncle makes those!" I wanted to yell to the officer. But that wasn't true. He only made the computer chips inside. I sank into Tito Boys hold and finally let go. Loose strands of blonde hair twined around my fingers. My head felt hot and my nose started to bleed. Just you wait, I thought to steel myself for the worse. Just you wait. We'll rise out of here. Then you'll truly be frightened. Blood started to trickle down my upper lip. I let it run and glared at Brittany. She was on the ground crying. Her face and hair were wet with tears and saliva. Next to her kneeled Colin, with one arm around her shoulder, head bent low, peering into her fucking ugly face.

To my surprise ma suddenly appeared next to me and Tito Boy. She gave me a frown and pinched my arm.

"We just come from church and this is what you do?" She asked.

This remark prompted me to cry. Not because I was ashamed or guilty. I pushed on Tito Boy so I could stand up straight. The traffic trembled above. I wondered if God was laughing at the scene before him. Why wouldn't he? He would think it was all silly kid stuff. A popularity contest I could never win.

The burning sunlight glared on both sides of the freeway. Tito Boy's chickens panted their tiny red tongues. It was almost one o'clock.

Gayle Romasanta is an artist based out of the SF Bay Area. Currently, she is the Artistic Director of the only Filipino American theater and arts space in the nation, Bindlestiff Studio. Her work has been featured at numerous venues and festivals, such as at the Gene Siskel Center for Film, San Francisco International Asian American Film Festival, National Public Radio and The Cultural Center of the Philippines. She graduated from the California College of the Arts with an MFA in writing and was the co-founder of CCA's literary arts journal, *Eleven Eleven*. She has been a resident artist with Bindlestiff Studio since 1998, as an actress/violinist with Tongue in a Mood, violinist for the Legendary Bobby Banduria, and founding member/writer/director of the Bindlestiff Pinay Collective. Her best work of art to date, and possibly ever, is creating Ruby Simona, her daughter.

Rey E. de la Cruz

DEAR SATU: LETTERS TELL
THE STORY OF OUR LIVES

For 40 years, a note from my pen pal could make my day. At last I met the woman behind the words.

Satu gave me a big hug and said, "It wasn't so hard to recognize you." Satu Vaverka and I had been writing each other since 1966, when we were 11 or 12 years old, and had exchanged so many pictures over the years that we could easily spot each other in a crowd. Now, at Finland's Helsinki-Vantaa airport, we were finally face to face.

Our correspondence had started when I was a sixth grader at San Beda College, a Roman Catholic boys' school in Manila. My friend Benjie had a pen-pal business with a children's organization, and I paid him a few centavos to register my name. I requested a female pen pal in Finland, a country that appealed to me because it was cold (in contrast with the tropical Philippine weather) and distant, and, therefore, different.

Writing to Satu made me more observant about my culture and environment. In an early letter I described *bibingka*, a Philippine rice cake cooked over an open fire. I wanted to make clear to Satu in what way it was different from the typical Western cake made of flour, sugar and eggs.

For Satu, writing to me meant paying more attention when the Philippines was mentioned, especially in the newspapers. She told me, "Anything Philippine fascinated me...Everything that came from you was exotic. Finland then was an isolated country." She admired my seemingly fluent written English, which then as now was spoken widely in the Philippines. "I had to ask my older sister to help me compose my letters to you," she admitted.

Satu had kept most of my letters, including their envelopes. I got goose bumps re-reading words I had written decades before. The letters told the story of my life—my anxiety at migrating to America, my excitement at becoming an uncle for the first time, my experiences as a special-education teacher with the Chicago Public Schools. In 1982 I had written: "Nothing remains the same. It's nice to know that you're always around when these changes occur." Then, in 2001: "Thanks for leaving a message on my voice-mail. It was wonderful to hear your voice for the first time after about 35 years of friendship."

I've kept Satu's letters as well, along with the pictures she had sent. In one photograph she posed with the postcards and pictures I had sent her in the background. She wrote on the back of the picture: "I am in my room in the country. I always bring your postcards and photos wherever I go." I also have pictures of her with her Czech-born husband, David, and her firstborn, Arto ("my little dictator"), who was born in 1984.

During my visit, we tested our memories on the things we had written about. When I asked to visit Turku (Finland's old capital) and Rovaniemi (a city in northern Finland, near the Arctic Circle), she asked me why I wanted to go there. I replied, "Because you sent me postcards of those places!" When I brought her to a Philippine fiesta organized by Filipinos in Helsinki, she instantly recognized the folk dance tinikling, exclaiming, "You sent me a postcard of this dance!"

My childhood pen pal and I were fortunate in having only one choice of mail when we started writing to each other. Because we had to sit down, compose our thoughts and physically mail the letters, there was commitment to our relationship. Technology as we know it now was absent in our lives, so we used our imagination in writing and reading each other's letters. Our correspondence inspired a host of emotions—the eagerness of waiting for a letter, the excitement in opening the envelope and, finally, the joy of reading it.

Nowadays, Satu and I e-mail each other and use the snail mail when sending cards on special occasions and postcards when we travel. I find the timelessness of our friendship rather incredible. We were children when we started writing to each other. Now we are adults, and at an age when we can truly appreciate the amazing quality of our lifelong correspondence. When I told my letter carrier, Craig, about my plans to visit Satu in Finland, I proudly raised the stack of letters he had just delivered and declared with a flourish, "The power of mail!"

The essay first appeared in the March 12, 2007 issue of Newsweek.

Rey E. de la Cruz's imagination lives in Ballesteros, Cagayan, where he spent a memorable childhood. A globe-trotter, he has the following degrees: A. B. in Broadcast Communication, University of the Philippines; M. A. in Communication and Theater, University of Illinois at Chicago; M.Ed. in Special Education, University of Illinois at Chicago; Master of Liberal Arts, University of Chicago; and Ed.D. in Special Education, Illinois State University.

Remé A. Grefalda

THE LOCUS OF OUR YEARNINGS

> "... Who are you, my soul's torment?
> And who am I to house
> The roaring
> Splendor of Your Name?"
>
> — *baring more than soul*

In an age when instant gratification is limitless, does the quixotic state of yearning have a place in our lives? Or is it passé—seeing as "yearning" seems to gestate during a time of waiting? Waiting, after all, is not what the 21st century is all about. The insistence on "instant" berates conditions that are not conducive to lightning speed response. One need not go that far back in time to realize that our lives never required "instant." The idea was mass-marketed and ingrained into our lifestyle until "instant" became a need and today, an addiction.

A yearning is more than just wanting. More than desire, if such is possible. And a yearning seems inextricably entwined and imbedded with waiting. Yearnings seem to make themselves known when one is whipped by an overwhelming sense of loneliness. A yearning moves in waves. Like seas gaining depth and turbulence, a yearning grows in proportion to some anticipation of fulfillment. But most times we yearn in mystery. We wait, not exactly certain, what it is we are waiting for.

To yearn and not know what one is yearning for is at the crux of our being human.

In the seventies, it was common practice for one to face the proverbial mirror and contemplate the ritual of escape. Escape from the frenzy of the daily grey. Move towards some clarity: into some form of discernment, albeit through distraction.

The phrase bandied about was the need "to search for oneself." So young adults, fresh from college campuses took to backpacking trips to temple cities in Asia, to ancient ruins in Europe, to deserts, to mountains; any place where the horizon was not jutting with golden arches or the interminable blinking of neon signs.

The so-called search began by stripping away hand-me-down ambitions, and questioning the familiar templates of success. However, after a few months buried in an Amazon forest, or having lingered along the fringes of Nepalese temples, entranced by monotones of chanting, one experienced a different awakening. It was as if one was urged to return with renewed interest in "conquering the world" thus, postponing the tedious process of discovery. What self-discovery? And why not within the cacophony of the familiar skyscraper metropolis? They who postponed the process were more honest and pragmatic.

But often heard were others who persisted; those who held their ground—who pursued their quest for the ultimate, exchanging their mindset and their life for what looked like windmills beyond our immediate understanding.

The immediacy of the human need to contribute to social order and high economic good became a guide and their life's direction. So much for well-meaning intent until within the frenzy of their altruism, a certain longing found an opening, lodged itself and stayed.

Where do longings come from? And is there a point to their existence?

This opaque state of wanting becomes slowly recognizable when one owns up to the common fear of confronting a pause; when one steps out of the treadmill of deadlines; when downtime makes us feel small pangs of guilt for doing nothing. We have all become inept at facing up to "free time." One responds instead to the legitimate call to be "doing," finding temporary fulfillment in being of service.

When altruism calls, who can ignore its demands? But altruism for its own sake and done far too long can become an empty pastime.

Can one, at the moment of confronting the wall, face an invisible mirror and say, "What is it, Self? What are you wanting?" One then realizes that longings never atrophy. True restlessness stirs and is unwilling to be stifled, comforted or distracted. The yearning demands its day in the sun.

Strange as it may seem, there are individuals for whom the state of yearning is ongoing. It is an anguish laced with anticipation—for what, they cannot say. The perennial question confronts them: What exactly do they want that cannot be met? If they knew what it was, they would be grateful just knowing. More likely, they haven't a clue. But the ache and the longing and the state of flailing in a vacuum tear at one's soul and gratefully there are the times when it subsides, but the yearning is an ember constantly glowing.

What is quietly amazing about this predicament is the discovery hidden within oneself that there is this willingness to wait out the longing, unknown though its goal may be.

For some of us, the yearning explodes into an ache beyond our surface wants. It feels as though our essential self, tears away layers of masks and superficial identities, and only asks to be named.

For some of us, the yearning calls out a self so recognizable—but in another, whose riveting look can blind us into seeing. Or it can be an echo of our own voice in someone else's timbre, in words we recall from a former time.

However startled we are, there is no calm for the jolt reverberates through our days, months, years till we are forced to come forth naked with only the Unnamed Self—battered but intact. Then and only then, does the ineffable longing emerge from the shadows. Here and again "moments of Now" take place and we experience ongoing time with no end, until our intense awareness bursts into points of dizziness. The longing palpitates and becomes its own Source of life. The Yearning clothes a searing hollow of ache. Straining to touch, a feel, a wall . . . as our fingertips reach for nothingness.

We confront the height and breadth of our yearning for it is now tinged with clarity.

Our reason for existing suffuses our entire being.

It is the Twin transmitting waves to match our own exquisite anguish. Here is the moment of the burning bush. To approach, more than sandals must be shorn. Quietly, breathe . . . Take a moment to withdraw . . . Creature that you are, reach for the fingertip of your Creator whose small spark of hunger first fastened itself on you.

Remé A. Grefalda is the founding editor of **Our Own Voice**, a literary/arts online journal http://www.ourownvoice. com. She was an active consultant in the Planning Board of the National Conference on Establishing an Asian Pacific American Collection in the Library of Congress (Oct 4-5, 2007). In 2006, **Our Own Voice** partnered with the Asian Division Friends Society of the Library of Congress to coordinate the Carlos Bulosan Symposium. She is co-editor and co-author of a groundbreaking report funded by The Ford Foundation, "Towards A Cultural Community: Identity, Education and Cultural Stewardship in Filipino American Performing Arts," a project of the National Federation of Filipino American Associations (NaFFAA). Grefalda is a recipient of the Philippine Palanca Memorial Literature Award for her full-length play, *In the Matter of Willie Grayson*.

Helen Dizon

Let There Be Light

Not too long ago, I chanced upon a friend, in fact, she was one of the active members of the support group for divorced women I headed in the late eighties. We shared a similar predicament then. We were both victims and survivors of domestic violence—with a little deviation though. Hers was more physical than emotional abuse. As far as I can recall she had been in and out of the hospital emergency room a dozen times and each time she would let her husband go scott-free. But the last time, she was so physically battered that the police had to intervene. In the end, her batterer wound up in jail.

Now materialized before me was a sad-eyed and pale-faced wisp of a woman who appeared to have no life in her at all. I was petrified. What's going on with her? She had the same lifeless look when she had just fled her perpetrator. After that, I remember she was always present in our support group sessions. And a few weeks later, she had gradually metamorphosed into an energetic and vibrant person, taking on a renewed interest in life. So whatever happened to that courageous survivor? This I had to find out.

With some time hanging in our hands, we walked into the delicatessen nearby to get a bite to eat and in the same vein, chat to keep each other abreast. Twenty years of estrangement seemed an eternity.

Ravenously digging into my scrumptious Mediterranean stuffed peppers, I tested the uncharted waters—I asked if she had news about her former spouse. In an instant, her brows knitted, her eyes turned ferocious and her jaws tightened. Then erupted her fiery words, scathingly harsh, heavily spiced with expletives.

"I don't give a @#&! to what became of him. I'm not f------ interested. He could have rot in jail for all I care." Then she began to unravel her "Pandora's Box." Endlessly she went on and on about his abuse and her pathetic life with him. Her tirade lasted for half an hour. Helplessly, I listened. This was nothing new to me. She had already divulged the exact, same story before with the other members of our support group as her audience.

"No, no, no, no," she said with finality. An emphatic, resounding *NO!* She concluded that she could not and would not forgive nor forget what he had done to ruin her life, as well as her children's.

Dumbstruck, I shot her a long look of disbelief. Now, that explained the sorry sight that had unfurled before me. Transparent in her demeanor was rage and anger that had consumed her entire being. So, this is a woman who has not forgiven her perpetrator. This is a woman who has not left her past.

Suddenly remembering she had to run an important errand, we said our quick good-byes. I came away with a heavy heart. The whole incident stayed with me for some time and had me delving into a lengthy self-analysis.

I realized that my friend had resonated the rage and bitterness I had internalized some three years after I had left my abuser. My silent, imploding anger, resentment and hatred for my ex-husband had completely overpowered me. Though I was often engaged in a flurry of activities and projects, somehow I would still find myself alone with thoughts and flashbacks: memories of his controlling looks, verbal put-downs, negative criticisms, demeaning accusations, constant threats of abandonment, his flagrant womanizing, ad infinitum. The more I indulged in those thoughts, the angrier I grew and the deeper I wallowed in self-pity. I had become so obsessed with replaying the tapes in my mind over and over again that it had taken a toll on my physical and emotional health. I would lose sleep, suffer from intense headaches, stomach upset and agitated nerves. What a vicious cycle. Enough!

Finally, I went to seek professional help. Grueling sessions with my therapist, specifically, working on my rage and anger issues were the staples in the ensuing weeks, months and years. I came to understand that anger, resentment, and hatred could be poisonous to one's physical, emotional, mental and spiritual well-being, more so, if allowed to rankle persistently. Had I not dealt with my anger and resentment early on, I could have gone on digging up more hurtful memories, thereby, compromising my sanity.

I have a very strong suspicion that my friend had inadvertently stayed in the anger and resentment stages of her grief. In "Solo Plight," an article I have written for the *Philippine News* (the week of September 14-20, 1994), I indicated that "in any kind of loss, one goes through the seven stages of grief—denial, shock, anger, guilt, resentment, acceptance and healing. No one is exempted from this painful process and there is no cutting corners about it." And that "...Getting stuck in one stage or moving smoothly onto the next stage of grief depends on the psychological makeup of an individual."

True, my friend and I had gone through enormous psychic pain but the difference is that I have worked hard and walked an extra mile to move on from anger and resentment. Essentially, I took a leap of faith. I have anchored myself in God through ceaseless prayers, deep meditation and yoga. Paramahansa Yogananda, who was a great Hindu yogi and one of India's renowned spiritual leaders, had introduced the Kriya Yoga, an advanced technique of Raja Yoga in America in 1920. Through his nonprofit organization (Self-Realization Fellowship based in Los Angeles) he had led thousands of spiritual seekers find the Truth. Yogananda had declared that, "Everything else can wait but your search for God cannot wait." Further, he attested that, "...He is with you every minute of your existence yet the only way to realize this is to meditate."

By "re-discovering" and acknowledging God in my life, I have, in the same breath, surrendered and entrusted my spirit, soul and body to Him. Gradually, the positive changes I have gone through have shown me the Light. As Yogananda observed, "Change yourself and you have done your part in changing the world. Every individual must change his own life if he wants to live in a peaceful world. The world cannot become peaceful unless and until you yourself begin to work toward peace. It is only by removing hate from our hearts that we can live a Christ-like life."

Forgiveness played a weighty role in my healing. When all the anger, resentment and hatred were expunged I found it in my heart to forgive my perpetrator. I was ready to forgive when I had come to terms with myself and gotten off the victim stance. I was ready to forgive when I put an end to finger pointing and owned up part of the blame. I was ready to forgive when I felt compassion for my perpetrator. And I was ready to forgive when I opened my heart to the grace of our heavenly Father by forgiving myself.

It is written in the Bible, "For if ye forgive men their trespasses, your heavenly Father will also forgive you. But if ye forgive not men their trespasses, neither will your Father forgive your trespasses. [Matthew 6:14,15]."

Then one beautiful Spring day, I headed for the phone and dialed my former spouse's work number. The once familiar voice came on. I broke the ice.

"How are you?"

"I had waited for this in a long time," he replied, with surprise and confusion evident in his voice. "I'm doing well. And you? I'm sorry for what I have caused you."

Heart sinking and voice slighting quivering, I answered, "Never felt better. You know, I no longer have ill feelings for you." I hesitated for one brief second, "...I Forgive You."

In the next ten minutes, we got comfortable and talked about other mundane things.

A heavy weight had been lifted off of me after I hung up. I felt I had received full Divine forgiveness. At last, I had unchained my soul!

That was so freeing. How I wished my friend could have reached this ecstatic phase of my healing. But all I could do for her is pray that she be enlightened the way I have been. I know it will come to her when she's ready.

As I continue with my enthralling spiritual journey, I acknowledge with endless gratitude God's gift of inner peace. And above all, I am so grateful to have walked out of my dark past, to be led into the path of the calming, Cosmic Light.

Helen Dizon is a journalist, publicist and author of *Patterns and Cages* (Sulu Books, 1997). She is one of the founding members of PAWA.

Marie I. Romero

MAN OF LE MURIA

*I*t was a slow afternoon when "The Colonel" came. He was in a KGB-like trenchcoat and marched in with the air of military sharpness. He took in the whole bookstore with a 360 degree appraisal and a curt smile formed on his lips. He zeroed in on the Rizaliana corner and methodically went through each of the books on the Philippine national hero with his neatly trimmed, long, snake-like fingers—one of which flaunted a stone-encrusted humongous ring. He browsed the books with the intensity of someone who knew exactly what he was looking for.

We shall call him *Col. Bravo*. His face was vaguely familiar but we couldn't pinpoint when and where we have crossed paths. He introduced himself by name and signed the mailing list making sure we saw that it matched the driver's license that he deftly fished out from his wallet. The license showed he resides in a middle-upper class community up the peninsula.

"I have come to show you my book," he says. He brings out a well produced self-published work. *More on that later.*

After his departure and the distraction of other patrons, I did a research on him on the computer and found out that he was actually who he was. I further confirmed with a couple of people who as it turned out were familiar with him. He was a product of the highly esteemed Philippine Military Academy. Assigned to the southern Philippine front of Mindanao and eventually making it to the Philippine contingent sent to help the United States army during the Vietnam War, he rose to the rank of colonel during the time of Philippine President Ferdinand Marcos.

He came back and soon was making a regular showing at the bookstore where he would regale us with his escapades as a military man in the Philippines and Vietnam. Skeptics as we are, we found ways to check out his stories and everything seemed to corroborate with what we learned and read. There was a time he was the team leader in charge of the security for the Beatles during their ill-fated Manila concert. The backlash was so harsh and mobs started stalking the group that they had to be secured aboard the presidential yacht.

"After they snubbed the invitation from the First Lady Imelda Marcos to show up at the palace and entertain the children from the government-run orphanage, a plan was hatched by my team to throw them into the Manila Bay and let them float around before being fished out," Col. Bravo said.

He decided against it for fear that it would create a more negative image of the country in the eyes of the international community. Photos taken then shows Col. Bravo and his team trying to prevent the mobs from hurting the Beatles. At the airport, it was a different story; he relented and let the mob get their hands on a few members of the group. They ended up running for their lives into the safety of the plane. Talk about a bad trip.

One time he came in with large shopping bags appearing like a street person just kicked out of a shelter. He pulled out wads and wads of 100 dollar bills from the bag. My mind raced to recollect if any banks nearby had any incidents recently. With Col. Bravo, anything is possible. Apparently these bills represent part of his savings which he doesn't deposit with any bank.

"The way I look, nobody thinks of robbing me. Actually, here is a sandwich a passerby just gave me," he quipped.

He was a member of a military tribunal handling the court-martial of another Philippine colonel. "He was accused of rape by three women simultaneously...that could not happen, one woman alone is hard to fight off...so I voted not guilty. Most likely he was just guilty of seduction," he justified.

Now back to his book. He used his military and personal resources to come up with an exhaustive research which took him all over the globe. In his book he ties up the passages in the Bible to actual events, landmarks, languages and dialects used.

"All this points to the Philippines as the seat of the most ancient civilization of Lemuria," he concluded.

For those who are not aware, Lemuria considered by many people around world as one of the earliest civilization whose people, the Lemurians, were supposedly highly evolved and very spiritual. Although scientific research has not pinpointed it's physical location, many people feel they have very strong roots with "Mu"—as it is referred to—most specially people who feel they have some kind of extra-sensory or healing powers.

Colonel Bravo proceeded to show how his research was able to back up the connection. One thing I could not deny was the amount of hardwork and resources that must have been put into this "mission," as he calls it. The book was unlike anything I have seen in print, almost "out-of-this-world" would be more apt.

"I personally gave copies of this book to various world leaders and politicians, including Marcos, a couple of United States presidents and even Condoleeza Rice," he declared beaming his trademark toothless smile. Lest you think the recipients are in good company, he also said he gave copies to Saddam Hussein and Moammar Khaddafy.

*A*wed by how much a man can dedicate his whole life to finding the answers to his existence, I was really in admiration of his "outwordly" show of tenacity. He left a good standing as a commissioned officer in the Philippine military, left two wives and gave up all of his personal possessions to pursue his light at the end of the tunnel.

It was more for him that I felt a sense of relief that his book is done and his life's work is done. Or so I thought. He pulled out a well-kept notebook and sheafs of paper.

"I am now ready to come out with the latest documentation that has taken me all over the world again...the Philippine National hero, Dr. José Rizal was in Austria at the time that a one night stand caused the birth of a baby that went on to become the corporal who was responsible for the Holocaust," he explained.

As he melted into the night, my heart can't help but root for the underdog and wished that along with his new adventure, the man from Lemuria would find his own Sancho Panza. *Olé!*

❧

Marie Irving Romero is with ARKIPELAGO–The Filipino Bookstore, a community-based specialty bookstore. It is also a gathering place for the young and the old to share and learn more about the culture as well as a venue for emerging writers, artists and educators to showcase their works. Arkipelago was recently awarded the *Most Innovative Small Business Award* from the City and County of San Francisco and in 2002, Mayor Willie Brown declared December 2 as "Arkipelago Books Day in San Francisco" in recognition of the bookstore's place in the community.

James M. Constantino Bautista

ANOTHER SIMPLE DEFINITION

*A*t nineteen years old, I may not know a whole lot. But I do know that when I call myself Pinoy, I'm referring to something that no dictionary, encyclopedia, website or scholarly article can properly define. I'm Filipino-American, the first generation in my family to be born in the States, and Pinoy is my personal history, my character, my biorhythm, and the structure that connects my branches to my roots. Pinoy could equally be expressed through a copper statue in Imus, Cavite, a vibrant mural in South City, or the unadorned flesh of a Filipino, a simple yet remarkable canvas painted by the toil of ancestors and the unique hues of the Pacific sun. Pinoy is a constant reminder of where I came from—an identity compass of sorts that is always there to prevent me from getting lost in the diaspora.

Pinoy is a concept that King Philip II could never understand or hope to dominate, and a place that Magellan could never truly discover. As a child in California, Pinoy was embodied by annual gatherings by the Marina, where the kisses of a dozen aunties saturated kids with potent fragrances, right before we were served *pancit palabok* and a multitude of meat dishes from aluminum trays. It was the feeling of being completely unencumbered, of seeing footballs whizzing through the air, and fantasizing about a colorful popsicle with bubble-gum eyes whenever the ice cream truck's sirenic melody rounded the corner. Pinoy was getting my Velcro shoes filled with sand and my T-shirt stained by wet grass, and hearing someone's *lola* hiss *"ingat ka!"* even though there was nothing there to bring us harm.

To me, Pinoy was greasy food, in the days before clogged arteries and high blood pressure. It was cross-legged brown and yellow children slamming pogs on a plastic-covered floor, spending endless days with *pinsan* whose exact blood relation to me mattered less than the exact size of our *tsinelas*. Pinoy was having intense crushes on dark-haired girls who failed to realize their perfection; it was schoolyard fights, and laughter at sensitive guys whose hard exteriors dissolved in tearful streams when their hearts were broken.

Pinoy was a fridge filled only with *gulay*, and a cabinet stocked with spam, vienna sausages, and corned beef. It was the familiar odor of raw seafood as it wafted through the Asian market, in a whirlwind of incomprehensible dialects and imported sweets. Being Pinoy meant hours of basketball on scorching summer days, when pricey kicks were the only indication of class differences. Pinoy was wiping sweat with washcloths, not being embarrassed to carry the scent of baby powder like an aura, and waiting for Kool Aid to freeze in an ice tray, while cartoons played in the background of our improvised games.

Being Pinoy meant hearing Mama's stories about Oakland in the 60's, or *tsismis* about dysfunctional relatives, as we sat with our small elbows sticking to the table, our backs turned toward large wooden utensils on the wall, and an image of "The Last Supper," displayed long before Da Vinci's secrets were revealed in novel and film. Pinoy meant reading invisible directional arrows that protruded from pursed lips. It meant listening to chilling tales of *kapre* and *aswang*, of monsters from across the Pacific, described in hushed tones beneath a light-skinned *Santo Niño* with a knowing gaze.

Pinoy meant having leftovers from Goldilocks, balanced on two plates that were separated by an inverted cup or bowl, surrounded by water, to form a moated fortress that no crawling *langgam* could hope to breach. Pinoy was having to perform, even if you didn't want to, in front of dozens of visiting relatives who seemed to be perfectly content with setting up camp in a two-bedroom apartment. It was my *Ate* on karaoke, trying her best to sing like Lauryn Hill; and it was tedious piano lessons, and learning to dance by observing trendy cousins. For me, Pinoy was having severe allergies, and ziplocked ice pressed against bruised flesh. It was cheap, cylindrical-shaped soft-serve, *lumpia* pronounced with a glottal stop at the end, and tables of boisterous, guffawing men emptying carton after carton of San Miguel.

Pinoy represented a love for family that was penetrating and visceral, the kind of emotion that was agonizing and elating at the same time. It was the kind of feeling that made me never doubt for a second what I was fighting for, the kind of feeling that brought strikingly clear images to my mind of my kin, whose lives would forever be a greater motivation than any flag, government, ideology, or creed I sought to defend.

Pinoy is like my conscience; it is the reason I cannot buy expensive shoes without thinking briefly of Imelda, it is the reason I cannot scrape uneaten food into garbages, and the reason I cannot stomach the taste of blatant or subtle oppression, even in jest. Pinoy is familiar to me; it emanates from the withered but firm fingers of our matriarchs clutching rosaries, just beginning to see God in themselves as they exit the *simbahan*, and it radiates just as much from the harlequin-like grins of TV personalities during long blocks of entertainment on TFC.

Growing up Pinoy, I understood the profoundness of *balikbayan*, beyond the enormous cardboard boxes filled with *pasalubong*, and I quickly developed a transnational sense of belonging. I was burdened by the awareness that I would forever be torn between two homes, stretched painfully across the Pacific Ocean in a desperate attempt to form a bridge. Pinoy pulsated within me as I played for the first time with cousins in a familiar, humid corner of Luzon, until linguistic and economic barriers melted away, just as quickly as the violet tubs of *ube* and sticky *kutsinta* that lay beneath insect-proof netting. Pinoy was almost tangible in the last meal I had with my cousins, as we hungrily ate the same food at the same table, hearing nothing but the scraping of forks against Nanay's dishes.

On these trips, Pinoy lingered in the aromatic stenches and intolerable perfumes that I inhaled in the kitchen. It urged me to improve my Tagalog, my peers' forgotten tongue, in the hope that I might someday hear it in my wife's lullabies, and that I might experience my children being precocious and *makulit* in same way as all the kids I once knew. Pinoy was the reason that a handkerchief, an electric fan (subject to brownouts), and some good conversation could make blistering heat completely subside. Pinoy also meant having a witty, irreverent sense of humor, and allowing roaring laughter to cut through the pain like static interference.

To be Pinoy was to offer and receive often unmerited hospitality. It meant having complex emotions, insecurities, joys, and yearnings, mixed like a tangy *sinigang* concoction or the ethnic *halo-halo* of our Malay blood. Pinoy was flaunted unabashedly, like a ship's colors, by cousins wearing my old clothes over *lamok*-bitten legs and ribs visible through skin. And to this day, there will never be a banner or insignia that can adequately represent how proud I am to be counted among them, no matter how far I may be geographically.

Pinoy is a cache of memories that is deeper and more vast than the sea that separates us. It enables me to capture, in my mind, a world of labyrinthine shopping centers, dizzying *palengke* markets, and stray dogs dodging exhaust-spewing tricycles, while still being able to memorize the profoundness of every wordless social interaction. Pinoy is the quilt that we form as survivalists, sewn together through our personal struggles, and pulled taut but never torn in the chaos that we live in. Pinoy is the set of common values that no amount of greed, thievery, and back-stabbing can permanently shatter.

As a Pinoy, I witnessed the burial of my grandfather and great-grandfather among the tombs of countless generations of our humble dynasty. I marched to escort the dead beneath the same scalding rays that they had felt on their backs in life, pained by the knowledge that I would never truly know them. As a Pinoy, I would stare at the open sky, just as they once had, without knowing exactly what existed beyond the firmament of endless *asul* and deep *bughaw* that swallowed me from above.

Pinoy is the ability to leave my family when a trip is over—to miss entire childhoods, funerals, and births, but to know that a combination of Friendster and a shared ancestry would allow us to continue where we left off when I returned in a couple of years. Pinoy is the unique bitterness that I felt as I was caught for the first time in this cruel cycle of *kumusta* and *paalam*, of incessantly forging and severing ties, and of learning so much in the islands, yet being forced to return to a world that did not accommodate a global perspective and a clear sense of identity.

For a Pinoy, a trip to the Philippines is always like a vivid dream, and once you awaken, you're left feeling heartbroken and numb, without being sure if it all really happened. Pinoy is the feeling I get after leaving, when I close my eyes, longing to teleport for a minute or two, just so that I can turn down an invitation to swim at Boracay, or shop at Makati, in order to spend time with my people, doing absolutely nothing—and everything at the same time.

Pinoy is the reason that my people are my deepest pride and happiness, and my deepest regret and worry. And Pinoy is undoubtedly unified with the Pinay, like the genderless pronouns of our mother tongues. The Pinay recalls a goddess archetype in her tenderness and toughness, and the way entire societies depend on her just to function. To be Pinay is to have cascading ebony hair, modeled after the sky at midnight, with a prick of starlight for every suppressed tear in her experience. To be Pinay is to be covered with majestic brown, like the shivering infant Christ's surrogate cradle, or the unbreakable, sea-weathered anchor of my *Lolo*'s naval ship. The diaspora's crashing waves can never fully wash away this coat of brown, and as a Pinay ages, her skin is etched with her family's history.

Pinay is everything I seek; it is confidence when I'm uncertain and wisdom when I'm foolish. Pinay is sexuality and innocence, insecurity and independence. Pinay is an embrace, it is an unwritten recipe, it is a nostalgic melody, and it is the mango-tinged scent of home. The Pinay adapts in desperate circumstances, and carries the weight of her family on her slender form. She exhibits the power of a queen unexalted, with intellect that classrooms cannot impart, and the scars of unparalleled sacrifice. I know Pinay well because it is my mother, *Lola*, sister, and aunt; it is my future wife and daughter. And it is my duty, as a Pinoy, to protect the Pinay's physical body, as she voluntarily protects every other facet of my being.

A Pinoy knows the feeling of *Lola* inhaling to kiss you, as if she wanted to retain a vestige of your spirit to carry with her while you're apart, or to preserve a memory in her mind that not even Alzheimer's could chip away completely. Pinoy is alive in the act of "blessing" an elder, hand to brow, as if no convalescent home could ever be worthy of them.

For me, Pinoy is a revulsion to skin lightening creams and other colonial poisons that seek to stifle our radiance. It is the dream of veteran's equity, of Clark and Subic cleaned of filth, of sex tourism eliminated, of hunger satiated. Pinoy, in José Rizal's words, is to have *"secos los negros ojos, alta la tersa frente... sin manchas de rubor."* Dark eyes dried, clear brow raised... without a spot of blush. To be Pinoy is to be unashamed, with the knowledge that we are perfect in our imperfections.

Pinoy can be seen in the indescribable beauty of a *sampaguita* flower or a transparent barong contrasting with caramel pigmentation. It can be felt in *kamayan* culinary interactions and meticulously extracted *tinik ng isda*. It can be smelled in my mother's embrace, and tasted in *adobo* and sweet *saging*. It can be heard in the sublime orchestration of my town's *Banda Kabataan*, or in the voice of my five-year-old cousin reading Tagalog and English better than most American toddlers can read familiar storybooks in their single tongue.

Pinoy can be detected anywhere Filipinos gather because we are Pinoy. We define the term just by living, and by remembering those who lived. We are vessels of history and culture that could shatter or empty if allowed to tip. Because of this, Pinoy is our constant voyage of rediscovery; it is the process of assimilating and then realizing that assimilation is not the answer. Each of us experience Pinoy differently, but we all perceive it as a mirror that is there whenever our reflection becomes distorted or foggy. For me, Pinoy has a simple definition because I know who I am, and I remember where I came from. And at any age—nine, nineteen, or ninety—this is the most important thing to know.

pancit palabok: one of the many Filipino noodle dishes
ingat ka!: be careful
pinsan: cousin
tsinelas: slippers
gulay: vegetables
tsismis(chismis): gossip
kapre: a mythical giant
aswang: a type of vampire
Santo Niño: the Christ Child
langgam: ant
ate: older sister
lumpia: a Filipino egg roll
simbahan: church
balikbayan: lit.—back to the homeland, Filipinos
          in the diaspora returning to the Philippines
pasalubong: gifts usually one gives upon arrival
ube: purple colored dessert made from a type of yam
kutsinta: a type of dessert
makulit: mischievous
sinigang: a type of tangy stew
halo-halo: a dessert consisting of its various ingredients
          mixed with shaved ice (lit.: mixture)
lamok: mosquito
palenque: market
asul, bughaw: blue
kumusta: How are you?
paalam: farewell, good-bye
lolo/lola: grandfather/grandmother
kamayan: use of fingers when eating
tinik ng isda: fish bone
adobo: marinated meat dish
saging: banana
Banda Kabataan: youth band

James M. Constantino Bautista is a writer from the East Bay, California, and Imus, Cavite. As of 2008, he is a third-year Language Studies major at UC Santa Cruz. In high school, Bautista co-edited a literary magazine called *Sea Changes* and contributed his own thirty-stanza poem, entitled "Ang Naka-limutang Pamilya." He has volunteered for several summers at his public library's reading program for children, and his travels, before the age of twenty, have spanned a dozen countries on four continents. Bautista's writings about Filipino identity and social change have appeared in {m}aganda magazine at UC Berkeley and *Alay* at UCSC.

Allen Gaborro

WHY PHILIPPINE HISTORY

It was as a college student that I first found the inspiration to conduct my own in-depth study of Philippine history. After a few fitful first steps and unavoidable diversions, I gradually felt myself reconnecting with my Filipino heritage as I unearthed for myself many of the invisible truths that had been secreted from the mainstream—i.e. colonial—discourse of Philippine history. As a matter of fact, the more I dug, the bigger the countertide of emotions I experienced in realizing how ignorant about the Philippines I had been all this time.

I have pored over resource after resource in my quest to learn about the events, individuals, forces, and ideas that have shaped the Philippines. This quest will never come to an end, for there is so much to discover and resolve about Philippine history, contrary to what many Filipinos, both in America and in the home country, believe. The moment I tell myself that I have learned everything there is to learn about Philippine history will be the same moment that I place myself in the long queue of Filipinos who have chosen to put the past behind them, thinking that it is of no practical value to them in today's hyperactive era of technological advances and unbridled consumerism.

A Filipino American friend of mine observed in a discussion I had with him about Philippine history that Filipino Americans from wide sections of society question the need to improve their knowledge of Philippine history. They after all, as my friend sagely pointed out, have already achieved the American Dream and have therefore taken an indifferent, if not unreceptive, attitude towards understanding their homeland's history. As he put it, "They have a nice job, a nice house, a nice car, and their kids are getting the best education. So they ask themselves, *Philippine history? What for?*"

When mentioning the subject of Philippine history among Filipinos, the run of the mill questions come cascading out of their mouths: How can you make any money from learning about Philippine history? Will it ever be as fun as watching American Idol or Dancing With the Stars or Eat Bulaga or Wowowee or watching Manny Pacquiao beat someone's brains out? Why should I care about things that happened a long time ago?

About a year ago, my family and I were spending Thanksgiving at our uncle's house in Pittsburg, California. At that gathering, I began a conversation with my Filipino American niece, who was studying as a freshman at San Francisco State University. Knowing that the school offered some respectable Philippine courses, I was curious to find out if my niece was taking any classes on Philippine studies. Before she could answer, my older cousin contemptuously interjected that "Don't waste your time. You won't get anything out of studying the Philippines. Filipinos are screwed up. You're an American aren't you? So study American subjects."

I wasn't sure what he meant exactly by "American subjects," but my cousin, because he was born and raised in the Philippines, was confident that he knew what he was talking about and insisted that my niece listen to him. Just for good measure, my cousin added that he refused to teach his children any Tagalog whatsoever. It was a useless language he told my niece, "Why don't you study French? It sounds nicer."

Not only was I appalled by my cousin's attitude, I was also disaffected by his subconscious expression of what can be called the "colonial mentality." It is a man-made affliction that has alienated Filipinos' collective connection from their cultural traditions and historical past and rationalized in their minds America's colonial and neocolonial domination of the Philippines. It is a perception that paints any Filipino perspective as potentially inferior against the backdrop of a presumably superior American ethos.

The effort to articulate a more authentic Filipino identity has been undermined by the colonial mentality. Philippine history, with all of its triumphs and tragedies and everything else in between, is a pillar of that precious identity without which Filipinos wouldn't be Filipinos. That singular identity sustains Filipinos' social and psychological bearings and affirms their indisputable place in the global community of nations, cultures, and people.

However, against the backdrop of the colonial mentality, there is both a subliminal and conscious push and pull tendency among far too many Filipinos to act and to think as white America does. In more extreme cases, this involves the familiar "coconut" syndrome: brown on the outside, white on the inside. There is simply no room, nor any aspiration, for a more comprehensive understanding of the Philippine past in this context.

Filipinos and Filipino Americans should be made aware that they have a great deal of cultural and historical capital to draw on. The Philippine historical tradition is rich with indelible narratives that together create a sort of shared parable not only about where Filipinos have been, but where they are now and where they could be headed in the future. By reorienting themselves to the past, without losing touch with the present and the future, Filipinos and Filipino Americans can recast their common identity in a more autonomous light and convey to self-hating, cultural naysayers such as my misguided cousin an important message: if only they knew what they have been missing.

※

ᴄ**Allen Gaborro** is a resident art and book reviewer for the San Francisco-based Philippine News weekly. As a freelance writer, Allen has composed articles on Philippine history, culture, and politics. He is currently working on a manuscript for a novel about the Philippines.

Antonio K. Joaquin

HEADLINE: TO REACH THE UNREACHABLE STAR

Tribute to a Filipino hero — Jose W. Diokno
on his Feb. 26th death anniversary.

The two men, unusually well dressed in dark suits in a typically warm Manila evening, were ushered into the lobby of the house by the maid. They asked to see the American master of the house. The maid motioned them to take a seat in the plush receiving room in Dasmariñas Village, Manila. They smiled but remained standing.

Inside were men playing poker.

Upon learning of the guests, the American, cigar in hand and apparently affected by whisky in his masterly voice, ordered the maid to escort the two men into their poker room where the players were all Filipinos of stature — from the upper level of government, and private Philippine business.

Smartly in their suits, the men appeared and stopped a few feet from where the men were enjoying their poker game.

"What can I do for you, gentlemen? Asked the American as he took a puff from his cigar.

"Mr. Stonehill," stated one who was probably a senior of the two in rank, "We came to arrest you and we have the warrant with us."

Taken aback, he guffawed while the others echoed his forced laughter.

"Who sent you? Pepe? " asked the American. Summarily, Stonehilll ordered his secretary to phone Pepe Diokno, Secretary of Justice and added, "use his direct line!"

The other man hastily interrupted. "Sir, Secretary Diokno issued the warrant of arrest."

Silence.

"Sir, you are under arrest and you must come with us this minute. Please dress up quickly."

Before too long, with complete and obvious puzzlement in the American's face, drained of blood, unable to utter anything, he disappeared to change into his street clothes. The two men led out Harry Stonehill before his surprised guests—politicians, law enforcement officers, businessmen, wheeler dealers all—out of the house and into detention at the NBI office on Taft Avenue.

That was the last time Harry Stonehill ever saw his residence. Soon after, Harry Stonehill was deported and declared persona non grata by the Philippine Government. He never came back to the Philippines up to his death sometime in the late nineties. For many years after WWII, the seeds of corruption had begun to grow permeating the middle and upper echelons of Philippine Society. Stonehill, ever the shrewd, sharp Jewish businessman, knew how to handle the Filipino businessmen and government officials. In no time at all, Stonehill had diversified his operations in the Philippines to glass, cotton, oil, insurance, newspaper publishing, cement, real estate, land reclamation, all of which resulted in a multimillion dollar conglomerate with property in eight countries and a personal fortune of over $50 million. Like Ferdinand Marcos who early in his political life knew the weakness of fellow politicians, Stonehill had virtually most powerful government officials in the Senate, Justice Department and the business sector "in his pocket." Except one—Jose Wright Diokno. As a matter of fact, many of the sad value systems that ruled crooked politicians then still prevail in the Philippines of today. "You can get anything you want in the Philippines...anything...if you know who to see" still rings true, sad to say.

Harry Stonehill was a young American Army lieutenant who saw the vast possibilities in the Manila of 1945. Following his discharge he dumped his American wife and child and returned to Manila alone. Together with Marcos, both found common interests and value systems but became silent partners.

His job was to introduce bright-leaf tobacco cultivation to the Ilocos—Marcos' home province. In 1950 Stonehill linked with another partner in the person of Peter Lim, a member of the Chinese Chamber of Commerce in the Philippines. Their gimmick was to buy cheap inferior tobacco and sell it to the Philippine government at bright-leaf prices. Soon the tobacco monopoly found itself with a lot of high-priced trash. Many cigarette manufacturers in the Philippines lost their leverage and had to close down. Stonehill's profits were smuggled out through devious channels to secret numbered accounts in Switzerland.

Once, Harry Stonehill was overheard saying that he can do anything that he wanted by hook or by crook because "Every one has a price..." He was right. But in those dark days, there still were virtuous men in the government, and one of the prominent ones who was not "in Stonehill's pocket" was named JOSE WRIGHT DIOKNO, who as Secretary of Justice, and even among Stonehill's' acquaintances, had to do his duty. And he had to enforce the law..

Jose W. Diokno, or "Ka Pepe," as he was popularly known, was born on February 26, 1922 to Ramon Diokno, a former associate justice of the Supreme Court, and Eleanor Wright, an American who became a Filipino citizen. He graduated from elementary school with distinction, and finished his secondary education at De La Salle College as valedictorian in 1937. In 1940, he earned his Bachelor's Degree in Commerce, *summa cum laude,* also at La Salle. He topped the CPA board examination in the same year with a rating of 81.18 percent. In 1944, without finishing his Bachelor of Laws degree, he took and topped the bar examination, with a rating of 95.3 percent. In 1961, President *Doodad* [Diosdado] Macapagal appointed him Secretary of Justice. Diokno believed in the sacredness and dignity of the human personality. Diokno was again voted outstanding senator in 1969 and 1970, thus earning the distinction of being the only senator so honored for four consecutive years beginning in 1967.

At that time, President Marcos was bending towards dictatorship in preparation for the declaration of martial law. Diokno, seeing the increase in human rights violations in the Marcos regime, bolted from the Nacionalista Party in the early part of 1972. His crusade for human rights so irked Marcos that, when martial law was finally declared on September 21, he was the first member of the opposition to be arrested. He was imprisoned without any charges being filed against him. Upon his release in 1974, Diokno immediately organized the Free Legal Assistance Group, which gave free legal services to the victims of military oppression under martial law.

After the EDSA Revolution, President Corazon C. Aquino appointed him chairman of the Presidential Committee on Human Rights, with the rank of minister and chairman of the government panel which tried to negotiate for the return of rebel forces to the folds of the law. However, after the "Mendiola massacre" of January 22, 1987, where 15 farmers died during an otherwise peaceful rally, Diokno resigned from his two government posts in protest of what he called "wanton disregard" of human lives.

From the time he was released from prison in 1974, Diokno fearlessly and with grim determination, fought for the restoration of Philippine democracy. He was a towering figure in opposition rallies denouncing the Marcos regime from 1974 up to the "EDSA Revolution" in February 1986. During the incarceration of Ninoy Aquino, Diokno was in constant contact with him through Mrs. Aquino, who acted as confidante of the two foremost oppositionists of the Marcos regime.

At 2:40 a.m., on February 26, 1987, Diokno died on the same date he was born. The cause of his death was "acute respiratory failure due to cancer." Diokno was married to the former Carmen Icasiano, by whom he had 10 children: Carmen Leonor, Jose Ramon, Maria de la Paz, Maria Serena, Maria Teresa, Maria Socorro, Jose Miguel, Jose Manuel, Maria Victoria, and Martin Jose.

President Aquino declared March 2-12, 1987 as a period of national mourning for Diokno. During this period, flags of all government buildings and installations throughout the country were flown at half-mast. Expressing her grief over the passing of Diokno, the President said: "Pepe braved the Marcos dictatorship with a dignified and eloquent courage our country will long remember."

Tony Joaquin, starting with an acting role at the age of 11 in the historical Metropolitan Theater during the Japanese Occupation, he went on to appear in Manila radio plays (in English and Tagalog). When TV came to the Philippines, Tony was installed as production manager of a new TV channel—in charge of both live and canned shows.

Pulsating with the genes of a dramatist mother, Sarah and Jazz pianist father, Ping, Tony completed his college at the Ateneo de Manila and taught what he practiced—Mass Communications at the FEU.

Spreading his wings out of the education field—fulltime that is—he set up his own atelier in Makati City, offering public relations, publications management, and industrial training program design and implementation, among other services.

He has written his autobiography, *Simple Glories* (Anvil Publishing, Inc., 2000), and edited his mother's *Of Laughter and Tears* (Carayan Press, 2007). In the twilight of his years, Tony says that he still feels energized to do video productions, drama and more. He is married to Chita Mendoza with whom he has five children. Tony was among the early PAWA members.

Benjamin Pimentel

LEAN ALEJANDRO'S MIDLIFE CRISIS
The short incredible life of a Martial Law Baby

In late 2006, Lean Alejandro got a fresh new look in San Francisco. A group of artists called the Haight Ashbury Muralists had decided it was time to refurbish a 20-year-old mural honoring him and other activist icons of the 1980s. The painting had started to fade, and there were even a few marks of vandalism.

But longtime visitors to the "Educate to Liberate" mural on Masonic Avenue will notice something different in the revised painting. Lean looks like he has started to grow white hair.

No, the artists had not intended to portray an older, Lean, said Jane Norling, one of the members the Haight Ashbury Muralists. The artists had used the original painting as a base. They added white streaks on Lean's head to add depth.

"But it really appears as white hair," she added. "So it adds another dimension—(like) he is forever alive."

It's been 20 years since Lean died. On September 19, 1987, he was shot dead in front of his Quezon City office. He was 27.

Speaking at a memorial in July to mark what would have been Lean's 47th birthday, activist JV Bautista noted that Lean was spared having to endure what many of us of his generation, now in our 40s, are going through or will likely go through: midlife crisis.

Lean will not have to bear with the physical signs of aging, like expanding waistlines or thinning hair, or agonize whether he made the right decisions in his personal and professional life, or whether he has led a meaningful existence. None of that.

Despite his unintentional aging on the San Francisco mural, in the minds of many, he will forever be the young, confident and brilliant activist who led us in the movement against dictatorship. He will forever be the symbol of the Martial Law Babies, as our generation is called.

We were children when Ferdinand Marcos imposed martial law in 1972, and the regime tried to shape us into an obedient army of blind followers. The dictator failed. By the 1980s, the Martial Law Babies were out in the streets, rebelling against the regime, with Lean at the forefront.

He wasn't exactly the epitome of the dashing mass leader. Tall and skinny, he spoke in a high pitched, sometimes shrill, voice. But he was charismatic, and it quickly became evident to those who watched him in action that he was intelligent, passionate and, most important, sincere.

FilAm activist Francis Calpotura, a former UC Berkeley student who founded the League of Filipino Students-USA, recalled the first time he heard Lean speak in Makati in 1984.

"This lanky guy gets on top of a flatbed truck and proceeds to explain to the throng of white collar workers and businessmen, the common cause of students and professionals against the Marcos dictatorship" he said. "I remember saying to myself, 'Not exactly my image of a mass leader, but he's good.'"

Lean defied the stereotype of the rabble rousing, sloganeering student leader. His friend Jojo Abinales said Lean showed how "to be an activist and an intellectual at the same time."

He was a voracious reader, and his interests cut across many fields. Lean was a fan of "Lord of the Rings," and he drew inspiration from the story of a peasant Jewish family that fought tyranny in the film version of the Broadway musical, "Fiddler on the Roof." The day he was killed, he was reading a book by Italian socialist Antonio Gramsci.

Abinales jokingly speculated that Lean would have dealt with his midlife crisis by spending more time in the library or returning to the University of the Philippines campus in Diliman. "He will try to finish what he failed to accomplish as a UP student—to graduate!"

As chairman of the UP Student Council and later secretary general of the Barong Alyansang Makabayan, Lean became a prominent figure at protest rallies at Liwasang Bonifacio and at Mendiola Bridge near the Malacañang Palace. He debated Marcos' allies and lackeys on national television and worked closely with such revered political figures as Senators Pepe Diokno and Lorenzo Tañada, as well as the *trapos* (as we called the traditional politicians) in trying to build a broad political alliance against Marcos.

The Left's heavy handed approach to coalition-building led to a personal crisis for Lean. He became controversial for advocating the boycott of the 1986 presidential election in accordance with the position of the underground left. The boycott campaign caused him nightmares, according to Abinales.

"He became the personification of the boycott position," he said. "Lean was being accused of being a dogmatic and a hardliner, and thus cannot be trusted when it came to coalition building."

Still, after the fall of Marcos, Lean continued to play a high-profile role in the social change movement, and even ran for congress in his hometown of Malabon. He was such an effective advocate for social justice that he apparently was considered a threat by rightwing forces seeking to preserve the old order. They saw the need to have him eliminated.

More than 60,000 people attended his funeral. Many of us honored his memory by naming our children after him.

In San Francisco, which Lean visited several times, news of his death shocked many of his admirers in the FilAm community and the broader activist movement. "Disbelief, disgust," was how Calpotura described how many of them felt.

The Haight Ashbury Muralists led by Miranda Bergman and Jane Norling had just started painting "Educate to Liberate" when Lean was killed. "Moved by Lean's dedication to justice and enraged by his death, we immediately brought him into our mural for the people of San Francisco to know and honor," Norling recalled.

The mural shows arms linked with other activist icons. On his right, is South African leader Winnie Mandela, ex-wife of Nelson

Mandela, and on his left, a Salvadoran mother of a *desaparecido* (disappeared, i.e. abducted). Also in the portrait were Benjamin Linder, the American engineer who was killed by U.S.-backed Contras in Nicaragua, Native American activist Leonard Peltier and the Puerto Rican nationalist Pedro Albizu Campos.

Around their portraits was a tapestry of political images depicting a hodgepodge of causes—from the fight against global hunger and colonialism to the battle for the rights of minorities and the elderly. Beneath Lean's portrait is his famous quote: "The place of honor is the line of fire."

For those of us who knew Lean—former Manila-based activists like myself, and Bay Area based FilAms who took part in the U.S.-based anti-Marcos dictatorship struggle—the mural was a source of pride, a landmark that we eagerly showed to visitors or friends.

The mural also underscored the importance of the FilAm activist movement, especially in San Francisco. The mainstream activist community came to know of Lean because of the Filipino Americans who made them aware of the fight against the Marcos regime, and who took part in and even spearheaded many community battles in the Bay Area, such as the struggle to save the International Hotel where many poor Filipino and Chinese elderly were evicted in 1977.

I wrote about the mural in the San Francisco Chronicle in 2002 to mark the 15th anniversary of Lean's assassination. At that time, I did not know anything about the artists who created it, so it was a pleasant surprise to get an e-mail from Norling.

"I loved remembering the enthusiasm we felt in painting Lean into our mural about liberation then, and today, the reminder of the relevance of public art in the great effort to build a just world."

After I wrote about the refurbished mural in August 2007, artist Nancy Pearson, who was active in Philippine solidarity work in the 1980s and sang Tagalog protest songs at rallies in the U.S. and in the Philippines, wrote me: "I remember that mural well. I'll look forward to going to see it the next time I'm in the Bay Area. Lean with white hair...how about that, aging right along with the rest of us."

Lean's legacy has remained strong in the United States. Calpotura, now a respected community organizer and activist based in Oakland, explained Lean's influence on his life. "The Activist as a Holistic Being—that's what Lean taught me," he said. "It's not enough to excel in activism (know how to explain, agitate, analyze, strategize), but being a good activist means that you model what it means to be a total human being—empathy with the plight of all, study and learn, listen to the truth laden in the stories of ordinary people, cook, wash clothes, and give your last penny to one that needs it more. It's a high standard."

A lot has changed since Lean's death.

The movement he once led went through major upheavals, including a bitter and painful split that at times turned violent. Many of Lean's former comrades, including his widow, Lidy Nacpil, eventually broke with the movement, rejecting what they increasingly saw as undemocratic, even totalitarian, tendencies.

Within the broader Philippine Left, there has been a push to rethink progressive politics based on more inclusive, undogmatic principles, and to de-mythify many of the movement's leaders, past and present. Even Lidy Nacpil appeared to do just that at the memorial for Lean in July. While she paid tribute to her late husband's courage and commitment to social change, she said Lean was nevertheless prone to the same narrow machismo of the typical Pinoy male. He once became upset when Lidy dared to challenge his views in public, she recalled, adding, *"Tao lang siya."* He was also human.

In San Francisco many activists and artists, including Jane Norling, also revisited their views of progressive political movements and the use of power. For it has become clearer that, while any political group calling for armed revolution can claim to represent "the people," that's not always the case. In not a few cases, armed revolutionaries eventually turned into tyrants.

"I firmly believe people have the right to take up arms for self determination as long as its for building justice," Norling said. "It's just that I was naïve about how armed force worked."

The changing view of progressive politics is manifested even in the mural on Masonic Avenue. Not only Lean's hair has changed. He is now seen also linking arms with a new comrade: Wangari Maathai, the Kenyan activist who won the Nobel Peace Prize winner for her work in empowering women, battling corrupt officials and planting millions of trees in ravaged lands in Africa.

The muralists painted Maathai's image over that of Winnie Mandela, who has become a reviled figure to many after she was accused of abusing her position and power during the struggle against apartheid. Norling said the muralists made the change principally because they wanted to honor Maathai—but also because Mandela, as an icon, has become "outdated and complicated."

That Lean did not suffer Winnie Mandela's fate on the mural is heartening for those of us who continue to remember him as a hero. His life and martyrdom remain relevant today. In spite of the changed attitudes and upheavals over the past 20 years, there is no debating that the young man who stood bravely in the line of fire deserves to be on any wall honoring those who fought for justice.

(Earlier versions of this essay were published in
Inquirer.net and *Filipinas* magazine.)

Veteran Bay Area journalist *Benjamin Pimentel* is a technology reporter at MarketWatch from Dow Jones and was a longtime staff writer of the *San Francisco Chronicle*. His book, *UG, An Underground Tale*, about the life of activist Edgar Jopson, was a bestseller in Manila in 2006. His first novel, *Mga Gerilya sa Powell Street* was published this year by Ateneo De Manila University Press. He lives in the East Bay with his wife Mara Torres and their son, Paolo and Anton.

Mga Gerilya sa Powell Street
(Excerpt from B. Pimentel's novel in Tagalog)

1. *Ang Makauwi Nang Buo*

Gaya ng bawat isa sa aming mga tambay sa Powell Street, ang pinakapangarap ni Ciriaco ay ang makauwi nang buo. Iyong nakahiga sa ataul. Nakasuot ng barong Tagalog o naka-Amerikanang may kurbata. Hindi iyong ginawang abo na, tapos e isinaksak sa garapon, kahit gaano pa ito kaganda o kakintab.

Isang araw, buong pagmamalaki niyang sinabi sa amin na siguradong ganoon nga ang mangyayari. Nasa labas kami ng estasyon ng BART sa Powell. Kahit papaano, sabi niya, makakabalik daw siya sa Angeles. Doon siya ibuburol. Makakapag-mahjong sa tabi ng kabaong niya ang mga kapatid niyát kamag-anak. At makakapaginuman habang tumitikim ng sitsaron at sisig ang mga dating kabarkada, o ang sinumang gustong makiramay o makikain.

Habang nagkukuwento, nakapatong ang isang paa niya sa isang bangkong bakal sa maliit na park sa laba ng BART. Nakapatong naman sa tuhod ang kanang braso niya. Suot niya ang lagi niyang suot noong mga araw na iyon. Botas na pangkoboy na gawa sa pekeng balát. Sombrero ng taga-Texas. "Tenggalong," kung tawagin niya. At pekeng *fur coat* na pambabae, kulay puti, at halatang masyadong maliit sa kaniya. Lahat ng ito ay nabili niya sa Salvation Army.

Kung maglakad ka nang ganoon ang suot sa Angeles, malamang mahimatay ka sa init at pawis o mabugbog ng mga siga sa kalye. Pero sa San Francisco, sa kanto ng Powell Street, walang problema. Walang papansin sa iyo. Siyempre, noong una namin siyang nakita na ganoon ang itsura, napatawa kami at kinantiyawan siyang mukhang koboy na bakla. Pero balewala ito kay Ciriaco. Nakitawa pa nga siya. Pobre kaming lahat at isusuot ang anumang mahihingi sa Good Samaritan o mabibili sa Salvation Army. Kahit punit-punit na sweater o, tulad ng lagi kong suot noon, isang *leather jacket* na amoy-kubeta.

Mayabang si Ciriaco, pero yabang na hindi nakakainis. Katuwaan pa nga namin ang pagiging mahangin niya. Naging libangan na namin ang isupalpal sa kaniya ang mga pagbibida niya. At pati siya e sumasali sa biro.

Itinuwid ni Ciriaco ang kaniyang tenggalong. "Kahit anong mangyari, Pare," sabi niya, "makakauwi ako at doon ako sa atin lalamunin ng mga uod. Mas gutom yata ang mga uod doon sa atin kaysa rito, kaya doon na ako tutulong sa kanila."

Humalakhak siyang parang matsing. Napatawa rin kami ni Ruben.

"E paano ka makasisigurong mananalo ka sa lotto?" tanong ni Ruben sabay kindat sa akin.

"Oo nga, Tex," sabi ko. Iyon ang tawag namin sa kaniya dahil sa itsura niya. "O baka naman may natisod kang biyudang mayaman na malapit nang mamatay."

"Kayo naman, mga Pare ko. Walang bilib sa akin."

"E paano nga," dagdag ni Ruben." Alam mo ba kung magkano ang magpadala ng bangkay na nasa kabaong sa Maynila? Kulang ang tentawsan dolyar."

"Baka naman ulo mo lang ang ipakakahon mo?"

"Oo nga, Tex. Baka iyong ulong mas maliit para iyon ang iburol."

Sumambulat ang laway ni Ruben sa kakatawa at napasabay kami ni Tex.

"Ay naku, wala kayong bilib." Ibinaba niya ang paa at naupo sa bangko." "Bumili ako ng *life insurance* na pag may mangyari sa akin e babayaran ng kompanya ang pagpapadala ng bangkay ko sa Filipinas. Mura lang, mga Pare. Mga beinte singko lang buwan-buwan. Nasa akin pa ang *calling card* ng ahente. Baka gusto ninyo."

"Beinte singko buwan-buwan?" tanong ni Ruben.

"Malaki na iyon para sa akin," sabi ko.

"Para sa akin din," sabi ni Ruben. "Palibhasa isa lang ang pinapadalhan mo ng pera sa atin kaya kaya mo iyon."

"E para kay Ignacia rin naman ang pambayad ko sa *life insurance*. Napakasakit naman sa kaniya kung ililibing na ako e garapon na lang na puno ng abo ang ibuburol niya."

"Kaya nga dapat e may pamasahe lagi tayo para kung alam mong padating na ang *long distance* mula roonó" tumuro sa langit si Ruben, "makakasakay agad ng eroplano pa-Maynila."

"Kung masuwerte ka at malaman mong padating na nga ang tawag," sabi ni Ciriaco. "E kung abutan ka habang naninilip ng mga tsiks na puti na palabas ng BART?"

Tawanan kaming sabay-sabay.

"O kaya habang nanunundot ng gintong talaba," dagdag ni Ciriaco sabay hampas sa likod ni Ruben. Lalong lumakas ang halakhak namin.

"Inggit lang kayo," sabi ni Ruben na medyo namula ang pisngi. Dahil siguro sa hiya sa biro ni Tex, pero alam kong malamang din e dahil naisip niya ang susunod nilang pagkikita ni Jessica ang nobya niyang *blonde* na mahilig sa maiigsing suot.

"Aruy, aruy, aruy," kanta ni Ciriaco nang may pasayaw-sayaw pa.

"Mga loko kayo. Hindi ninyo ba alam na ang pagiibigan namin e dalisay at walang kupas?" sabi ni Ruben na hindi mapigilan mapangisi.

"Aruy, aruy, aruy," tuloy ni Ciriaco. "Aruy ko po."

Patuloy ang tawanan habang umaapaw ang mga bagong dating mula sa BART station. Humihingal na si Ciriaco noong tumayo si Ruben para magpaalam.

"O sige na, mga ungas."

"O bakit, magkakaskas ka na naman ng gintong mais," hirit pa ni Ciriaco.

"Tang ina mo. Tumigil ka na at baka atakihin ka sa puso diyan e mapaaga pa ang burol ng maliit mong ulo sa Angeles. O sige na."

Tumatawa pa rin kami ni Ciriaco habang pinapanood si Ruben sa eskaleytor na paakyat ng Powell. Kahit malayo e halata sa nginig ng balikat na tumatawa rin siya.

Patuloy ang daloy ng mga tao sa estasyon: mga galing opisina, mga estudyante, mga nanay na hawak ang kamay ng kani-kaniyang mga anak.

"Anong oras mo na, Pare?"

"Alas-otso."

Dumidilim na rin. Sa wakas.

"Uwi na tayo, Pare."

♺

Matagal na kaming naglalakad ni Arnel. Nahiwalay kami sa yunit na-min. Ngayon, nagtatago kami sa mga Hapón. Pero dahil sa pagod, bumag-sak na lang kami sa lupa para matulog. Nasa gitna kami ng isang tubuhan. Madilim na. Mabilis kaming nakatulog. Yakap ko ang riple ko. Pero unti-unti kong naramdamang lumuwag ang kapit ko rito. Tinakpan ng mga ulap ang buwan at bitwin. Nagsimulang umambon. Lumakas ang ulan. Biglang tumindi ang lamig. Maski ang pagod ko, walang laban dito. Nanginig ako. Manipis na diyaket lang ang suot ko. Manipis na pantalon. Tsinelas na upod na. Lumakas ang ulan, tulak ng hangin. Lalo akong nanginig. Nagising ako at lumingon kay Arnel. Mahimbing pa rin siya sa pagtulog. Bakit parang hindi siya giniginaw? Sa tindi ng panginginig, kumiskis at humampas ang mga ka-may at katawan ko sa nakapaligid na mga dahon. Untiunti, lumalakas ang kalasikas dahil sa panginginig ko. Palakas nang palakas hanggang kumalat na sa buong tubuhan. Nilingon ko muli si Arnel. Pero hindi na siya si Arnel. Siya na si Pedring. Mahimbing din ang tulog niya. Paano siya nakakatulog sa lamig at ingay? Sa kabila ng ingay, mas tumitindi pa rin ang ginaw na sumasakal sa buong katawan ko. Gising na gising na ako. Kailangan ko nang gumalaw. Kailangang tumakbo para magpainit. Bumangon ako. Kinuskos ang mga braso. Pero mayroong hindi tama. Tumigil na ako sa panginginig, pero may naririnig pa rin akong kalasikas. Dahan-dahan, tumayo ako. May papalapit sa amin. Dahan-dahang lumalakad sa tubuhan. Doon nanggagal-ing ang mga kaluskos. Nakapalibot na sila. Papalapit nang papalapit. Saan kami tatakas?

♺

"Fidel! Hoy, Fidel."

Pagdilat ko'y una kong nakita ang mukha ni Ruben. Patay ang ilaw pero may kaunting liwanag mula sa neon layt ng Crazy Fog, ang bar sa tabi ng gusali namin.

"Sabi na sa iyong lubayan mo na ang Tabasco, e," sabi niya. "Hayan, hindi makatulog ang tiyan mo kaya binabangungot ka."

Bumangon ako at naupo sa kama. Mga kalahating hakbang lang ang layo ng higaan ko sa higaan ni Ruben.

"Ano naman ang humahabol sa iyo ngayon?" tuloy ni Ruben.

"Ano pa, e di mga Hapón noong panahon ng giyera," sabi ko.

"E, minsan, aso o mga parak doon sa atin ha."

"Napanaginipan ko si Pedring."

Kapatid ni Ruben si Pedring. Sabay-sabay kaming tatlo nina Ruben na sumali sa gerilya noong panahon ng Hapón. Huminga nang malalim si Ruben. Hindi muna siya nagsalita. Ay lintik, mali. Hindi ko na lang dapat sinabi, pero huli na.

"Sori, Pare. Hindi ko na lang dapat sinabi. Sige na, tulog na tayo."

"Hindi, hindi," sabi niya. "Napanaginipan mo noong napatay siya?"

"Hindi. Ewan ko ba. Noong una, siya si Arnel. Tapos naging si Pedring. Nasa gitna kami ng tubuhan, nagtatago. Gabi na. Doon na kami matutulog. Pero sa sobrang ginaw hindi ako makatulog. Nanginig lang ako kaya umingay ang mga tubuhan. Siguro dahil doon, nahanap kami ng mga Hapón."

Hindi ganoon ang nangyari. Minura ko muli ang sarili ko dahil alam kong umuulit sa utak ni Ruben ang eksena kung paano namatay ang kapatid niya. Napasubo kami sa sagupaan sa mga Hapón. Natamaan si Pedring sa dibdib at sa paa. Kitang-kita ko pa siya sa isip ko. Tinedyer na patpatin. Laging sumasama sa kuya niya sa pangingisda at pag-aalaga ng kalabaw. Idolo niya si Ruben kahit madalas namin siyang tuksuhin at pagkatuwaan ng kuya niya. Tapos noong araw na iyon sa gubat, duguan siya, nakasandal sa kuya niya.

"Kuya, natatakot ako," sabi niya.

"Huwag kang magsalita. Ako'ng bahala sa iyo," sagot ni Ruben.

Pero hindi nakatagal si Pedring. Namatay siyang hawak ni Ruben. Patindi na ang labanan. Nagbigay ng komand si Kapitan Olivares na umatras. Pero gustong dalhin ni Ruben ang bangkay.

"Naloloko ka na ba? Kailangan na tayong tumakbo!" sigaw sa kaniya ng kapitan.

"Hindi ko iiwan ang kapatid ko," sabi ni Ruben.

"Ilibing man lang natin."

Itinaas ng kapitan ang kaniyang riple at itinutok kay Ruben.

"Kung hindi ka susunod, papatayin na rin kita. Kasi kung mahuli ka puwedeng pigain sa iyo ng mga Kempetai kung nasaan ang kampo natin."

Lumapit ako at inakbayan si Ruben.

"Sasama na ho siya, Kapitan. Hali na, Pare."

Hindi na pumalag si Ruben. Tumakbo kami paloob ng gubat. Naiwan si Pedring. Hindi na nabura sa utak ko ang imahen ng batang iyon: nakahiga sa tabi ng punó, duguan at madungis. Alam kong hindi rin nakalimutan ni Ruben na iniwan niya ang bangkay ng kapatid niya nang hindi nakalibing. Noong matapos ang giyera, sinubok naming balikan kung saan naiwan si Pedring. Pero hindi na namin nahanap.

Kinuskos ko ang ulo ko.

"Pasensiya na, Pare, ha. Napaalala ko pa sa iyo."

Tinapik niya ako sa balikat. "Wala iyon. Araw-araw ko namang naaalala siya. Paminsan-minsan e binabangungot din ako. Hindi lang nga ako kasing-ingay mo."

Tawanan kami. May biglang kumalabog sa dingding.

"Si Madam Sungit," bulong niya. Tumuro siya sa kapitkuwarto naming biyuda na laging masungit sa amin.

"Alam mo ang nakapagtataka? Sa panaginip ko e halos mamatay ako sa ginaw. E noong dalawang taong nasa bundok tayo, ang naaalala ko e sobrang init at lamok, kahit sa gabi."

Tumayo si Ruben para pumunta sa maliit na mesa na pinagkakainan namin. Narinig ko ang buhos ng tubig.

Inabutan niya ako ng baso. "O, uminom ka o."

"Salamat."

"Baka naman dahil kulang ang suot kaya ka binabangungot.

Naka-sweater na makapal at sombrerong panlamig si Ruben. Tapos magkapatong na *jogging pants* at dalawang pares ng medyas at malalaking glab. Sweater, jogging pants, sombrerong panlamig, at medyas ang suot ko.

"Nanginginig ka, 'ika mo, sa lamig?" sabi niya. "E di dagdagan mo ang suot mong pantulog. Alam mo namang palyado ang *heater* natin."

Minsan parang repridyereytor ang kuwarto namin. Sa sulok e may-roon nang mga lumot—mga mold—dahil laging basâ.

"Kung magdamit ako nang tulad mo e mas lalo akong babangungutin. Paano ka nakakatulog nang balot na balot? Makapal naman iyang komporter mo ha."

"Kulang pa rin. Alam mo namang mahina ako sa lamig. Pati nga ang maupo sa kasilyas e *major operation* sa akin dahil parang umuurong ang etsas ko pag upo sa malamig na upuan. Kaya laging kailangan ng pampainit."

Nagkatinginan kami at sumambulat ang tawa. Pero naudlot ang kasiyahan namin nang may boses na tumagos sa dingding.

"Hoy! Magpatulog kayo."

"Sige na, at baka lumusob na si Madam Sungit," bulong ni Ruben, sabay senyas na matulog na kami.

Sandali lang bago narinig kong humahagok na si Ruben. Pero ayaw pa akong patulugin ng lamig. Inabot ko ang diyaket ko sa paanan ng kama. Sinuot ko ito at sinikap hulihin ang antok.

&

Reprinted, courtesy of the author and publisher, from
Mga Gerilya sa Powell Street by Benjamin Pimentel
Ateneo de Manila University Press
Copyright 2007 by Benjamen Pimentel
and Ateneo de Manila University
www.ateneopress.org

Evangeline Canonizado Buell

THE PAROL: A BAMBOO STAR OF HOPE

President Franklin Delano Roosevelt's voice blared on the radio, declaring war on Japan a day after its attack on Pearl Harbor on December 7, 1941. I felt the tension because of the gravity of the news coming from the grownups around me. I clung to my sister Rosita, as we gathered with our neighbors in the living room, our heads turned in the direction of the radio and the president's somber words.

"We're in for difficult times," our step-grandmother Roberta said to her husband, Manuel Unabia.

"This means Stanley will be going to war," he said. Stanley, my father had just been recalled to active duty in the U.S. Navy and left the month before for retraining in Pensacola, Florida. Rosita and I were still grieving over our wrenching farewell to him. We had huddled and clung together desperately before he boarded and departed on the Southern Pacific train at the old 16th street station in West Oakland. It would be months, then years before we saw him again.

Four months before that, on an August afternoon my mother had been taken away and locked up in Napa State Mental hospital. As the radio blared, my mind wandered back to the sight of the tall dark, gray towers that loomed over the entrance of the hospital when we visited her. I recalled the acrid smell of disinfectant that lingered through the narrow, cold, desolate corridors and clung to my screaming mother. I could still hear the caretaker's keys clanging as he slammed the huge iron doors, leaving Rosita and me with Mama and other people who acted strangely. We were terrified of Mama.

"Will she spank us again? Grandma stay with us," we yelled. "Please don't leave us." we cried.

Uncle turned off the radio jolting me back to our living room and the ensuing silence. President Roosevelt had completed his solemn speech. Then everyone was speaking at once. Grandma kept saying, "It will be a long time before Stanley comes home."

"No. No," I pleaded. "He's coming home soon."

"If there's going to be a war, I hope I don't have to go," Uncle shouted through the chatter. "I don't want to leave my new family."

His "new family" included Rosita and me. Daddy had turned to our step grandmother Roberta and her new husband Manuel Unabia for help after my mother's breakdown. They had been married only a year at the time.

Grandma Roberta was the second wife of my late grandfather Ernest Stokes, an African American who served in the American army in the Philippines in the 1898 Spanish American war and stayed until 1928. He married her shortly after my real grandmother died. Roberta was born in Pampanga, PI, and came to the U.S. with Ernest Stokes in 1928. When he died in 1936, Roberta moved to Salinas, Calif. where she met her new husband in 1940. She wanted us to call her Grandma out of respect for our late Grandfather. She was only 35 years old, a very young Grandma.

Manuel Unabia had been born and raised in Cebu, Philippine Islands, and was recruited to work on the pineapple fields of Hawaii. Then in the late 1930's he was sent to Salinas, California to work in the vegetable farms. During World War II he worked in the Naval Shipyards at Mare Island, Vallejo. We called him Uncle because he said he was too young to be a Grandfather. He was in his late thirties.

When we arrived at their house at ages eight and six years old, Rosita and I were black and blue all over from having been beaten and pinched by our mother. We were near starvation, because we had been locked in our bedroom for six months with only a small amount of crackers, sardines, and tea to eat and drink.

"*Susmariosep!*" What did your mother do to you?" Grandma Roberta said as she looked at us. "*Kay laki ng sakit ang nanay mo. O Dios ko!* How sick your mother is! O my God!" She immediately promised Dad that she would take care of us while he was gone. "I promise never to put a hand on them," she told him as Uncle Manuel stared in disbelief at our physically abused condition. He bent down and hugged us, "Stanley you need not worry about putting them in an orphanage. They can stay with us. Please children don't cry anymore."

After trying to eat dinner, we couldn't because we were too ill from not being fed for a long time, we were immediately put to bed. Grandma carefully undressed us. She gently bathed us and put on our old ragged nightgowns and said, "We will need to get new nightclothes right away." She then tucked Rosita and me side by side into bed and assured us that Daddy would spend the night with us. Then he and Uncle Manuel come in to kiss us good night.

Daddy hugged us saying, "Don't worry, I won't leave you."

"Where is Mamma, Daddy? What happened to her?" I cried.

"Don't worry, Mamma is in the hospital. She'll be okay."

"When will she come home? "

"When she is better. Now you go to sleep. I'll be right here in the next room."

The next day Daddy told us that we would go back to our own house on Magnolia Street to live and grandma and uncle would move in with us. Rosita and I, though confused and emotionally drained, were consoled by our new caring parents. Over the next few months they nursed us back to health. When we arrived Rosita had the measles, and I had impetigo, a painful bacterial disease on my face and head. We began to heal both inside and out, nurtured by the love of Grandma Roberta and Uncle Manuel.

"*Pasko* is coming," "Christmas is coming," Grandma announced one day, soon after President Roosevelt's broadcast. "We must make preparations." Christmas? I remembered my green tricycle and Rosita's red wagon, Christmas presents when I was five. Mama destroyed them in a fit of anger, denouncing Christmas and saying we couldn't have the toys that Daddy had given us.

Grandma interrupted my thoughts: "Evangeline, don't look so sad. Christmas is a special day. Now that I have you and Rosita for my family, the holidays will have more meaning for us."

She and Uncle spent the next two weeks cleaning the house,

which Mama had left a mess. They scoured and mopped, and washed the walls. They cleaned out the closets and took out all the junk. It was a wonderful transformation.

"Evangeline, Rosita how would you like to have a Christmas tree?"

"Really, Really!" We jumped up and down with joy. Perhaps we did have one before, but I could not remember and neither did Rosita. "My gosh, my first Christmas tree, just like the other kids at school." They brought us with them to buy a real Christmas tree. We chose a huge six-foot Douglas fir with flowing symmetrical branches. We were ecstatic as we placed it in its full majesty in the front window of our living room. "Lots of branches to hang ornaments on." Grandma exclaimed.

The next day Grandma invited some friends over for dinner and to help decorate the tree. Manangs (a term of respect for our elders) Rosaria, Agapita, Oping, Maria, Nene and a few manongs (men). Some of the women were widows of American soldiers who had fought in the 1898 Spanish-American War. Most of the manongs were brought over from the Philippines in the 1920s and '30s to work in the farms of California. Many of the manongs were not allowed to marry and have their own families here. Our home was open to them, and they treated us like treasures, as Filipino children were a rarity in those days. We were also the host family for many of the Filipino men who traveled through California from the farms to the Alaskan fish canneries. Discrimination barred them from staying in hotels and eating in restaurants. The manangs and manongs were mainstays of our lives for years, doting on us as their very own.

"*Masuwerte kayo.* You're so lucky to have these kids" Manang Nene said. "*Tutulungan kita*, Berta. We'll help you. The children are ours, too."

We all sat over a table groaning with pancit, chicken and pork adobo, pinakbet, baked fish, rice, vegetables, and salads. I loved it. Rosita and I got to cook the rice and prepare the vegetables. We learned to measure the water with our fingers to make perfect rice. We felt so proud to help the grownups in the kitchen.

They reminisced about Christmas in the Philippines. "We didn't have Christmas trees in my hometown," Uncle said. "It was customary to decorate with parols."

"What's a parol, Uncle?" I asked.

"It's a Christmas lantern in the form of a star made of bamboo and decorated with colored paper," he explained. "Can we have one too?" The other adults said it would be wonderful to have a parol in America, but where would we find one? Uncle proudly said "I'll make it if you help me find the bamboo."

"Yes" they all piped up.

"Will Santa come to our house on Christmas Eve?" we asked Grandma.

"Yes, as long as you believe in his spirit he will always come. There is a Santa in all of us. Some day you will understand what I mean."

Manang Oping said to Grandma in Tagalog, "Berta you and Manuel have a big responsibility taking the children to raise."

"Oo, yes, I want to have them. They are my first husband's grandchildren and their mother is my stepdaughter, so they are mine too. Their grandfather loved them—*Minamahal sila*—when they were babies. I have no other relatives here in America. Just like you, Oping, I left my family behind in the Philippines. Perhaps I will never see them again. Look at the children, they are so well behaved, sweet, and very smart little girls. They are feeling so much better now. I love them already like my own. I'm glad they found me again. We are their guardians while Stanley is in the war overseas."

We watched Uncle as he worked on the parol at night. He whistled and sang as he cut and split the bamboo. The manongs came over in the evenings to help him. They were his friends from Salinas where they worked as farm laborers.

When Christmas Eve arrived we went outside to see the tree lights flood the front window. The tree with beautiful glass fruits, musical instruments, animals and angels hanging from its branches was a welcome, dazzling sight as people passed by. Then with a grand entrance, Uncle brought out the parol. It was a three-dimensional star, six feet tall and four feet wide in blue, green, red and white crepe paper. He placed a green light in the center of the star and hung it in the front window next to the tree. It was awesome! There was no other Christmas decoration like ours in the city of Oakland.

Grandma helped us put on our new dresses for Christmas Eve mass. She braided my sister's curly hair and my long thick straight hair with ribbon bows. Our hair was badly matted and tangled from neglect by my mother. "Oh Grandma! It doesn't hurt anymore when you comb my hair." I exclaimed happily.

"Me too, me too," Rosita chimed in.

She bundled us off to hear Mass. "We'll pray for your mama to get well, and for your daddy to be safe and to come home soon," she told us at church. I cried as we lit the candles for them. I knew they wouldn't be home for Christmas with us.

When we returned home we each got to open one present. We received a new warm, soft nightgown to wear. Rosita wrapped hers around herself, squealing with delight. Then we stood at the front windows to enjoy the tree and the parol.

"The parol is a very special star because it is for my new family. You will be the only children I will ever have.

On Christmas Day, the manongs and manangs joined us for a feast. We gathered around the tree and each one took turns to open gifts. We all exclaimed over the presents and applauded one another."Oh Berta! Oh Children! What a pretty sweater."

Uncle exclaimed, "Thank you, children for my nice, warm slippers! They're the right size!"

It was a joyous day. Christmas wrapping lay in heaps all around the room and our wonderful presents were by our side. Brand new clothes for both of us, and from Santa Claus, roller skates for me! A little red car for Rosita! We could hardly wait to try out our new toys.

"*Maligayang Pasko*, Merry Christmas everybody." Grandma and Uncle said to us.

The kitchen hummed as the manongs and manangs helped prepare dinner. There was roast turkey with Grandma's special oyster dressing, as well as lechon [roast pork] lumpias [egg roll] pancit [noodles], sweet rice cakes and Grandma's lemon pie.

The New Year 1942 came with World War II looming dismally

over all of us. But my sister and I were secure and happy in our new home. The parol, a star brightly shining alone in West Oakland, was left in our front window as a guiding light for daddy and mama to find their way home to us.

From: Twenty-Five Chickens and a Pig for a Bride
(T'Boli Publishing, 2007)

Evangeline Canonizado Buell was born and raised in Oakland, California. She has been president of the East Bay Chapter of FANHS, a board member of the Berkeley Art Center and a member of the Asian Pacific Advisory Council of the Oakland Museum of California. She has written for newsletters, journals, *Filipinas Magazine* and San Francisco Bay Area newspapers. She wass co-editor of *Seven Card Stud with Seven Manangs Wild* (T'Boli Publishing, 2002) and author of *Twenty-Five Chickens and a Pig for a Bride* (T'Boli Publishing, 2007). Vangie lives in Berkeley, California with her husband Bill.

Penélope V. Flores

RUN, EBONY, RUN

*K*uya Pepito's birthday was coming soon. The air had a busy heady scent of surprise. The bodega had been cleared of rubbish. The living room walls had been slapped with a fresh coat of paint. Wispy sheer new curtains peeked at the capiz windowpanes. The scully maid, arms loaded, kept running up and down the stairs. The scrub maid hopped up and down the wooden floor with the *bunot*, the half portion of a coconut shell, cut cross-wise revealing a head of stiff brown bristles. At each worked area, the *narra* planks magically shone to sheen. Clearly, the suspense was worse. The best-kept secrets were most clear to those who were not supposed to know. I couldn't keep up the pretense any longer. It was too much. Something's got to give.

Then that following weekend, May 23rd to be exact, I was awakened by a loud scraping sound, accompanied by voices: "*Hala, bira.*" A burly man wearing a *buntal* hat was barking directions to several *camiseta*-clad men in various modes of tattered shirts. They were coordinating their movements unloading something from a horse-driven *cartanilla*. I noted it had a menacing red arrow sign. It read: THIS SIDE UP ^ in bold letters.

With my torso hanging out of the windowsill, my arm sleeves serving as banners, I spotted the cause of the cacophony of noise. "So, this is the birthday surprise we were all waiting for," I exclaimed, with a heavy tinge of envy in my voice. My brother's birthday present was in a crate carried by four muscularly burly *cargadores*.

Moises, our general man-of-the household service set up his headquarters by the ground floor. Opening the gate door wide to let the cargo in, the men inched to the stairs. They heaved and grunted upon reaching the first floor landing. Then a right turn on to the second floor brought them face to face with my father in the middle of the living room. My mother was holding on to the banisters, her eyes beaming with pride.

Opening the shipment was a huge operation. First, a crowbar piece by piece dismantled the wooden crates. Made of *palo china* or evergreen its dusty fragrance enveloped the entire house. Soon, a box of corrugated cardboard emerged from the crate. With a sharp *bolo* edge, this cardboard gave way to a mass enveloped by jute and fastened by *abaca* twine. It was like a *cine palabas*. The household members came out of the kitchen and dining rooms to watch.

"What a pain. Get on with it," I said to myself. I was so impatient to find out what was inside this enigma. My toddler brother discovered the empty carton boxes and gleefully played with the discard oblivious to the anticipation building up.

The speckled light from the window pervaded the room. The texture of the drawn curtains played eerie shadows on the floor. With her shears, mom dramatically cut off the twines. Down dropped the jute cloth and out came a shimmering *mantón de Manila*. It was a silk embroidered shawl with silky fringes. It was like peeling an onion where each layer exposed the bulb. Finally covering this object was a black shiny ebony console table.

"It's only a table," I observed with waning interest. "Wait! It is a... it's a... PIANO!" I exclaimed in wild excitement as I focused on the surprise. My sister Carrie edged near. "I got to see this first," she announced.

I turned to my mother. "Is it a toy piano?" I asked.

"No, it is a real piano, only smaller. Violins have the adult size, the half size and the three-fourth size versions. This piano here is a three/fourths size of a true regular musical instrument."

Although slightly smaller, the piano was a complete instrument with two pedals, a music sheet pullout, regular hammer and damper mechanisms and had the musicality of up to intermediate level piano pieces. An octave from the top and another octave from the bottom were truncated. Never before had a 3/4th piano been made. This *Lyric* brand piano was specially constructed as a promotional one-of-a-kind. It was built for a young classically trained piano player. It was for window display only and not for sale. I have no idea how my father convinced the store manager to sell it to him. He surely paid the price of a regular upright piano, and a special add-on for being a Young Musician version. It was meant for a child 10 to 12 years old.

"Come over here, Pepito," Dad beckoned *Kuya*—the birthday boy. "Well what do you know? The ivory keys fit your short stubby fingers. Now you can reach your octaves. Go on. Try it out. Play your favorite piece."

Kuya had been taking private piano lessons and had completed *Streabog's Book One.*

"Wow, just right. Look at it swivel. I can adjust it," he exclaimed. He seemed piqued by the mechanics of the piano stool's capacity to be elevated. He was Baby Bear trying the piano stool for size. The piano's knee space ergonomically fit a boy over four feet tall. Because his feet rested flat on the floor, his shoulders naturally relaxed. Carefully he poised his correctly curled fingers over the keys and lightly came down for the beginning phrase of Schumann's "Happy Farmer." What a delightful tumbling little brisk number. Applause, deep bow, smug self-satisfaction.

A standard piano has a keyboard of fifty-two white and thirty-six black keys. This one had thirty-four whites and twenty-six blacks. With easy playability, size of its keys narrowed to about 5 inches long, and less than an inch wide--it could sustain notes beautifully with the damper pedals. The sound was not at all tinny. It carried a rich brightly nuanced, *moderato* voice like Leopoldo Salcedo's baritone. It can play *fortissimo* and *pianissimo* and all the intervals in between like Rogelio de la Rosa and Carmen Rosales in their title roles singing "*Nasaan ka Irog.*"

For days, this piano special edition was the talk of Calapan, Oriental Mindoro. Friends dropped in. Acquaintances multiplied ten-fold. All of a sudden, hordes of people would pass by the house. My friend Aurora called it a "freak," a real piano *wanna be.* Although no one could see it, they knew it was there. The neighbors saw it actually arrive on the scene, like they were witnesses to a birth. With a baby, you don't have to see the infant, but you know it is there by its cries. They did not have to see the baby piano; Kuya essaying "Over the Waves" and "Minuet" could be heard down the street. My brother Pepito continued his private piano lessons. My sister and I started ours. I played my scales and exercises daily because of the novelty piano. Mr. Jareño, the music teacher, reported our amazing progress to our parents.

Once, Kuya thought he could dismantle the instrument. It was peanuts. Putting it back required stamina and persistence. But he did it. Maybe the tinkering had an effect because the piano sounded brilliant According to Carrie, it was "a *kumpuni* job" a local term for "repair."

Virginia, a classmate, complimented my sister. "Carrie, you are so smart; you can read music," she said. My sister acknowledged her with a nod and a knowing smile. Then outside of her hearing distance she turned to me and said:

"Whenever Mr. Jareño gives me piano lessons, he sings out the notes: "Mi mi sol, mi mi do." So I really didn't have to read the music. I just listened to him sing the notes. I played by *oido* [by ear]. That's how I learned to play," Carrie said with pride. She sure fooled my mother because mom made a special trip to Manila and purchased two music books: *The Children's Music Series the Whole World Plays*, and *Opera for the Young*. My mother, she was unreal.

Then World War II broke out and our peaceful bucolic and pastoral life changed. During the Japanese occupation of the Philippines, my family was forced to move a lot. My parents were on the Japanese "Wanted" list, and we were always on the go, always just a day ahead of the Japanese patrol that was out to get my father (a guerilla sympathizer). Off and on, we evaded the Japanese: to the mountains of Pasi in Pola, off to Biga, back at Kilometro Once (Eleven), on to the meadows at Cuatro (Kilometer 4), through the back west entry to downtown Calapan near Adriatico Elementary Farm school, at the house opposite the town square and to our domicile house on San Vicente street.

The piano accompanied the family wherever we went. It was borne up on the shoulders of two muscularly built *cargadores* to whenever and wherever it was time to move. Mom would wrap it in banig, the woven mat *pandan* kind, which is soft and not scratchy. While everyone walked, this piano was carried on a large reed hammock.

A spectacular event defined our trips. Guerilla groups traveled incognito while my mother's idea of evading the enemy was creating a public spectacle. Village farmers lined up the village dikes admiring this piece of furniture. A retinue followed our camp wherever we hid. At Biga, (Kilometro 17 interior) our log house had a platform of wooden planks, not logs, for the baby piano.

In the middle of the war, at Village Cuatro, people organized little moonlight parties. Kuya and I had learned simple waltzes, polkas and *kundimans*. The young men bravely put on their shoes, which for the most part of the year remained, tucked away in their local woven suitcase *tampipis*. The young ladies lost their shyness and danced with them. I learned to play bass (pah ump pah pah) while Kuya played the melody line of current song hits. Together we played mostly American pop songs: "Paper Moon," "Over There," "Danny Boy," which we heard over the ham radio. The villagers danced till morning, courtesy of our music and then proceeded to the fields at break of dawn to plow the field,

Lalud village had a modest asphalt road. On our way there my mother hired a carabao cart. The piano sat on the cart while my cousin Eli, who taught himself piano, played such jaunty cowboy pieces like "Deep in the Heart of Texas," "Vaya con Dios," and "Adiós Muchachos." As the cart rolled along, I remembered a motley ragged scene! The mad piano player of Calapan had attracted a following.

"The Japanese will see us." I cried in despair. But the townspeople and the village farmers enjoyed having a respite from hard labor and couldn't care less. Here was a built-in entertainment system, free of charge.

Never before had the word *evacuate* (locally pronounced *bakwet*) turn tragic-comic. We were running away from Japanese control but we can easily be traced. When it was time for another *bakwet*, none of our belongings were packed. But the piano made it. Everyone knew where we were, the direction we were going and the location where we would hide. This piano created such a buzz. It actually announced our whereabouts negating traveling in disguise. The Japanese patrol sergeant must have admired my mother's spunk. He strategically allowed her just a walking day headstart. What a farce! Our *bakweting* trips gained a phrase: *Heto Na!* (Here it comes.)

These peripatetic moves with the piano were taking its toll. It was rumored that I developed a serious mental condition. Like a *loca-loca*, I had been seen and heard talking to myself. My only constant friend was the piano. I talked to her often. When I was in a good mood, I would call her "Whitie" from the ivory keys. Otherwise, she was "Ebony" because of her rich black ebony finish.

"How do you feel? Are you tired of *bakweting* like me? It's always run, Ebony, run. Didn't you wish you could play some modern pieces? And with real sheet music instead of the copies scratched out on brown butcher paper available for sale? Aren't your sides and top bruised and scratched with all that jostling around in the hammock? Don't you abhor the smell of those sweaty porters? How do you find the smell of fresh carabao dung splashing in the middle of the road? What about the grubby hands of curiosity seekers? They press and depress your keys. Wouldn't you want to give them a kick with your foot pedals? Wouldn't you wish this war would end? Then I could get me new clothes with lace-trimmed collars, and long sleeved dresses with cuff buttons."

Every single day as I practiced my pieces and murmur; "Little Ebony," when will you grow up?"

Kuya had already outgrown the piano. My sister and I were quickly outgrowing it too. I began dreaming of playing on a full-grown upright. But the Japanese Occupation made it hard for many to live normally, let alone comfortably. Meanwhile my baby brother had reached up to the ivory keys with his sticky index finger and could play the first phrase of "Jingle Bells: *mi mi mi; mi mi mi.*"

The war years were painfully dragging on. "When will this terrible war end?" I cried as I pounded the piano keys.

⁊

Far Above Cayuga's Waters

"*I* always felt an occasional down-time in college—a certain gentle melancholy of quiet presence. So did Dwayne, my dorm roommate. Maybe it's a congenital disease among college freshmen. I'm glad I'm home," Norman told me.

Norman had spent an entire year doing things on his own and the corresponding responsibility for making tough college decisions. His face had become tanned by exposure to the bright glare of up-state New York's harsh winter in the open large campus.

He sauntered in with a streak of confidence and self-assurance. What a change two semesters of undergraduate Cornell university units made in a person! What were most impressive about him are his boyish good looks, his openness, and his interest in learning everything. Moreover, he had become more curious about our family history back in the home country.

Having earned high grades to land him among the first ten percent of his senior class at Kenwood Academy, Hyde Park, Chicago, Norman applied to several colleges and universities across the country. The University of Wisconsin, University of Illinois, Cornell University, University of Pennsylvania and University of Chicago admitted him.

My preference was the University of Chicago. "You can save on dormitory fees," I advised him. "You can just walk to the library and into your classes."

However, the idea of flying out to a campus located as far as possible from his meddling mother clinched the deal. "It's not just an escape, Mom," he insisted. "It's what I can do with life change—mine."

The following morning, I heard his slippers slowly shuffle to the kitchen. He reached to the top shelf cabinet and got the pancake mix.

This is the type where you mix plain water and presto, a golden brown pancake is ready. This behavior is the by-product of a son's independence as a function of having emptied a parent's nest. As he flipped his pancake, he sang the first line of a Cornell freshman college song:

"Far above Cayuga's waters...with its waves of blue,"

It is the tradition in the university town of Ithaca, up-state New York, that at the football match's half time, all freshmen on the stands are expected to race across the entire field and run as if the bulls of Pamplona were programmed to gore the greenest and freshest butt in the whole campus. The more the freshmen cohort actively took part in this ritual, the more likely the home team was expected to win. On many occasions, the uncaring and stubbornly heavy-footed freshmen had been severely blamed for Cornell's narrow loss against Brown.

Norman's baritone voice filled the kitchen. His membership at the Chicago Children's Choir gave justice to the college song hit. Then, out of nowhere came a gravely but clear riposte:

"Stands our noble alma mater...Glorious to view."

Norman and I looked at each other with stunned silence. Grandma Villarica was the sort of person who was practical in all situations where most people were sentimental. She was the sort of mother who returned letters from her offsprings writing from college with red corrections marks and marginal comments on grammar and punctuation. She was the sort who would raise her voice in answer to a hymnal response during Sunday's high mass, as she just did a minute ago.

"Lola, how did you learn that song?" Norman asked in wonderment.

"Mr. Johnson taught that to us at San Isidro High School in Nueva Écija, Philippines," my mother replied matter-of-factly.

"I attended the provincial high school where our teacher arrived from America. I was among the few original female students taught by the Thomasites," she continued to explain.

"But Lola, that's our Cornell college song," Norman said emphatically.

"No, no, *hijo*. That's our high school cheering song," she insisted.

The grandmother/grandson tandem burst out in lively duet. Their voices wafted over the steaming pancakes. However, while Norman's lyrics were "Cayuga's waters," my mother sang "Pampanga's waters."

"Lift the chorus...Speed it onward..."

"What a nice interesting coincidence. I bet Mr. Johnson went to Cornell," I remarked.

"You really think so?" Norman noted in surprise.

Sure enough. A quick reference from my library indicated that the first American teachers to the Philippines in 1901 came from several universities and colleges. Among the institutions that contributed to the Thomasite teaching pool was Cornell University. The original American teachers were increased until 1927 when the entire public school system was taught entirely by trained Filipinos who studied under the Thomasites.

"Does Thomasite mean the teaching orientation was held at Santo Tomás University?" Norman was curious. Santo Tomás of course, is the oldest university in the Philippines, founded by the Dominicans in the late 1500. It had a prestigious education department.

"Nothing like that. There was this Philippine Commission that established a public school system all over the Philippines. They recruited teachers from the US to teach English in the newly opened Philippine schools. Those pioneer teachers—540 strong—arrived on the US Army transport, USS Thomas. These American teachers were deployed to the various provinces," my mother lectured. She was in her comfort zone. After all, she was a college professor at a private college in the Philippines.

"Lola, my sense is this. From the USS Thomas, they were called *Thomasites*. Had the transport ship been named USS Para, then I suppose your teachers would have been called *Parasites*," he chuckled, so full of himself.

"Norman José Flores Villarica, don't be impertinent," my mother gently reprimanded him. "This is no joke."

I knew that when my mother uttered out your full four-name patronymics you're in for a lot of trouble. However, they both enjoyed the exchange and laughed together. I could feel a three-generational bonding going on. My mother never talked about her reminiscences of her early school days. That was because in her vanity, she hid the fact she was born during President McKinley's time when the administration of the Philippines passed from Spain to the US. That period was at the cusp of the introduction of mass public education to the Filipinos under the tutelage of the Thomasite teachers.

No one was interested in her schooling history. That was ancient history. Nor was I interested in her colonial experience. Here, finally, my mother found a captive audience—this Cornell smart-ass freshman who, having been raised in the US knew *nada* about Philippine history.

Admission practices/Rizal associations

My mother picked up her crochet bag, sat on her favorite armchair took out her half-finished doily, and worked on it without dropping a stitch. She began:

"Admission was through personal references and a strong record of having gone successfully through the public elementary school system taught in English. My uncle, Señor Juan Parungao, an educated town functionary, recommended me to the high school principal."

"Marcela is smart and very intelligent," he proudly reported.

"Juan Parungao and José Rizal, the Philippine national hero, were classmates at San Juan de Letrán in Manila. During their Letran student days, Rizal would be Uncle Juan's guest at the Gapan town fiesta celebration. May 1st was the feast day of the *Divina Pastora*. The farmers came to town bringing fresh produce. Carabao led carts festooned the streets. Gaiety reigned. In the evenings Rizal and the *binatillos* participated in the town square paseo, a good excuse for girl-watching."

"Uncle Juan was the town eccentric. He always wore a white *cerrada* suit (jacket with a high collar). If he were not writing poetry, composing music, whittling wood, constructing musical instruments from bamboo, and acting the general factotum that he was, he would be assigning ridiculous nicknames to the neighborhood kids: *Rubentusin for Ruben, Kalembang for Evangeline.*

Needless to say, those name labels stuck into adulthood to the recipients' agony and dismay.

"Another student was José Villarica Viola. He came highly recommended by his uncle, Dr. Máximo Viola of San Miguel de Mayumo, Bulacan, the next town from Gapan. The *médico* carried himself with great seriousness and dignity expected of a Spanish mestizo. He seemed to be forever washing his hands with Lysol. He smelled like an itinerant hospital ward." Dr. Viola said of his nephew:

"José is a nice, moral, upright lad and shows great promise."

"Máximo Viola studied medicine at the University of Barcelona. Whenever José Rizal visited this Catalan city by the Mediterranean, or was either on his way to Paris and Europe he would stay with his friend Viola who had a 3rd floor ritzy apartment on Calle Vergara. José Rizal started writing *Noli me Tangere* in Madrid. His money had been depleted when the manuscript was ready for publication. His monthly remittances from Calamba had oftentimes been delayed. He despaired of not having the novel published. Máximo Viola offered Rizal the three hundred pesetas needed to have the Noli manuscript printed but Rizal declined. Viola insisted, and Rizal accepted only if it was considered a loan. Months later when Rizal's money arrived, his friend Viola refused the repayment. Instead, the two friends—now armed with their brand new medical degrees earned in 1887—spent it on traveling throughout Europe."

"Hah Sim was an affluent Chinese merchant. He owned the biggest rice mill in Gapan, our hometown. He also had established general stores in several urban areas including Dapitan, where José Rizal was exiled. Rizal, in his letters to his family, complained about Sim's propensity to monopolize the Dapitan market to jack up prices. This was how Sim recommended his son to the public school officials."

"Behold, he will cheat with whomsoever he hath dealings with, from Pasig to San Fernando River. Of course, he takes after me, a charming swindler and a most exquisite liar."

Norman perked up. "Lola, be careful what you say in this society. I know you're not racist, but it can sound so to others. Can you back this up with a direct quote? You don't want to be politically incorrect."

"Thank you, Norman. Yes, I should be careful in my stories. Rizal, in his *Epistolarios* and letters to his sister Soledad, complained about being swindled for the price of a pair of socks and vowed not to buy from Sim because he was a liar...you know, as my story goes. No offense but in the context of those times, smart business meant taking advantage of the ignorant buyer and buyer beware practices. The Chinese were mainly the businessmen."

"To go back to my story: there was equity in the admission. The sons and daughters of farmers, merchant classes, town functionaries and the elite *ilustrados* had the same equal opportunity and access to the American universal public education."

"Also for the first time, unlike in the previous Spanish schools, we had a coed school. In the past the girls had a different school with a home arts curriculum and the boys had a separate school with an academic curriculum. Now, content-wise, we had equal footing with the boys, especially in the college prep core subjects in high school such as biology, chemistry, physics, geometry and calculus."

MARCELA DAYAO VILLARICA'S PERSONAL EXPERIENCE AS A THOMASITE STUDENT

"Our American teachers were amazed at the progress of our education and academic achievement taught in English. However, they were dismayed with our pronunciation. Our daily lessons always began with tongue twisters as exercises. Untrained tongues, especially those coming from the rural areas constantly interchanged their "e's" and "i's", and their "o's" and "u's.""

"Peter Piper picked a peck of pickled peppers" came out as
"Peetir Paper pecked a pick of peckold peeppirs."

"We drove those Thomasites close to insanity. All except Mr. Johnson, who sat with his shoes impolitely propped up on the desk, and who threw his tousled blond mane back roaring with laughter like a lion at our brave attempts in English. He always had a funny bone, that's why we loved this tall lanky teacher. Once he barked: "Answer me," although no question was asked."

"On one occasion, in our Arithmetic class, just to tell Mr. Johnson off, I overcompensated for the inaccurate claim that I could not say "f" properly. So I interchanged the p's and f's. Who said we didn't have "f" in the Filipino alphabet? Listen to this:

"Fedro had pifty fencils and sold hap of them at two centabos each. How much fesos did Juan fay for twenty-pibe fencils? How many fencils did Fedro habe lept?"

"Every English lesson revealed a new place for us to visit, bargains for us to find, stories for us to tell. Mr. Johnson's teaching showmanship was amazing. He was not like any of my old teachers of the *cartilla* method. There in the old school, I sang every syllable of the alphabet all day long. I was not used to this American Thomasite way of conducting a class."

Cartilla, is that a small cart, Lola?"

"Close. It was a small chart where we learned the phonetic method of reading by rote memory with nonsensical combinations of syllables."

"Uh-uh. That's no help."

"OK, the chart starts with *a-e-i-o-u*. Then a consonant is added:
Ba-be-bi-bo-bu.
Ka-ke-ki-ko-ku.
Da-de-di-do-du.

You go down the *Abakada* alphabet until you get down to the last consonant:
ya-ye-yi-yo-yu."

"Lola, lemme get this straight. You were taught in the Filipino language, right? "

"Certainly not. The American policy was to introduce English in all Philippine schools as the language of instruction. It was outrageous in the beginning. We spoke Tagalog at home, and Spanish was still the language of higher education. But there was definitely a change in the whole educational system. English was made the tool for learning at all levels, from first grade to high school and on to college."

"So, you took it without complaining, Lola? It seems strange to be such docile fools."

"Well, we were stupid fools alright, and we did complain a lot, but we truly believed their propaganda that learning English would open many doors of opportunity. We learned English diligently. All of a sudden our *cartilla* reading skills became obsolete. You see, English is not a phonetic language. Mr. Johnson introduced whole word recognition:

> *Autograph, polygraph; bake, cake, rake, take.*
> *Could, would, should; pasture, capture, rupture.*

"Then something unexpectedly intriguing happened. The more we resisted, the more we learned. The reason was this: Mr. Johnson asked us to teach him some Filipino proverbs and riddles. It worked because we would ask for the English word equivalents. Truth is, we taught ourselves how to learn."

> *Riddle: Isang bayabas, pito ang butas. (One guava, seven holes.)*
> *Answer: A face.*

"We didn't have any textbooks or paper supplies. One day, Mr. Johnson asked Lorenzo, a farmer's son, ways in which we could use some paper substitute so we could write our own text. He suggested banana leaves."

"At the next session, we came loaded with banana leaves. No, not the spread-out kind that you see proudly waving on banana trees. It was the rolled kind found unopened neatly tucked inside the trunk, getting ready to unfold within a day or two."

"We gingerly spread it out, treated every single leaf on an open fire coal, and made it supple and flexible. Then we cut, folded and bound each one neatly into booklets. It was easy to use a pointed stick as a pen and we wrote English translations of Philippine proverbs and special verse translations of the old Tagalog popular epic poem *Florante at Laura* written by Francisco Balagtas."

"The use of banana leaves for writing paper was not a new thing in the Philippines for it might be recalled that the ancient Filipinos used to write their extant script *Baybayin* on bamboo and banana leaves. We taught him something he did not know."

"Mr. Johnson was so delighted with our book project that he journeyed to Manila and talked to Mr. Barrows, the Director of Public Instruction:

*"Do you think it would be a good idea to send these banana
leaf copybooks to the United States and ask the American students to send to their Filipino counterparts some paper books and
other kinds of books needed by the people of Nueva Écija?"*

"He got the Bureau of Education's approval. Then he sent our banana leaf books to the School Superintendent of Cayuga Unified High
School District, New York. Mr. Johnson taught there before going
to the Philippines. He pressed the right button. The Cayuga School
District distributed the copybooks among the people of Ithaca, New
York. Soon big wooden crates and boxes arrived full of books. We had
a bonanza. Those boxes of books were the real peacemakers. Remember we were in the midst of the Philippine-American War."

"Well, I can personally attest to the hospitality of the Ithaca community at Cornell," Norman interjects. "If they could accommodate
the crazy antics of university students, they surely could accommodate the Filipino's need for serious education."

"I got my hands on textbooks in algebra, geometry and physics. It
was a bit advanced for me, but this started my love affair with becoming a trained and certified mathematics teacher."

"José Villarica got hold of the first edition of *The Merck Manual* a
handbook aimed at supporting medical education and practice. It was
leather bound and looked heavily used. It was dictionary-like, with
clinical descriptions of diseases arranged alphabetically, their symp-
toms, and common ways to treat them. This volume started your
grandfather on to the road of becoming a physician."

"We got many books about foreign, strange and confusing ideas. I
had no idea what a *ski* was. Was it pronounced *skee* or *sky*? I had absolutely no concept of snow, yet many stories talked about throwing
snowballs. In the illustrations, snow looked much like white refined
sugar. Well, I thought, how can I form balls out of sugar? Wouldn't it
pour off between my fingers?"

"Most of the books were not adapted to Philippine schools. However, I loved reading *The Song of Hiawatha* by Longfellow. I really identified with the American-Indian *Minehaha and the laughing waters*."

"Be that as it may, another important consequence of these banana copybooks was the fact that José Villarica inscribed 24 stanzas of a direct translation into English of Florante at Laura."

At this juncture, my mother gave a pregnant pause. She wiped her wire-rimmed eyeglasses with the sleeves of her blouse. I could see that she was wading through her stream of memory with an emotional staff. It was clear she was moving fast forward several decades with her Thomasite story. Suddenly I noted a shift in her story telling, the narrator changed from an individual perspective to a spouse and partner perspective.

"As we led our lives and practiced our professions, both of us were compelled to go back to that high school English assignment of translating the *Florante at Laura*. It became a family obsession. A boy in the family born during the project was named Florante, a reminder for us to get the book done. Finally after a lot of red Stops and yellow Waits and green Go's, in 1940, we completed the English version, a parallel line-by-line translation of the whole epic poem. Then WWII broke out. Everything came to a halt."

She rummaged through her crocheting bag for a trimmer. She had actually finished the lace doily during this session. Eyeing it carefully, she flattened the doily on the table. My mother makes those doilies everyday. My living room has doilies. Lots and lots, as head rests, pillow throws, napkins, towels, you name it. It's like one has entered doily heaven. While admiring her lace work, she turned to Norman and noted that he had pooped out. His head lay across the back of the sofa with the pale green lace, his mouth open.

"Norman," she nudged him. "Bear this in mind."

"Your grandfather was the first Filipino to publish an English translation of the famous Balagtas epic poem. The first edition came out in 1948. The following year, when I included some study guides and comprehension questions, the book was adopted by the Philippine Educational school system."

"After WWII, the high school curriculum required the teaching of the Pilipino language as a single subject. The text used was your grandfather's translation. It served as a venue for learning from the regional languages to Tagalog with English as the mediating language. You find it strange?"

"At that time, there were about 200 languages and dialects in the whole archipelago. There was no national language where the people could use to communicate with each other. Of course there were regional languages.

"Are these Ilocano, Visayan and Tagalog?" Norman rubbed his eyes. He knew of these because Tagalog is offered as a foreign language in the Liberal Arts program at Cornell.

"Yes, indeed. When the Americans introduced English in all public schools, a language interface was created. English became that bridge where Tagalog-based Pilipino evolved as a national language. There was a strong regional linguistic transference. The Villarica text with an English line-by-line parallel translation played an integral part in binding the Filipino people together with one language of communication. Several students of mine who spoke Bicolano became proficient in Tagalog because of the English-Tagalog referents from that epic poem translation."

"Is that right! Here I am sitting at the edge of my seat developing some goose bumps thinking of the ghost of the vanished past, " he stood up from his seat.

"Lola, *salamat po*. I'm hungry. I need to get me a big whopper hamburger sandwich," he announced.

"But, *hijo*, didn't you just have breakfast?" his grandmother inquired.

As Norman left the room, my mother said to no one in particular: "Well, this generation wants to stuff themselves with fast food. We, original students of the Thomasites ate sparsely and learned our English well. It passed the test of time."

My father, José Villarica Viola, MD. was at the peak of his career as a physician and was a budding literary poet-writer in English when in 1942, World War II and the Japanese occupation short-circuited his life at age 48. My mother, Marcela Dayao Villarica earned her Master's degree in Education and became an outstanding educator.

It was José who saw Florante at Laura as a Filipino literary piece written in pure Tagalog, which should earn the appreciation by all Filipinos regardless of home language. He was the ultimate poet artist. It was Marcela who recognized the instrumental value of the translation as an approach to language acquisition across all schools in the Philippines. She took advantage of the right time, and the best teaching strategy. She was the effective teacher educator, a legacy of being the student of a Thomasite.

She lived to be one week short of her 105th birthday in 2004. Let's do the math; she most likely was one of the last original Thomasite student.

Penélope V. Flores is a professor at the College of Education, San Francisco State University. Her research interests are on the correlates of Filipino-ness and the Filipino American family. She was the president of the Philippine American Writers and Artist, Inc from 1998 to 2004. During her tenure as PAWA president she established the "Calatagan Awards" for literary and art contribution to Philippine culture and society, and introduced the Anthology series publication. She is the author of *Goodbye Vientiane: The Untold Stories of Filipinos in Laos, 1957-1973.*

She has a Ph.D. in Comparative and International Education from the University of Chicago, a Master of Science in Education at the University of Pennsylvania, and a Bachelors of Science degree from the Philippine Normal University, Manila. Penélope and Manuel Flores have two sons, Norman and Ivan.

J. Mark Muñoz

Strategies for Filipino migrant entrepreneurs in the United States

Abstract

The Philippines is one of the countries that have the largest number of overseas workers and immigrants. Migration from the country has been millions, and will likely grow even larger in the future. This article explores factors that shape entrepreneurship among Filipinos in America. Based on gathered literature, workable strategies are offered.

Introduction

Global metropolises are being transformed by entrepreneurs. Not just local entrepreneurs, but international and migrant entrepreneurs as well.

A new breed of cosmopolitan, cross-cultural entrepreneurs are emerging and transforming societies. The role of ethnic entrepreneurs in societies is expanding (Cui, 2001). According to the US Census Bureau (1997), out of 21 million firms in the country, 3 million are minority-owned, and about one third of the minority-owned ventures are operated by Asians and Pacific Islanders. Saxenian (1999) indicated that in 1998, ventures operated by immigrants contributed over $16.8 billion in sales and helped create close to 60,000 jobs in the US.

Minority entrepreneurs have the ability to make a positive impact in societies where they operate in. Kurklantzick (2004) characterized minority entrepreneurs in the US as : 1) evolving and growing as more women and minority ventures are expected to be created by 2010, 2) spurred by changes in demographic compositions, 3) perceived favorably due to the existence of successful role models, and 4) increasing in visibility and involvement in community affairs. In addition, ethnic minorities may comprise over half of the US population by 2060 (Feagin & Feagin, 1996).

Zhou (2002) pointed out that ethnic entrepreneurs facilitate community building, information flow, and enhance relationships. Eaton (1998) suggested that in the case of smaller cities, immigrants absorb professions that would not have been filled if their absence. A good number of Asian ventures in the US are successful (Le, 2004).

Research suggests that there is a confluence of factors that affect entrepreneurial propensities of immigrants. For instance, Waldinger et al (1990) pointed out that the interplay of characteristics relating to premigration conditions, migration circumstances, and the postmigration situation leads to variations among ethnic enterprises. In addition, Portes & Rumbaut (1990) attribute entrepreneurship propensities among immigrants as being shaped by environmental factors like human capital access, community integration, economic opportunities, and government policies.

Ethnic entrepreneurship is driven by either internal or external factors. Aldrich & Waldinger (1990) observed that the interconnection of social characteristics inevitably impact behavior, relations, and economic advantages among immigrants.

Internal factors refer to underlying circumstances, personal motivation, or conditions that encourage immigrants to engage in entrepreneurship in order that an economic advantage may be gained. Light & Bonacich (1988) cited resources such as wealth, values, and knowledge as drivers of ethnic entrepreneurship. The presence of support networks, as well as prior business experiences further encourage migrants to engage in entrepreneurial activities (Massey et al, 1994 ; Portes & Bach, 1985). In addition, emerging opportunities may open up as immigrants see avenues to bridge trade gaps across regions (Saxenian & Edulbehran, 1998).

External factors refer to circumstances, conditions, or other forces that force immigrants to engage in entrepreneurship as a means of survival and in coping with a new environment. Portes & Rumbaut (1990) pointed out that some immigrants pursue entrepreneurial activities in order to survive or improve their economic situation, while Mata & Pendakur (1999) noted that immigrants undertake entrepreneurial activities due to constraints in status, language, and human capital limitations. Economic growth and institutional factors such as governance can motivate immigrants to strive towards new directions (Frey & Stutzer, 2002). When educated immigrants are hindered by language proficiencies they would be more likely inclined to engage in entrepreneurship (Tienda, 2001).

Entrepreneurial activities of migrants can change lives and lead to prosperity. Galster et al (1999) pointed out that ethnic entrepreneurs have the ability to prosper in their host countries by capturing local market niches, engaging in trade arbitrage between the host and home countries, and establishing ventures in enclaves in the host country. Basch et al (1994) pointed out the concept of "transnationalism" where immigrants build upon multi-faceted social links between their country of origin and present residency, while Saxenian (1999) observed the expanding entrepreneurial role of highly skilled immigrants and their ability to establish business ties between domestic and foreign enterprises.

Minority groups, however, take on different approaches. In the case of Asian immigrants in the US, Le (2004) attributes the expansion of entrepreneurial propensities to: 1) labor market penetration challenges, 2) cultural factors and work ethics, 3) resource availability in the form of capital and skill sets, and 4) economic opportunities derived from ethnic support, location, and venture availability. Tienda (2001) observed that Asian entrepreneurs perceive business ownership as a way to generate more income and achieve prosperity.

Filipinos starting businesses in the United States or internationally, are in the position to make a positive impact their own way, and help shape the economy of their host nation.

Opportunities and Challenges
of Minority Entrepreneurs

*An entrepreneur in a foreign country is exposed to
several opportunities as well as risks.*

Potential opportunities include the following: informal networks
contribute to business success (Masurel et al, 2002); through the strategic use of support networks there are gained knowledge in industry
practice and management, capital acquisition, and human resources
development (Smart, 2003); ethnic support networks expands entrepreneurial contacts, facilitates training and business advice, and access
to loans and credit including money pools and loan clubs (Chotigeat
et al, 1991; Ginsberg, 2003); gain support from co-ethnic members
due to trust, ease of communication, credit privileges, and cultural
compatibility (Tienda , 2001); and spurs the formation of economic
clusters that reinforce value systems (Portes & Zhou, 1992).

Potential challenges are: limitations on class resources (Ram et al,
2000); non-usage of formal business loans and tax credits from the
government (Ginsberg, 2003); language barriers and non-transfer-
ability of degrees acquired in their home countries (Tienda, 2001);
existence of quasi-legal structures and taxation challenges (Ginsberg,
2003), poor personnel practices and low rate of utilization of institu-
tionalized training programs (Ram et al, 2000); non-awareness of new
venture government support programs and benefits (Tienda, 2001);
segregated in certain locations and lack capitalization (Louie & Ong,
1995); face the challenge of capital acquisition (Kurklantzick, 2004);
and the existence of internal diversity (Crane, 2004).

A key issue relates to how operational activities are conducted. Le
(2004) identified typical challenges of Asian immigrant ventures in
the US as: 1) having overworked owners putting in long hours, 2) exposed to inter-racial tension, 3) experiencing low profit margins, and
4) undergoing high rates of failures.

Evidently, there also seems to be a common thread among minority ventures. Ethnic ventures tend to be more common in industries such as restaurants, personnel services, and retailing, due to the fact that entry barriers are lower (Butler & Greene, 1997).

While there are several daunting challenges confronting migrant entrepreneurs, strategic approaches can lead to gains. Advantages may be derived from co-ethnic support networks through entrepreneurial contacts, acquisition of business advice, training, and loan or credit access (Masurel et al, 2002; Smart, 2003; Chotigeat et al, 1991; Ginsberg, 2003) and participation in activities in economic clusters ((Portes & Zhou, 1992). The path toward self-employment may be the way to overcome obstacles in job acquisition and financial betterment (Srinivasan, 1992).

A keen understanding of the implications of the opportunities and challenges, as well as implementing strategic approaches are critical in the pursuit of an entrepreneurial venture in a foreign country.

CHARACTERISTICS OF FILIPINO MIGRANT ENTREPRENEURS

Migrant entrepreneurs from the Philippines have indeed travelled far. The Philippines is located in Southeastern Asia, in an archipelago between the Philippine Sea and the South China Sea. The country has a population of around 91 million, and is slightly larger than the state of Arizona with a total land area of 300,000 square kilometers (CIA World Fact Book, 2007).

Despite being a beautiful tropical country, millions of people have left the country. Mercado (2002) depicted the Philippines as the largest labor exporter in Asia, having sent over 7.4 million or 22% of its entire labor force of 30 million to over 120 countries. In addition, over one million Filipinos emigrated to other countries in the past 20 years and more than 70% of the migrants headed towards the United States. Table 1 on the following page shows the migration destination of Filipinos.

TABLE 1

NUMBER OF REGISTERED PHILIPPINE EMIGRANTS (1981-2001)

Country of Destination	No. of Emigrants	Percentage	Annual Average
USA	799,501	71.0	36,582
Canada	151,127	13.4	6,733
Australia	81,397	7.2	3,782
Japan	56,756	5.0	2,416
UK	5,732	0.5	265
Germany	8,464	0.8	379
Others	23,100	2.1	988
TOTAL	1,126,077	100.0	53,623

Source : Commission on Filipinos Overseas (2004)

Several reasons have been identified to explain this excessive migration. Crane (2004) pointed out that Filipinos migrated to the country in the '70s and '80s as a result of experienced economic difficulties during the regime of President Ferdinand Marcos, and in the '90s as a response to the proliferation of labor intermediary agencies. Other explanations attributed to migration include: enhancement of socio-economic position in relation to another location (Stark & Bloom, 1985), optimization on investment on education (Tan & Canlas, 1989), and diversification of income streams (World Bank, 1995). Scarcity of jobs and higher income abroad has triggered the mass exodus in the Philippines, resulting in a scenario where the total number of overseas Filipinos exceeded 10% of the total population (Mercado, 2002; Ravanilla & Robleza, 2003).

Much of the Filipino migration into the US has been attributed to family related reasons. Data from the US Department of Homeland Security (2004) indicate that out of the 45,397 Filipino immigrants in the US in 2003, 20,498 (45%) were immediate relatives of US citizens, while 14,974 (32%) were family-sponsored.

Table 2 highlights the emigration volume in 1981-2001 according to occupational groups.

TABLE 2
PHILIPPINE EMIGRANTS
ACCORDING TO OCCUPATIONAL GROUPS (1981-2001)

Occupational Group	Number	Percentage
EMPLOYED		
Professional, technical and related workers	118,185	10.50
Managerial, Executive and Administrative workers	11,849	1.05
Clerical workers	48,276	4.29
Sales workers	47,035	4.18
Service workers	28,623	2.54
Agriculture, Animal husbandry, Forestry workers, and Fishermen	26,762	2.38
Production process, Transport Equipment Operators, and Laborers	46,124	4.10
Members of the Armed Forces	3,868	0.34
UNEMPLOYED		
Housewives	240,867	21.39
Retirees	36,690	3.26
Students	272,979	24.24
Minors (below 7 years old)	89,288	7.93
Out of school youth	1,908	0.17
Refugees	3	0.00
No occupation reported	153,620	13.64
TOTAL	1,126,077	100.00

Source : Commission on Filipinos Overseas (2004)

The data suggests that while about 30% of Philippine emigrants during the period had some form of employment, 70% were unemployed. In addition, the emigrants are mostly female with a ratio of 100 females for every 67 males, and have an average age of 32.

In the case of migration into the United States, the Philippines had a long history. Since the early part of the 1900's, Philippine laborers have been documented as workers in pineapple plantations in Hawaii, fruit pickers in California farms, and fish canners in Alaska (Morada, 2004).

The Filipino community in the US has been described as : 1) the second largest Asian population and fast growing, 2) predominantly in the California area with 49% of US Filipinos living in the state, and 3) one of the most educated among the US ethnic groups (Inquirer News Service, 2004).

Since 2003, the Filipinos constitute the third largest immigrant group in the US, with 45,397 migrants accounting to 6.4% of the total of 705,827 persons granted lawful permanent status (US Department of Homeland Security, 2004). Data from the National Federation of Filipino American Associations (NaFFAA, 2004) shows large Filipino communities in California (918,678), Hawaii (170,635), Illinois (86,298), New Jersey (85,245), and New York (81,681).

Filipino migrants offer unique skills to their new adopted countries. Crane (2004) characterized the Filipino migrants as : 1) well-liked, 2) polite, 3) dependable, 4) optimistic about the future, 5) possessing a wide range of skills, 6) flexible with the demands of the job market, and 7) uncomplaining on tasks assigned.

In the US, several Filipino migrants have started their own business. Data from the US Census Bureau (1997) show that Filipinos operate close to 85,000 ventures, have more than 100,000 employees, and have generated sales exceeding $10 billion. Table 3 presents relevant data on Philippine business ownership in the US.

TABLE 3
PHILIPPINE VENTURE OWNERSHIP IN THE US (AS OF 1997)

Category	Number
ALL	
Firm Number	84,534
Sales Receipts ($1000)	11,077,885
FIRMS WITH PAID EMPLOYEES	
Firm Number	14,581
Sales and receipts ($1,000)	8,966,386
Employees	110,130
Payroll ($1000)	2,667,333

Source : US Census Bureau (1997)

The data further suggest that most of these ventures are in the service industries, retail trade, and real estate. Table 4 shows the categories of Philippine-owned ventures in the US.

TABLE 4
PHILIPPINE-OWNED VENTURES IN THE US
(ACCORDING TO CLASSIFICATION) – 1997

CATEGORY	NUMBER	SALES RECEIPTS ($1,000)	MAJOR ACTIVITIES
Agricultural services, forestry, and fishing	831	38, 673	Agricultural services
Construction industries, subdividers, & developers	2,990	551,610	Special trade contractors
Manufacturing	1,615	932,452	Apparel & textiles, Printing & publishing, Food
Transportation, communication, & utilities	3,628	334,354	Motor freight transportation & warehousing, Transport services, & Local interurban passenger transport
Wholesale trade	2,672	2,013,297	Mostly in durable goods
Retail trade	9,323	764,361	Eating and drinking places, Food stores, Other retail
Real estate industries	8,356	628,532	Real estate & insurance agents
Service industries	46,629	5,375,426	Health, Business, & Personal, Engineering, Accounting, & Management Services
Other industries not classified	8,493	439, 180	
Total	84,534	11,077,885	

Source : US Census Bureau (1997)

From this data, the following are gathered about Philippine ventures in the US: 1) While the wholesale sector constitute among the lowest number of participants, it has posted one of the highest sales receipts, 2) While the service industry has the highest sales receipt contribution, there is likely a saturation in the sector, and 3) As shown in Table 2, only 2.54% of departing migrants in the Philippines were involved in the service sector, yet in the US a majority of ventures were in the service category. This suggests that several immigrants are likely pursuing service-oriented ventures in the US without having prior training or experience in the field.

Research also suggests that many Filipinos are taking jobs rather than starting ventures. Philippine entrepreneurs in the US have among the lowest number of ventures as compared to immigrants from other Asia-Pacific countries. The ease of finding jobs, and closer cultural assimilation with the mainstream society has inhibited Filipino migrants from pursuing avenues for self-employment and has dampened the urgency to pursue entrepreneurial activities (Min, 1986 ; Crane, 2004).

Filipinos are also known to adapt well in foreign locations, such as the United States. Min (1986) pointed out the advantages of Filipino migrants as: 1) proficiency in English, 2) commonality with US educational approaches, 3) possess high level of cultural integration.

As venture managers in foreign locations, Filipinos are likely to implement their own brand of management. Henderson (1999) identified the key attributes of traditional Philippine management as: formal (need to use titles, formal names, and handshakes); punctual (need to prepare for delays due to traffic congestion), relaxed (allow time for small talk); sensitive (avoid raising voices or implication of incompetence); paternalistic; dense with close work networks; emphasizes group loyalty and social harmony; indirect and elusive communicative responses (executives tend to use a variety of approaches to say "no" to soften the blow and prevent embarrassment); leave projects uncompleted (*ningas cogon*); and anchored on trust building (*tiwala*), a key ingredient in building a successful relationship. Andres and Ilada-Andres (2001) cited the Philippine culture as possessing attributes such as personalism, familism, and particularism, while Mendoza (2001) pointed out that these attributes are misaligned with certain Western values that emphasize objectivity, professionalism, and goal orientation. These cultural differences can lead to misunderstandings and work conflicts with employees, business partners, and other stakeholders.

The Philippine value system shapes entrepreneurial behavior and propensity. The Philippine culture possesses a favorable disposition towards entrepreneurship, except on the aspect of individualism. Hofstede (1991) in his cross-cultural study has shown that the Philippine culture has high power distance, high masculinity, low uncertainty avoidance. These attributes have been identified by McGrath et al (1992) as traits typically present among entrepreneurs in various cultures. However, as shown in Hostede's (1991) study Filipinos scored low on individualism, high individualism rating typically characterize entrepreneurs (McGrath et al, 1992). The culture's low level of individualism can adversely impact entrepreneurial tendencies. Furthermore, Mueller and Thomas (2000) uncovered that cultures possessing high individualism and low uncertainty avoidance created a succeeding generation with stronger entrepreneurial attributes.

The entrepreneurial propensity of Filipino immigrants can be dampened by the cultural perspectives such as fatalism and long-term orientation. Sison (2003) pointed out the culture's short-term perspective and fatalistic or "*bahala na*" attitude, where fate is ultimately left to God. Hofstede (1991) indicated that Filipinos scored low on long-term orientation (Hofstede, 1991). A short-term rather long-term focus translates into the immediate desire for financial gains that are not often attainable in self-employment or in start-up entrepreneurial ventures. Additionally, many Filipinos view their immigration as a temporary period and eventually dream of returning to their home country (Crane, 2004). This perspective, therefore discourages the formation or acquisition of concrete and long-term business infrastructure in foreign locations.

Despite potential cultural drawbacks, numerous business opportunities exist in the US. Motivated Filipino migrants have the ability and the potential to overcome these shortcomings and create dynamic ventures in their host country.

Strategies for Filipino Entrepreneurs

Based on the research findings, the author offers a few strategies for Filipino entrepreneurs in the US.

Explore opportunities in the wholesale sector. As seen in Table 4, the wholesale sector constitutes the lowest level of participation among Philippine businesses in the US. Ironically, it has posted one of the highest sales receipts. New opportunities in this sector deserve closer examination.

Pursue opportunities in the service sector. As seen in Table 4, the majority of Philippine ventures in the US are in the service category. This is one sector where Filipinos can excel. Develop skills in this arena and explore relevant opportunities.

Embrace an entrepreneurial mindset. In Hofstede's (1991) study Filipinos were determined to have scored high on the masculinity index and low on the uncertainty avoidance index. Both characteristics were determined by McGrath et al (1992) to be indicators for an entrepreneurial predisposition. Culturally, there are entrepreneurial tendencies among Filipinos, it is important to convert these tendencies into business realities.

Be patient. Hofstede's (1991) study suggests that Filipinos tend to have a short-term orientation. In start-up ventures, a long-term focus is essential. Postponing the attainment of gains, keeping faith, and being patient is key.

Know the business environment well. The business and economic environments of the Philippines and America are different. Understanding where differences lie, and strategizing accordingly is important.

Arbitrage cross-cultural opportunities. There are product, service, and price gaps that exist between the US and the Philippines. Finding these gaps and creating business opportunities from them would be an excellent way forward. Saxenian & Edulbehran (1998) pointed out that immigrants are in the position to identify and bridge trade gaps across countries.

≈Learn from mentors. There are several successful Filipino migrant entrepreneurs in the US. Meet with them and solicit advice and guidance. Ibrahim & Galt (2003) pointed out the merits of tapping into the expertise of migrant mentors.

The influx of Filipino migrants into the US would likely expand into the future. Through proper research, courage, and strategic approaches, there is much that can be achieved by current and future migrant entrepreneurs.

J. Mark Muñoz is an Associate Professor in the Tabor School of Business at Millikin University, Illinois. He is also the Chairman of an international market research and consulting company, Muñoz and Associates International. He has conducted international research on globalization and business spanning 35 countries. His research won two Best Research Paper Awards in international business conferences. He is published in international management journals, and commercial business magazines. He is the author of *Land of My Birth* (2005), *Winning Across Borders*, and *In Transition* (2007).He lives in Decatur, Illinois. E-mail : jmunoz@mail.millikin.edu

Works Cited from

Against the Winter Sky: The Figurative Use of Winter in Philippine and Philippine American Poetry by Jennifer Macagba

Angeles, Carlos. "Washington D.C." A Native Clearing: Filipino Poetry and Verse from English since the 50's to the Present: Edith L. Tiempo to Cirilo F. Bautista, ed. Gemino H. Abad. (Quezon City: University of the Philippines Press, 1993), 120.

Bautista, Cirilo F. "The Archipelago." A Native Clearing, 456.

Bulosan, Carlos. "A Child Dying in a Tenement." Man of Earth: An Anthology of Filipino Poetry and Verse from English, eds. Gemino H. Abad and Edna Zapanta Manlapaz. (Quezon City: Ateneo de Manila University, 1989), 192.

Concepcion, M. de Gracia. "Ili-na." Man of Earth, #.

Daguio, Amador T. "Bloom of Waters Call." Man of Earth, 204.

Feria, Dolores Stephens. "Filipino Writers in Exile." Likhaan Anthology of Philippine Literature in English, ed. Gemino H. Abad. (Quezon City: University of the Philippines Press, 1998), #.

Francia, Luis. "An Arctic Archipelago." A Habit of Shores: Filipino Poetry and Verse from English, 60's to the 90's, ed. Gemino H. Abad. (Quezon City: University of the Philippines Press, 1999), 131.

Lim-Wilson, Ma. Fatima V. "Bride of Okura." A Habit of Shores, 404.

Lim-Wilson, Ma. Fatima V. "Luzviminda, or Filipinos Makes Such Good Maids." A Habit of Shores, 407.

Lim-Wilson, Ma. Fatima V. "A Sestina Written in a Cold Land, or There is No Word for Snow in My Language," A Habit of Shores, 406.

Manuud, Antonio P.G. "On the Baltica's Leaving for a Northern Port." A Native Clearing, 228.

Pacis, Donel. "Photographs of an Exile." A Habit of Shores, 126.

Santos, Bienvenido N. "Pagan." The Wounded Stag. (Quezon City: New Day Publishers, 1992), #.

Tonogbanua, Francisco G. "Tranquility." Man of Earth, 44.

Viray, Manuel. "Washington Morning." A Native Clearing, 47.

Viray, Manuel. "A Winter Walk." A Native Clearing, 49.

Bibliography for *Strategies for Filipino Migrant Entrepreneurs in the United States by J. Mark Muñoz.*

Aldrich, H.E. & Waldinger, R. (1990). Ethnicity and entrepreneurship. Annual Review of Sociology 16 : 111-135.

Andres, T.D. & Ilada-Andres, P.C.B. (2001). Understanding the Filipino. New Day Publishers : Quezon City, Philippines.

Basch, L., Glick-Schiller, N., & Blanc-Szanton, C. (1994). Nation Unbounded : Transnational Projects, Post Colonial Predicaments, and Deterritorialized Nation States. Langhome, PA : Gordon and Breach.

Butler, J. & Greene, P. (1997). Ethnic entrepreneurship : The continuous rebirth of American enterprise. In Sexton, Donald L. and Raymond W. Smilor, (Eds), Entrepreneurship 2000 (267-289). Chicago, IL : Upstart Publishing Co.

Chotigeat, T., Balsmeier, P.W., Stanley, T.O. (1991, July). Fueling Asian immigrants entrepreneurship : A source of capital. Journal of Small Business Management 29 (3) : 50-61.

CIA.(2007). The Philippines. World Fact Book [available at https://www.cia.gov/library/publications/the-world-factbook/geos/rp.html]

Commission on Filipino Overseas.(2004). Number of registered Filipino emigrants by major country of destination : 1981-2001 (accessed Sept 2004), [available at : http://www.cfo.gov.ph/stat_bod.htm]

Crane, K. (2004, Feb). Governing migration : Immigrant groups' strategies in three Italian cities Rome, Naples, and Bari. Psychoanalytic Institute for Social Research, Rome, (accessed Sept 2004), [available at : http://www.feem.it/NR/rdonlyres/6D92E1D5-F3B4-4727-A5C6-ADC8BBF58E41/1081/3704.pdf]

Cui, G. (2001). Marketing to ethnic minority consumers : A historical journey (1932-1997). Journal of Macromarketing 21 (1) : 23-31.

Department of Homeland Security. (2004). 2003 Yearbook of Immigration Statistics, (accessed Sept 2004), [available at : http://uscis.gov/graphics/shared/aboutus/statistics/IMM03yrbk/2003IMM.pdf]

Eaton, A.L. (1998). Immigration and the structure of demand : Do immigrants alter the labor market composition of US cities. Working paper 98-11, Seattle Population Research Center, University of Washington, Seattle.

Feagin, J.R. & Feagin, C.B. (1996). Racial and Ethnic Relations (5th edition). New Jersey : Prentice Hall.

Frey, B. and Stutzer, A. (2002, June). What can economists learn from happiness research ? Journal of Economic Literature 40 (2) : 402-435.

Galster, G.C., Metzger, K., Waite, R. (1999). Neighborhood opportunity structures and immigrants' socioeconomic advancement. Journal of Housing Research 10(1) : 95-127.

Ginsberg, T. (2003, Nov. 17). Immigrants pool money, find success. The Philadelphia Inquirer, (accessed Oct 2004), [available at : http://www.philly.com/mld/inquirer/7279815.htm?1c]

Henderson, C. (1999, July). Filipino business norms, etiquette, and style. Asia Pacific Management Forum (accessed June 2004), [available at : http://www.apmforum.com/columns/orientseas6.htm]

Hofstede, G. (1991). Culture and Organizations : Software of the Mind. London : Mc Graw-Hill.

Inquirer News Service (2004). Filipino business leaders share secrets to success, (accessed Sept 2004), [available at : http://inq7.net/globalnation/ser_ann/2004/jul/30-01]

Kurklantzick, J. (2004, January). About face. Entrepreneur.com, (accessed Oct, 2004), [available at : http://www.entrepreneur.com/Magazines/Copy_of_MA_SegAr ticle/0,4453,312260,00.html]

Le, C.N. (2004). Asian small businesses. Asian-Nation : The landscape of Asian America, (accessed Oct 2004), [available at: http://www.asian-nation.org/small-business.shtml]

Light, I., & Bonacich, E. (1988). Immigrant Entrepreneurs : Koreans in Los Angeles. Los Angeles : University of California Press.

Louie, W. & Ong, P. (1995). Asian immigrant investors and the immigration act of 1990. California Policy Seminar Research Project Report. Berkeley : California Policy Seminar.

McGrath, R., McMillan, I., & Scheinberg, S. (1992). Elitists, risk-takers, and rugged individualists ? An exploratory analysis of cultural differences between entrepreneurs and nonentrepreneurs. Journal of Business Venturing 7 : 115-135.

Massey, D., Arango, J., Hugo, G., Kovaovci, A., Pellegrino, A., Taylor, J.E. (1994). An evaluation of international migration theory : The North American case. Population and Development Review 20 : 699-752.

Masurel, E., Nijkmamp, P., Tastan, M., Vindigni, G. (2002, Spring). Motivations and performance conditions for ethnic entrepreneurship. Growth & Change 33 (2) : 238-260.

Mata, F. & Pendakur, R. (1999). Immigration, labor force integration, and the pursuit of self-employment. International Migration Review 33 (2) : 378-402.

Masurel, E., Nijkmamp, P., Tastan, M., Vindigni, G. (2002, Spring). Motivations and performance conditions for ethnic entrepreneurship. Growth & Change 33 (2) : 238-260.

Mendoza, M.L. (2001). The crisis of management culture in the Philippines : Neither East Asian nor Western. A paper presented at the 3rd EUROSEAS Conference in London, IK and the 4th European Philippine Studies Conference in Alcoba, Spain on September 2001.

Mercado, J.L. (2002, Oct 14). Chatting up Filipinas in airport queues. Philippines Today Online edition, (accessed Oct 2004), [available at : http://www.philippinestoday.net/ofwcorner/ofw11_3.htm]

Min, P.G. (1986). Filipino and Korean immigrants in small business : A comparative analysis. Amerasia Journal 13 (1) : 53-71.

Mueller, S., & Thomas, A. (2000). Culture and entrepreneurial potential : A nine-country study of locus of control and innovativeness. Journal of Business Venturing 16:51-75.

NaFFAA. (2004). Filipino Americans in each state based on the 2000 US Census (accessed Oct 2004), [available at http://naffaa.org/census2000]

Portes, A. & Rumbaut, R. (1990). Immigrant America : A Portrait. Berkeley & Los Angeles : University of California Press.

Portes, A. & Zhou, M. (1992). Gaining the upper hand : Economic mobility among immigrant and domestic minorities. Ethnic and Racial Studies 15 (4) : 491-522.

414

Ram, M., Sanghera, B., Abbas, T., Barlow, G. (2000). Training and ethnic minority firms: The case of the independent restaurant sector. Education & Training 42 (4/5) : 334-341.

Ravanilla, N.M. & Robleza, E.J.P. (2003, March). The contribution of OFW remittances to income inequality : A decomposition analysis. A paper submitted to the University of the Philippines School of Economics : Manila, Philippines.

Saxenian, A. (1999). Silicon Valley's new immigrant entrepreneurs. Public Policy Institute of California (accessed Sept 2004), [available at : http://www.ppic.org/content/pubs/R_699ASR.pdf]

Saxenian, A. & Edulbehran, J. (1998). Immigrant entrepreneurs in Silicon Valley. Berkeley Planning Journal 12 : 32-49.

Sison, A.J. (2003). Business and culture in the Philippines : A story of gradual progress. [available at: http://www.unav.es/empresayhumanismo/2activ/seminario/miembros/sison/ii26/default.html]

Smart, J. (2003, Fall). Ethnic entrepreneurship, transmigration, and social integration: An ethnographic study of Chinese restaurant owners in rural western Canada. Urban Anthropology and Studies of Cultural Systems & World Economic Development 32 (3/4) : 311-342.

Stark, O. & Bloom, D.E. (1985). The new economics of labor migration. American Economic Review 175 : 173-178.

Tan, E.A. & Canlas, D.B. (1989). Migrants savings, remittances, and labour supply behaviour : The Philippines case. in Rashid Amjad ed., Into the Gulf and Back : Studies on the Economic Impact of Asian Labour Migration. Geneva : ILO-ARTEP. 223-254

Tienda, M. (2001, November). Comparative perspectives on ethnic and immigrant entrepreneurship and business development in Chicago. A paper prepared for the Illinois Coalition for Immigrant and Refugee Rights (accessed Sept 2004), [available at: http://www.roosevelt.edu/ima/pdfs/ethnic-immigrant-entrepreneurship.pdf]

U.S. Census Bureau (1997). Economic census minority and women owned businesses United States, (accessed Sept 2004), [available at : http://www.census.gov/epcd/mwb97/us/us.html]

Waldinger, R., Aldrich, H., Ward, R. and associates. (1990). Ethnic entrepreneurs : Immigrant business in industrial societies. Newbury Park : Sage Publications.

World Bank. (1995). Workers in an integrating world. World Development Report 1995. New York : Oxford University Press.

Zhou, M. (2002, Dec). How neighborhoods matter for immigrant adolescents. CPRC Brief 14 (8), accessed (Sept 2004), [available at http://www.ucop.edu/cprc/neighborhoods.pdf]

PHILIPPINE AMERICAN
WRITERS AND ARTISTS, INC.
(PAWA, INC.)

PO Box 31928
San Francisco, CA
94131-0928

www.pawainc.com
pawa@pawainc.com

Reflections: Readings for the Young and Old
A Collection of Scripts and Narratives
Edited and Introduced by Penélope V. Flores
2002

Whisper of the Bamboo
An Anthology of Philippine American Writers and Artists
Edited by Penélope V. Flores, Allen Gaborro
2004

Good-bye Vientiane
Untold Stories of Filipinos in Laos
Penélope V. Flores
2005

The Philippine Jeepney, A Filipino Family Metaphor:
Understanding the Filipino American Family
Penélope V. Flores with Araceli N. Resus
2008